Twenty Years of Legal Marriage for Same-Sex Couples in the United States

EVIDENCE REVIEW AND NEW ANALYSES

BENJAMIN R. KARNEY
MELANIE A. ZABER
MOLLY G. SMITH
SAMUEL J. MANN
MARWA ALFAKHRI
JESSIE COE
JAMIE L. RYAN
CATRIA GADWAH-MEADEN
CHRISTY MALLORY
BRAD SEARS
CHANDRA GARBER

RAND SOCIAL AND ECONOMIC WELL-BEING

For more information on this publication, visit **www.rand.org/t/RRA2912-1**.

Published by the RAND Corporation, Santa Monica, Calif.

Library of Congress Cataloging-in-Publication Data is available for this publication.

ISBN: 978-1-9774-1322-2

Cover design by Katherine Wu.

Cover image: ekhi/Adobe Stock

About This Report

Twenty years after the first marriage licenses were issued to same-sex couples in Massachusetts, this report provides a review of evidence and new analyses describing the effects of granting legal status to the marriages of same-sex couples in the United States. For the evidence review, we assembled and evaluated existing research that has examined how any form of legal status (e.g., marriage, civil unions, domestic partnerships) affects well-being in lesbian, gay, bisexual, and transgender individuals; their children; and the general public. For the new analyses, we leveraged data from multiple national datasets (e.g., the American Community Survey, the Current Population Survey, the Panel Study of Income Dynamics, the Monitoring the Future main study) to examine how changes in the legal status of same-sex couples within and across states affected trends in family formation (e.g., marriage and divorce) between 2000 (before marriage was available to same-sex couples in any state) and 2014 (when the last cohort of states chose to issue marriage licenses to same-sex couples before all restrictions on marriage for same-sex couples nationwide were lifted by *Obergefell v. Hodges*). This report should be of interest to researchers and policymakers considering how to promote the well-being of relationships, U.S. families, and members of gender and sexual-minority groups. Preparation of this report was supported by Centerline Liberties, Inc., a 501(c)3 focused on advancing policy solutions that defend core constitutional freedoms and liberties.

Social and Behavioral Policy Program

RAND Social and Economic Well-Being is a division of RAND that seeks to actively improve the health and social and economic well-being of populations and communities throughout the world. This research was conducted in the Social and Behavioral Policy Program within RAND Social and Economic Well-Being. The program focuses on such topics as risk factors and prevention programs, social safety net programs and other social supports, poverty, aging, disability, child and youth health and well-being, and quality of life, as well as other policy concerns that are influenced by social and behavioral actions and systems that affect well-being. For more information, email sbp@rand.org.

Acknowledgments

We are grateful for communications assistance provided by Kate Giglio and administrative assistance from Rosa Maria Torres. Our analytic approach benefited early on from comments from Lowell Taylor, Laurie Martin, and Julia Rollison. We are thankful for the astute review of the final report from Lowell Taylor, Christopher "Kitt" Carpenter, and Laura Bellows. We thank Katherine Wu for design support, Emily Ward for editorial expertise, and Babitha Balan for overseeing the publication process for this report.

Summary

The Research Question

Prior to the Supreme Court's *Obergefell v. Hodges* decision in 2015, the United States had been divided by heated debates over the merits of legalizing marriage for same-sex couples. Those who were in favor argued that granting same-sex couples access to marriage would strengthen commitment for same-sex couples, extend the financial benefits of marriage to same-sex households, and improve outcomes for children being raised by same-sex parents. Those who were opposed argued that granting legal status to marriages between same-sex partners would alter the foundation of marriage and thereby diminish its value for different-sex couples, ultimately harming children by making them less likely to be raised in stable, two-parent families.

It has now been 20 years since Massachusetts became the first state to issue marriage licenses to same-sex couples in May 2004. The consequences of extending legal recognition to same-sex couples need no longer be a topic of speculation and debate; researchers have had two decades to study the consequences of legalizing marriage for same-sex couples on lesbian, gay, bisexual, and transgender (LGBT) individuals; their children; and the general public.

The broad goal of this report is to document those consequences. We pursued this goal in two ways. First, we conducted a comprehensive review of the existing research literature on the effects of legalizing marriage for same-sex couples. Second, we conducted new analyses to evaluate the specific prediction that rates of marriage, divorce, and other aspects of family formation would be adversely affected by marriage policies that afforded equal treatment to same-sex and different-sex couples.

Approach

For the evidence review, we conducted a comprehensive search of existing empirical studies of the impacts of legal marriage for same-sex couples on LGBT individuals, their children, and the general population. The 96 studies identified in our search employ a wide variety of methods and designs, including cross-sectional surveys, repeated comparisons across state policy environments, and longitudinal research. Furthermore, this substantial literature incorporates diverse perspectives and scholarly disciplines and examines a broad variety of outcomes potentially influenced by legal marriage for same-sex couples.

For the new causal analyses, we drew on multiple national datasets to evaluate how changes in marriage policy across states relate to changes in marriage rates, divorce rates, and cohabitation rates in the general population. We also examined attitudes toward marriage among young adults. For these analyses, we used the latest advances in difference-in-differences methodology to estimate the effects of state-level policy changes in the legalization of marriage for same-sex couples on each outcome. We replicated our analyses across a variety of data sources with different sampling structures and tested the sensitivity of our findings across a variety of approaches to modeling each outcome of interest.

Key Findings

Evidence Review

Across 96 published or soon-to-be published empirical studies conducted over the past 20 years, the consequences of extending marriage and other forms of legal recognition to same-sex couples have been consistently positive for same-sex couples and LGBT individuals, their children, and the general population.

For LGBT individuals and same-sex couples—the populations who were most directly affected by legalizing marriage for same-sex couples—the benefits of access to legal marriage were unambiguous. Without exception, research has found that the well-documented advantages associated with marriage in different-sex couples are reliably observed in same-sex couples as well:

- When states legalized marriage for same-sex couples, same-sex households in those states experienced more-stable relationships, higher earnings, higher rates of homeownership, and better preparation for retirement and end-of-life care.
- When states legalized marriage for same-sex couples, the physical health of LGBT individuals in those states improved, demonstrated by higher levels of health care use, higher levels of health insurance coverage, and declining rates of sexually transmitted infections and problematic substance use.
- Multiple studies have found that married same-sex couples report lower psychological distress than same-sex couples with other forms of legal status (i.e., civil unions or domestic partnerships) or no legal status.
- After states legalized marriage for same-sex couples, social support, particularly family support, improved for LGBT individuals and perceived stigma declined.
- When states legalized marriage for same-sex couples, sexual orientation–motivated hate crimes and employment discrimination against LGBT individuals declined.
- In contrast, when states banned marriage for same-sex couples, LGBT residents of those states reported higher anxiety and lower life satisfaction than residents of states without bans, even after controlling for other elements of the state political climate.

Although extensive research has consistently found that children raised by same-sex couples experience similar levels of well-being to children raised by different-sex couples, few studies have directly examined the effects on children when their same-sex parents are granted access to legal marriage. Of the studies we identified that addressed this question, all found that children of same-sex couples benefited when their parents were granted access to legal marriage:

- Access to legal marriage greatly reduced or eliminated disparities between the children of same-sex couples and the children of different-sex couples, with respect to access to health insurance and progress through school.
- After controlling for socioeconomic variables, there were no reliable differences in the emotional and physical health of children of married versus cohabiting same-sex parents.

Despite the concerns of opponents of legalizing marriage for same-sex couples that doing so would bring harm to different-sex couples and households, the existing research has found the effects of legal access to marriage for same-sex couples to be uniformly beneficial for these groups as well:

- Although some feared that judicial and legislative actions granting same-sex couples access to marriage would provoke a backlash in public opinion, no evidence of lasting negative changes in public opinion have been found. On the contrary, nationally representative polls find that more than 70 percent of Americans now approve of marriage for same-sex couples.
- When states legalize marriage for same-sex couples, state-level rates of syphilis, HIV, and AIDS fall significantly, resulting in billions of dollars in savings to the nation's health care system each year.
- Extending legal recognition to same-sex couples affects state-level adoption rates, which rise by between 4 percent and 6 percent after marriage between same-sex partners becomes legal.
- There is some evidence that the economies of states that granted legal status to same-sex couples improved as a result, as measured by higher rates of patents awarded in those states and higher market values for corporations headquartered in those states after marriage for same-sex couples was legalized.

As notable as these significant findings are, it is also worth noting what has *not* been found in the past two decades of research. Across 96 studies conducted over 20 years, the existing literature has not identified any reliable adverse consequences of policies granting same-sex couples access to legal marriage. In particular, prior research has not found any evidence of any effect of these policies on trends in family formation among different-sex couples.

New Analyses

To evaluate the specific impact of policies legalizing marriage for same-sex couples on family formation among different-sex couples and the general population, we leveraged advances in research methodology and multiple data sources to examine the causal effects of such state-level policy changes between 2000 and 2014 on different-sex couples' marriage rates, divorce rates, and cohabitation rates.

- We found no evidence of a retreat from marriage. In fact, the only evidence of change that we discovered is a possible *increase* in marriage resulting from legalization of marriage between same-sex partners. Importantly, we can identify that this is not driven solely by newly marrying same-sex couples.
- When we compared states that legalized marriage for same-sex couples earlier with states that legalized it later (but still pre-*Obergefell*), we found no evidence that our results are unique to the states that were earlier adopters of issuing marriage licenses to same-sex couples.
- In the datasets in which we were able to examine cohabitation, there is no evidence of a statistically significant increase in cohabitation by unmarried different-sex couples, and there is limited evidence of a decline.
- We similarly found no consistent evidence of an increase in divorce as a consequence of legalizing marriage for same-sex couples, regardless of potential changes in who was getting married.
- Finally, across a variety of attitudes toward family formation assessed among high school seniors, we found no evidence of a negative shift in attitudes toward the institution of marriage, and we observed some evidence of an improvement.

Opponents of granting marriage licenses to same-sex couples predicted that doing so would undermine the institution of marriage and result in fewer couples marrying, more couples divorcing, and an overall retreat from family formation. In examining this question, we used analytic approaches designed to maximize the chances of observing a statistically significant effect, if one exists. Yet these analyses reached the same conclusions as the other studies of this issue: Permitting legal marriage among same-sex couples had no adverse effects on marriage, divorce, or cohabitation among different-sex couples. On the contrary, the few significant effects observed in our analyses suggest a slight increase in marriage rates and potentially improved attitudes toward marriage after same-sex couples were granted legal status by a state.

Contents

Together, these rights and privileges, sometimes accompanied by corresponding duties and obligations, afford married couples an elevated status in the United States compared with other intimate relationships and family forms (Cherlin, 2020).

For most of the history of the United States, same-sex couples have not been eligible to receive the social and economic benefits associated with marriage. Although throughout history there have been same-sex couples that identified as married and were treated by their communities as married (Cleves, 2015; Dynes and Donaldson, 1992; Eskridge, 1993), these instances were rare. More commonly, legal status was granted only to the marriages of different-sex couples. In the latter years of the 20th century, with the rising visibility of lesbian, gay, bisexual, and transgender (LGBT) individuals, same-sex couples were occasionally offered other forms of legal status (e.g., domestic partnerships, civil unions). Yet through the end of the 20th century, marriage remained reserved for one man and one woman.

How Marriage Became Legal for Same-Sex Couples in the United States

The path to legalizing marriage for same-sex couples proceeded in four phases:[1]

- 1970s to 2002: Initial steps were taken toward legal status in some states, along with efforts to restrict marriage to different-sex couples.
- 2003 to 2011: Several states legalized marriage for same-sex couples, while a greater number of states passed bans on marriage for same-sex couples at the ballot box.
- 2012 to 2014: There was a rapid expansion of states issuing marriage licenses to same-sex couples.
- 2015: The U.S. Supreme Court's decision in *Obergefell v. Hodges* required all states to issue marriage licenses to same-sex couples.

[1] This section briefly describes the timeline of the extension of marriage licenses to same-sex couples in the United States from the 1970s to the present, but it is important to acknowledge that the broader path to marriage access for same-sex couples was much more complex and involved organizing by lesbian, gay, bisexual, transgender, and queer or questioning (LGBTQ) communities and their allies; the work of social movement organizations; and growing support from government institutions, civil society, religious denominations, the business community, and others. Important highlights in that broader discussion include changes in public opinion, leadership by elected officials and others, executive branch policies, and other contributing forces. For a discussion of the fuller history of the decades-long path toward marriage equality, see Eskridge and Riano (2020).

1970s to 2002: Initial Steps Toward Marriage Access and Efforts to Restrict Marriage to Different-Sex Couples

Discussion of granting same-sex couples the same legal status as different-sex couples can be traced to the earliest days of the modern LGBTQ rights movement in the United States,[2] but the first recorded attempts to have marriage licenses issued to same-sex couples occurred in the years after the Stonewall Riots in 1969, when same-sex couples unsuccessfully sued for the right to marry in Minnesota (*Baker v. Nelson*, 1971) and sought marriage licenses in other states.[3]

Starting in the 1970s, states began passing laws expressly defining *marriage* as a union between "one man and one woman," effectively barring same-sex couples from legally marrying. In 1973, Maryland became the first state to pass such a law (Maryland Laws Ch. 213, 1973). In the subsequent decades, other states followed suit. State legislatures enacted statutes that barred same-sex couples from marrying, and voters approved constitutional amendments limiting marriage to different-sex couples.

The pace of these enactments accelerated in 1990 after several same-sex couples sued for the right to marry in Hawai'i (*Baehr v. Miike*, 1996). In response to that case, new laws and amendments specifically stated that marriages (and other forms of legal status, such as civil unions and domestic partnerships) were unlawful for same-sex couples. In Hawai'i, new laws gave the legislature the exclusive power to determine who could marry, taking decisionmaking away from the courts (e.g., Nebraska Const. Art. I, § 29, 2000; Hawai'i Const. Art. 1, § 23, 1998). In 1996, the federal government followed suit when Congress passed the Defense of Marriage Act, which upheld states' right to not recognize the marriages of same-sex couples granted in other states and preemptively denied federal recognition and benefits to married same-sex couples (Pub. L. 104-199, 1996).

Starting in the late 1990s, some states began to pass laws that provided forms of legal status to same-sex couples, but these laws stopped short of marriage. In 1997, for example, Hawai'i passed "reciprocal beneficiary" legislation granting same-sex couples a limited set of marital rights and responsibilities (Hawai'i H.B. 118, 1997). California followed suit in 1999 with a "registered domestic partnership law" that also initially provided a limited set of rights (California S.B. 75, 1999). In 2000, Vermont became the first state to grant same-sex couples nearly all of the protections and obligations of marriage through its "civil union" legislation (Vermont H.B. 847, 2000). California expanded its domestic partnership legislation in a similar way in 2003 (California A.B. 205, 2003), and Maine (Maine H.P. 1152, 2004) passed a comprehensive domestic partnership law in 2004.

[2] The Mattachine Society is widely seen as the first sustained LGBT organization after World War II. One of its initial issues of *ONE Magazine* in 1953 was temporarily held by the Los Angeles Post Office because it was focused on "homosexual marriage." See ONE Archives at the USC Libraries, undated.

[3] In 1972, in response to a report from a clerk of court that "an increasing number of persons of the same sex [were] seeking marriage licenses," the Maryland Attorney General issued an opinion stating that only different-sex couples were permitted to marry (57 *Opinions of the Attorney General* 71, Maryland, 1972).

By 2002, although a few states offered some form of legal status to same-sex couples, married same-sex couples in those states were still unable to access federal benefits associated with marriage because of the Defense of Marriage Act (California Fam. Code §§ 297–299.6, 1999). Moreover, almost every state had statutes expressly limiting marriage to different-sex couples,[4] and four states also passed amendments to their constitutions reiterating that restriction or otherwise limiting the availability of marriage for same-sex couples.[5]

---

[4] Most states had laws that expressly defined marriage as between one man and one woman: Alabama, Alaska, Arizona, Arkansas, California, Colorado, Delaware, Florida, Georgia, Hawai'i, Idaho, Illinois, Indiana, Iowa, Kansas, Kentucky, Louisiana, Maine, Maryland, Michigan, Minnesota, Mississippi, Missouri, Montana, Nebraska, Nevada, New Hampshire, North Carolina, North Dakota, Oklahoma, Oregon, Pennsylvania, South Carolina, South Dakota, Tennessee, Texas, Utah, Virginia, Washington, West Virginia, Wisconsin, and Wyoming (Alabama Laws 98-500, Alabama Marriage Protection Act, 1998; Alaska Laws Ch. 21, 1996; Arizona Legis. Serv. Ch. 348, 1996; Arkansas Laws Act 144, 1997; Cal. A.B. 607, Leg., 1977-78 Sess., 1997; Colorado Legis. Serv. Ch. 233, 2000; 70 Del. Laws 375, 1996; Florida Sess. Law Serv. Ch. 77-139, 1977; Georgia Laws § 1, 1996, p. 1025; 1994 Haw. Sess. Laws Ch. 217, 1996; Idaho Laws Ch. 104, 1995; Illinois Law 504, Public Act 89–459, 1996; Indiana Pub. L. 1-1997, § 3, 1997; Acts Iowa Ch. 1099, § 1, 1998; Kentucky Laws Ch. 258, 1998; Louisiana Laws Act No. 890, 1999; Maine Laws Ch. 65, 1997; Maryland Laws Ch. 213, 1973; Michigan Comp. Laws § 551.1, Public Act 1996 No. 324, § 1, 1996; Minnesota Laws Ch. 441, sec. 1, 1977; Mississippi Laws Ch. 301, sec. 2, 1997; Missouri Legis. Serv. S.B. 768, 1996; Montana Laws Ch. 424, 1997; New Hampshire Laws Ch. 218:1, 1987; North Dakota Laws Ch. 145, 1997; Oklahoma Laws Ch. 39, 1975; Pennsylvania H.B. 1996 Legis., 2022; South Carolina Laws Act 327, 1996; South Dakota Laws Ch. 161, 1996; Tennessee S.B. 2305, 99th Gen. Assem., 2nd Reg. Sess., 1996; Texas Sess. Laws Ch. 7, 1997; Utah S.B. 24, 2004 Gen. Sess., 2004; Virginia Laws Ch. 354, 1997; Washington S.H.B. 1130, 55th Leg., Reg. Sess., 1998; West Virginia H.B. 2199, 76th Leg., 2001; Wisconsin Stat. Ann. § 765.001, 1975; Wyoming Laws Ch. 70, 1977, p. 228).

In Massachusetts, New Jersey, New York, Rhode Island, and Vermont, state statutes did not expressly define marriage to be "between a man and a woman" but often used gendered language, such as "husband" and "wife," and were interpreted by state officials to preclude same-sex couples from marriage. See, for example, Massachusetts Gen. Laws Ch. 207 § 1 & 2, 2023 (which used the gendered language of "husband" and "wife" or "man" and "woman"); *Lewis v. Harris*, 908 A.2d 196, 208, New Jersey, 2006 (which said, "Plaintiffs do not dispute that New Jersey's civil marriage statutes, New Jersey Stat. Ann. §§ 37:1–1 to 37:2–41, which were first enacted in 1912, limit marriage to heterosexual couples. That limitation is clear from the use of gender-specific language in the text of various statutes"); *Hernandez v. Robles*, 855 N.E.2d 1, 6, New York, 2006; Rhode Island Gen. Laws §§ 5-1-1 to 5-2-11, 2003 (which used the gendered language of "bride and groom" and "male" and "female"); and *Baker v. State*, 744 A.2d 864, Vermont, 1999 (which said that "the common understanding that marriage under Vermont law consists of a union between a man and a woman"). Marriage statutes in New Mexico have never been gender-specific (New Mexico Stat. § 40-1-1, 2003).

[5] These states were Alaska, Hawai'i, Nebraska, and Nevada (Alaska Const. Art. I, § 25, 1998; Hawai'i Const. Art. 1, § 23, 1998; Nebraska Const. Art. I, § 29, 2000; Nevada Const. Art. I, § 21, 2000). Hawai'i's amendment did not expressly limit marriage to different-sex couples but gave the legislature the exclusive power to determine who could marry. In effect, the amendment took the decisionmaking power away from the courts.

2003 to 2011: Legalization of Marriage for Same-Sex Couples in Several States, amid a Wave of Restrictions on Marriage in Other States

In 2003, the Massachusetts Supreme Judicial Court held in *Goodridge v. Department of Public Health* that the state constitution guaranteed same-sex couples the right to marry (*Goodridge v. Department of Public Health*, 2003). In its decision, the court wrote, "Limiting the protections, benefits, and obligations of civil marriage to opposite-sex couples violates the basic premises of liberty and equality under law protected by the Massachusetts Constitution" (*Goodridge v. Department of Public Health*, 2003, p. 342). The court delayed implementation of its decision for 180 days to give the state legislature time to prepare; in that time, opponents of marriage for same-sex couples unsuccessfully attempted to block the ruling from taking effect (*Goodridge v. Department of Public Health*, 2003, p. 344). On May 17, 2004, Massachusetts became the first state in the United States to issue legal marriage licenses to same-sex couples statewide (Belluck, 2004).[6]

After Massachusetts extended marriage to same-sex couples, efforts to bar same-sex couples from marrying intensified in other states across the country. During the 2004 presidential election, voters in 13 states approved amendments to their state constitutions that specifically barred marriage for same-sex couples, reinforcing existing statutes that defined marriage as "between one man and one woman."[7] Within four years of the *Goodridge* decision, an additional 13 states had similarly amended their constitutions to prohibit marriage between same-sex partners.[8] In 2008, the merits of recognizing or prohibiting marriage for same-sex couples were the subject of a heated national debate due to the presidential election and the passage of California's Proposition 8 (California Const. Art. 1, § 7.5, 2008), which overturned a California Supreme Court decision striking down restrictions on marriage for same-sex couples (*In re Marriage Cases*, 183 P.3d 384, California, 2008).

---

6 During this period, several efforts were made by local elected officials to grant marriage licenses to same-sex couples. For example, then–San Francisco Mayor Gavin Newsom declared marriage for same-sex couples legal on February 11, 2004. Nearly 4,000 licenses were issued in San Francisco before the California Supreme Court halted the issuing of marriage licenses to same-sex couples and then invalidated the marriages on August 12, 2004.

7 These states were Arkansas, Georgia, Kentucky, Louisiana, Michigan, Mississippi, Missouri, Montana, North Dakota, Ohio, Oklahoma, Oregon, and Utah (Arkansas Const. Amend. 83, 2004; Georgia Const. Art. 1, § IV, 2004; Kentucky Const. § 233A, 2004; Louisiana Const. Art. XII, § 15, 2004; Michigan Const. Art. 1, § 25, 2004; Mississippi Const. Art. 14, § 263A, 2004; Missouri Const. Art. 1, § 33, 2004; Montana Const. Art. XIII, § 7, 2004; North Dakota Const. Art. XI, § 28, 2004; Ohio Const. Art. XV, § 11, 2004; Oklahoma Const. Art. 2, § 35, 2004; Oregon Const. Art. XV, § 5a, 2004; Utah Const. Art. 1, § 29, 2004).

8 These states were Alabama, Arizona, California, Colorado, Florida, Idaho, Kansas, South Carolina, South Dakota, Tennessee, Texas, Virginia, and Wisconsin (Alabama Const. Art. I, § 36.03, 2006; Arizona Const. Art. XXX, § 1, 2008; California Const. Art. 1, § 7.5, 2008; Colorado Const. Art. II, § 31, 2006; Florida Const. Art. I, § 2, 2008; Idaho Const. Art. III, § 28, 2006; Kansas Const. Art. 15, § 16, 2005; South Carolina Const. Art. XVII, § 15, 2006; South Dakota Const. Art. XXI, § 9, 2006; Tennessee Const. Art. XI, § 18, 2006; Texas Const. Art. 1, § 32, 2005; Virginia Const. Art. 1, § 15-a, 2006; Wisconsin Const. Art. XIII, § 13, 2006).

By the end of 2011, more than 40 states had passed statutes prohibiting marriage for same-sex couples,[9] and the majority of states had also enacted constitutional amendments restating those prohibitions.[10] Only six states and Washington, D.C., provided marriage licenses to same-sex couples.[11]

2012 to 2014: Rapid Expansion of States Issuing Marriage Licenses to Same-Sex Couples

The national election in 2012 marked a critical turning point for legal marriage for same-sex couples. For the first time, voters in three states—Maine, Maryland, and Washington—approved measures to extend marriage to same-sex couples (Maine Question 1, 2012; Maryland Question 6, 2012; Washington, Ref. 74, 2012). Voters in Minnesota rejected an attempt to ban marriage for same-sex couples (Minnesota Amend. 1, 2012). In the first six months of 2013, five more states—Delaware, Hawai'i, Illinois, Minnesota, and Rhode Island—passed legislation extending marriage to same-sex couples, and New Jersey's Supreme Court lifted restrictions on marriage for same-sex couples in that state (79 Delaware Laws Ch. 19, 2013; Hawai'i Act 1, 2013; Illinois S.B. 10, 98th Gen. Assem., enacted, 2013; Minnesota H.B. 1054, 88th Reg. Sess., 2013; Rhode Island H.B. 5015, 2013-14 Leg. Sess., 2013; *Lewis v. Harris*, 908 A.2d 196, 2006). In less than a year, the number of states issuing marriage licenses to same-sex couples doubled.

In June 2013, the U.S. Supreme Court struck down part of the Defense of Marriage Act. In *Windsor v. United States* (2013), the Court invalidated the provisions denying federal recognition of marriages that had been validly recognized by states, ensuring that any legally married same-sex couples would have access to the same federal rights and benefits that were available to married different-sex couples. This decision ensured that the more than 1,000 federal laws that regulated marital rights and benefits would apply to the marriages of same-sex and different-sex couples equally, but it did not require states to issue marriage licenses to same-sex couples or to recognize the marriages of same-sex couples performed in other states (*Windsor v. United States*, 2013, pp. 752, 761). As a result, same-sex couples continued to face a patchwork of legal rights and protections depending on where they lived.

The Court's decision in *Windsor* paved the way for challenges to state-level bans on recognizing marriages between same-sex partners. One legal scholar tracked 21 lawsuits challenging state marriage bans filed in the second half of 2013, after *Windsor* was decided, and

[9] See states listed in footnote 4; Connecticut Legis. Serv. P.A. 05-10, S.S.B. 963, 2005; Ohio H.B. 272, 125th Gen. Assem., Reg. Sess., 2004.

[10] See states listed in footnotes 5, 7, and 8.

[11] These states were Connecticut, Iowa, Massachusetts, New Hampshire, New York, and Vermont (Ct. S.B. 899, Gen. Assem., Jan. Sess., 2009; *Varnum v. Brien*, 763 N.W.2d 862, Iowa, 2009; *Goodridge v. Department of Public Health*, 440 Mass. 309, 2003; New Hampshire H.B. 436, Gen. Ct., 161st Sess., 2009; New York A.B. 8354, 234th Leg., Ann. Sess., 2011; Vermont S. 115, 70th Bienn. Sess., 2009).

another 28 suits filed in 2014 (Kreis, 2018). After *Windsor*, same-sex couples in many states gained access to marriage as a result of federal circuit and state supreme court decisions striking down the bans.[12] By March 2015, federal judges had invalidated marriage bans in 18 states (Kowal, 2015). Some of these cases eventually made it to the Court and were consolidated in a single case, *Obergefell v. Hodges* (2015). By the time the Court heard the case, legal marriages between same-sex partners had been established by statute, court ruling, or voter initiative in the majority of states and the District of Columbia (Denniston, 2015).

2015 to the Present: Legalization of Marriage for Same-Sex Couples Nationwide

In the *Obergefell* decision, announced on June 26, 2015, the Court held that state-level bans on marriage for same-sex couples violate the Constitution of the United States, thereby extending the right to marry to same-sex couples nationwide (*Obergefell v. Hodges*, 2015). In the majority decision, Justice Anthony Kennedy wrote:

> There is dignity in the bond between two men or two women who seek to marry and in their autonomy to make such profound choices. . . . Especially against a long history of disapproval of their relationships, this denial to same-sex couples of the right to marry works a grave and continuing harm. The imposition of this disability on gays and lesbians serves to disrespect and subordinate them. And the Equal Protection Clause, like the Due Process Clause, prohibits this unjustified infringement of the fundamental right to marry. . . . No union is more profound than marriage, for it embodies the highest ideals of love, fidelity, devotion, sacrifice, and family. In forming a marital union, two people become something greater than once they were. As some of the petitioners in these cases demonstrate, marriage embodies a love that may endure even past death. It would misunderstand these men and women to say they disrespect the idea of marriage. Their plea is that they do respect it, respect it so deeply that they seek to find its fulfillment for themselves. Their hope is not to be condemned to live in loneliness, excluded from one of civilization's oldest institutions. They ask for equal dignity in the eyes of the law. The Constitution grants them that right. (*Obergefell v. Hodges*, 2015, pp. 666, 675, 681)

Since 2015, in light of the judicial rulings in *Windsor*, *Obergefell*, and other, lower court cases, some states have repealed their marriage bans (e.g., Oregon Laws 629, 2015; Virginia Acts 195, 2020; Nevada Question 2, 2022). However, 35 states still have statutory or consti-

[12] Examples are *Baskin v. Bogan*, 766 F.3d 648, 7th Cir. 2014; *Bishop v. United States*, 962 F. Supp. 2d 1252, N.D. Okla., 2014; *Bostic v. Schaefer*, 760 F.3d 352, 4th Cir., 2014; *Condon v. Haley*, 21 F. Supp. 3d 572, D. S.C., 2014; *Garden State Equality v. Dow*, 82 A. 3d 336, N.J. Super. Ct. Law Div., 2013; *Geiger v. Kitzhaber*, 994 F. Supp. 2d 1128, D. Or., 2014; *Griego v. Oliver*, 316 P. 3d 865, N.M., 2013; *Guzzo v. Mead*, No. 14-CV-200-SWS, WL 5317797, D. Wyo, 2014; *Latta v. Otter*, 771 F.3d 456, 9th Cir., 2014; and *Whitewood v. Wolf*, 992 F. Supp. 2d 410, M.D. Penn., 2014.

tutional marriage bans on the books, though none of these bans can be enforced (Movement Advancement Project, 2022).

On June 24, 2022, when the U.S. Supreme Court overturned its 1973 *Roe v. Wade* decision that protected the federal right to abortion, Justice Clarence Thomas, in a concurring opinion, explicitly suggested that the Court revisit other previous decisions that he believed were decided incorrectly, mentioning the *Obergefell* decision by name. Partially in response to Justice Thomas's concurring opinion, Congress took additional steps to protect marriage equality in 2022 by passing the Respect for Marriage Act (Pub. L. 117-228, 2022). The Respect for Marriage Act repealed the Defense of Marriage Act and required all states to recognize marriages between same-sex partners that were validly performed in other states.[13] In essence, the Respect for Marriage Act codified the *Windsor* decision, guaranteeing that same-sex couples would continue to have these protections and cross-state marriage recognition even if the *Windsor* decision were overruled in the future. As a result of these various court decisions and statutes, same-sex couples are guaranteed the right to marry in every state and have access to all state- and federal-level privileges and benefits of marriage.

Debating the Consequences of Legalizing Marriage for Same-Sex Couples

During the heated debates over the legal status of marriage for same-sex couples, many of the disputes involved competing empirical predictions about the most-likely consequences. Those in favor of legal marriage for same-sex couples argued that the social and economic effects of granting same-sex couples access to marriage would be positive, in that the ability to marry would strengthen commitment for same-sex couples, extend the financial benefits of marriage to same-sex households, and improve outcomes for children being raised by same-sex parents.

Those opposed argued that granting legal status to marriages between same-sex partners would alter the foundation of marriage and thereby diminish its value for different-sex couples, ultimately harming children by making them less likely to be raised in stable, two-parent families. Justice Samuel Alito, in his dissenting opinion on the *Obergefell* decision, voiced this perspective:

> There are those who think that allowing same-sex marriage will seriously undermine the institution of marriage. Officially abandoning the older understanding of marriage may contribute to marriage's further decay. (*Obergefell v. Hodges*, 576 U.S. 644, 2015, pp. 739–740)

[13] Pub. L. 117-228, 2022. The law does not, however, require all states to offer marriage to same-sex couples. Thus, the statute would not prohibit states from enacting and enforcing state-level marriage bans if the *Obergefell* decision were to be overruled, but it does require states to recognize marriages performed legally in another state.

Justice Thomas, in his own dissent, expressed concerns about children being raised in same-sex households:

> [Marriage] arose in the nature of things to meet a vital need: ensuring that children are conceived by a mother and father committed to raising them in the stable conditions of a lifelong relationship. . . . [F]or the good of children and society, sexual relations that can lead to procreation should occur only between a man and a woman committed to a lasting bond. (*Obergefell v. Hodges*, 576 U.S. 644, 2015, p. 689)

Other groups advocating for prohibiting marriage for same-sex couples elaborated on these arguments, predicting that "Licensing same-sex marriage severs the connection between natural procreation and marriage" and will lead to "fewer opposite-sex marriages" (*Obergefell v. Hodges*, 576 U.S. 644, 2015, p. 679). The Family Research Council (undated) developed materials suggesting that

- marriage for same-sex couples would de-gender marriage, "marriages typically thrive when spouses specialize in gender-typical ways," and "couples are less likely to divorce when the wife concentrates on childrearing and the husband concentrates on breadwinning"
- "same-sex 'marriage' would further isolate marriage from its procreative purpose" and "fosters an anti-natalist mindset that fuels population decline, which in turn puts tremendous social, political, and economic strains on the larger society"
- both parents having "a biological connection to the child would increase the likelihood that the parents would identify with the child and be willing to sacrifice for that child, and it would reduce the likelihood that either parent would abuse the child."

Considering all of these predicted negative consequences (e.g., lower rates of marriage, higher rates of divorce, harms to children), the state governments of 15 states jointly submitted a brief to the U.S. Supreme Court in the *Obergefell* case in which they warned, "the amici States . . . highlight the negative consequences that will flow from a decision that the Fourteenth Amendment compels recognition and adoption of same-sex marriage. Those consequences would be *severe, unavoidable,* and *irreversible*" (*Obergefell v. Hodges*, Brief of Louisiana, et al. as Amici Curiae, p. 13, emphasis added).

At the time that these arguments were being made, other countries had already legalized marriages between same-sex partners for a decade or more (e.g., the Netherlands in 2001, Belgium in 2003, and Canada in 2005). Since as far back as the late 1980s, several other countries throughout Europe—including Denmark (in 1989), Norway (in 1993), the United Kingdom (in 2005), and Sweden (in 2007)—had offered same-sex couples the option of entering *registered partnerships*, granting them most of the rights extended to different-sex married couples. By 2015, none of these laws had any observable effects on marriage rates among different-sex couples (Trandafir, 2014a; Trandafir, 2014b; Trandafir, 2015). Yet opponents of legalizing marriage for same-sex couples in the United States argued that the fact that granting legal recognition to same-sex couples had no effects on different-sex couples in European countries did not bear on the question of whether such effects would occur in the United States. Without reliable empirical data on the consequences of issuing marriage licenses to same-sex couples in the United States, opponents argued that granting legal status to the marriages of same-sex couples would be taking a dangerous and unacceptable risk (Sprigg, 2011).

Rationale and Organization of This Report

Upon the 20th anniversary of the first legal marriages between same-sex couples in the United States, there is no longer a lack of empirical data on the consequences of extending legal recognition to same-sex couples. On the contrary, research on the impacts of marriage between same-sex partners has been going on for longer than 20 years. This substantial literature covers a wide variety of perspectives and scholarly disciplines and an even wider variety of outcomes potentially influenced by legal recognition. Moreover, enough time has passed that there are sufficient data available to directly test how rates of marriage, divorce, and cohabitation were affected by changes in policy over the past two decades. Whereas the national debates leading up to the *Obergefell* decision in 2015 revolved around what the consequences of extending legal recognition to marriages between same-sex partners might be, the accumulated research and data can now provide a strong foundation for evaluating what the actual consequences of legal recognition for same-sex couples have been.

Thus, the overarching goal of this report is to assemble existing research and conduct new analyses that address what we can now say with confidence about the impacts of legalizing marriage between same-sex partners. We pursued this goal in two ways. First, we conducted a comprehensive review of existing empirical research on the impacts of granting legal status to same-sex couples on LGBT individuals, their children, and the general population. Second, we conducted new causal analyses that draw on multiple national datasets to evaluate how changes in marriage policy across states relate to changes in marriage rates, divorce rates, cohabitation rates, and other outcomes in the general population.

In pursuit of these goals, the rest of this report is organized into three chapters. Because the language used to describe sexuality and gender has evolved over time, this chapter ends with a box in which we explain how we selected the language used throughout this report. Chapter 2 presents the results of our review of prior research. Chapter 3 presents the results of our new analyses. Chapter 4, the concluding chapter, discusses the implications of this work for future policy and jurisprudence and highlights priorities for future research.

Notes on Language

In the past 20 years of research addressed in this report, the language scholars have used to discuss sex, sexuality, and gender has evolved substantially. The research cited in this report has used a wide variety of terms to refer to a few concepts, and some of the older articles use language that is considered imprecise, insensitive, or inaccurate today. In this box, we describe and provide a rationale for the language we have elected to use throughout the report.

Sex* vs. *gender. Throughout the social sciences, the word *sex* is typically used to refer to biological differences, whereas *gender* is used to refer to differences in identity and culturally assigned social roles. If we had been guided by this distinction, then it would have been most accurate to refer to *same-gender* and *different-gender* couples. However, because national discussions of marriage policies uniformly refer to *same-sex couples*, and because we wish the results of this report to inform those discussions, we have elected to use the language of *same-sex couples* throughout this report.

Different* vs. *opposite. If a pair of individuals who both identify with the same gender is a *same-sex couple*, what is a couple in which each partner identifies with a different gender? The commonly used term *opposite-sex couple* falsely implies that men and women are opposites and so has fallen out of favor. In this report, we use the term *different-sex couple* to contrast with *same-sex couple.*

Sexual orientation* vs. *gender identity. We acknowledge that gender identity and sexual orientation are distinct and independent concepts. Most research reviewed in this report does not directly measure sexual orientation. Thus, the fact that a couple consists of two individuals who both identify as men or two individuals who both identify as women does not mean that either partner identifies as gay or lesbian. Similarly, the fact that a couple consists of an individual who identifies as a man and an individual who identifies as a woman does not mean that either partner identifies as heterosexual. Throughout this report, we have been careful not to use terms, such as *gay marriage* or *heterosexual marriage*, that make such assumptions. Instead, the labels *gay*, *lesbian*, and *bisexual* are used only when we are describing studies that measured sexual orientation directly. In all other cases, this report refers more precisely to marriage for *same-sex couples* or *different-sex couples*, terms that focus on the gender identities of the partners and not their (unmeasured) sexual orientations.

Legal status is an umbrella term used to describe any way in which a state can grant privileges to a couple, including marriage, civil unions, and domestic partnerships. The report uses the term *legal marriage* or the phrase *issue marriage licenses* to refer to marriage specifically. Civil unions and domestic partnerships are other forms of legal status that in many states preceded legal marriage. These alternatives granted most of the same state-level rights and benefits as marriage but not the federal responsibilities or the cultural or social recognition of marriage itself.

LGBT individuals is an umbrella term used to refer broadly to people whose sexual orientation or gender identity places them in a sexual- or gender-minority group.

CHAPTER 2

Evidence Review

For decades, scholars interested in intimacy and families have examined how the gender composition of a romantic couple (i.e., a man and a woman, two women, or two men) shapes the partners' outcomes (e.g., physical health, emotional well-being, relationship stability). Over the past 20 years, this literature has been the subject of numerous systematic and scholarly reviews (Biblarz and Savci, 2010; Herek, 2006; Kurdek, 2005; Peplau and Fingerhut, 2007; Reczek, 2020), all of which have reached the same straightforward conclusion: Interpersonal processes like connection, commitment, and satisfaction are fundamentally similar and serve similar functions across same-sex and different-sex couples (e.g., Chen and van Ours, 2018; Joyner, Manning, and Prince, 2019; Rostosky and Riggle, 2017). When differences between same-sex and different-sex couples are observed, they arise primarily because LGBT individuals, on average, confront challenging circumstances (e.g., stigma, discrimination) that heterosexual cisgender individuals do not (Frost, Fingerhut, and Meyer, 2022).

For most of the history of this research, same-sex couples were prevented from marrying. As legal marriage gradually became available to same-sex couples, scholars were able to ask new questions about the consequences of such policy changes. This new research focused less on comparisons between same-sex and different-sex couples and more on differences between the outcomes of same-sex couples granted access to marriage and those prohibited from marrying (a comparison across states) or on differences between same-sex couples before and after access to marriage was granted or withheld (a comparison across time).

To date, the consequences of extending or withholding marriage for same-sex couples have been studied in three different populations: (1) same-sex couples and LGBT individuals (e.g., how has the availability of marriage affected same-sex couples?), (2) children being raised by same-sex couples (e.g., are children affected when their same-sex parents have access to or are prevented from marrying?), and (3) the general population (e.g., are different-sex couples affected when same-sex couples obtain the right to marry?). In each of these groups, research has examined the possible impacts of marriage for same-sex couples on several outcomes, including

- mental health (e.g., rates of depression, life satisfaction)
- couple well-being (e.g., the quality and stability of intimate relationships)
- physical health (e.g., rates of sexually transmitted infections [STIs])
- access to health insurance

are consistent with the idea that changes in policy cause changes in outcomes, but they are subject to alternative explanations as well if the outcome being measured is already changing over time. To evaluate the causal effects of changes in policy on changes in outcomes, there exists a powerful design known as a *difference-in-differences* approach (Lechner, 2011). This analytic technique, originating in econometrics, exploits differences in the timing of a policy change across states to compare changes in outcomes in states that enacted a change in policy with changes in those same outcomes in states that did not enact a change in policy, thereby estimating the causal influence of those changes on other time-varying variables. More than one-quarter of the studies in this review (26 percent) employed a difference-in-differences approach.

Many of the studies identified in this review also make use of large national datasets, including the U.S. Census Bureau's American Community Survey (ACS), the Bureau of Labor Statistics' Current Population Survey (CPS), the Centers for Disease Control and Prevention's (CDC's) National Health Interview Survey (NHIS), and Gallup polls, as well as online samples, medical records, and financial data. One advantage of drawing on datasets such as these is that their large sample size provides sufficient statistical power to detect smaller effects if they exist. Another advantage is that these datasets are generally weighted to be representative of the general population. A noteworthy disadvantage of these datasets, especially for the purposes of the current review, is that they generally do not ask about respondents' sexual orientation, leaving scholars who are using these datasets having to infer sexual orientation from the gender composition of a couple. An additional challenge, for scholars focused on assessing impacts on different-sex couples and non-LGBT individuals, is that the sex and/or gender of the respondent's partner is not tracked in some datasets, making it difficult to focus analyses on particular subpopulations. (For more details about the characteristics of the data sources most commonly used to address issues related to same-sex couples and households, see Appendix C).

As shown in Figure 2.1, publication rates for research on the consequences of granting legal status to the marriages of same-sex couples have increased steadily over the past 20 years. Of the studies we identified, 70 percent were published after 2015, reflecting increased interest in understanding the consequences of allowing same-sex couples to marry after the *Obergefell* decision lifted restrictions on marriage between same-sex partners throughout the country.

The articles we reviewed can be divided into three categories based on the populations they assess: research on LGBT individuals or same-sex couples, research on the children of same-sex couples, and research on the general population. Within these three groups of studies, articles were grouped by theme according to the outcomes assessed in each study. These themes range widely, from psychological outcomes obtained through self-reports to economic and demographic trends derived from census data. In the rest of this chapter, we summarize and evaluate the accumulated research grouped by population and outcome categories. Because several of the studies included in this review assess outcomes that fall into multiple categories, those studies appear multiple times in the text and tables that follow.

FIGURE 2.1
Frequency Histogram of Publication Dates of Reviewed Studies

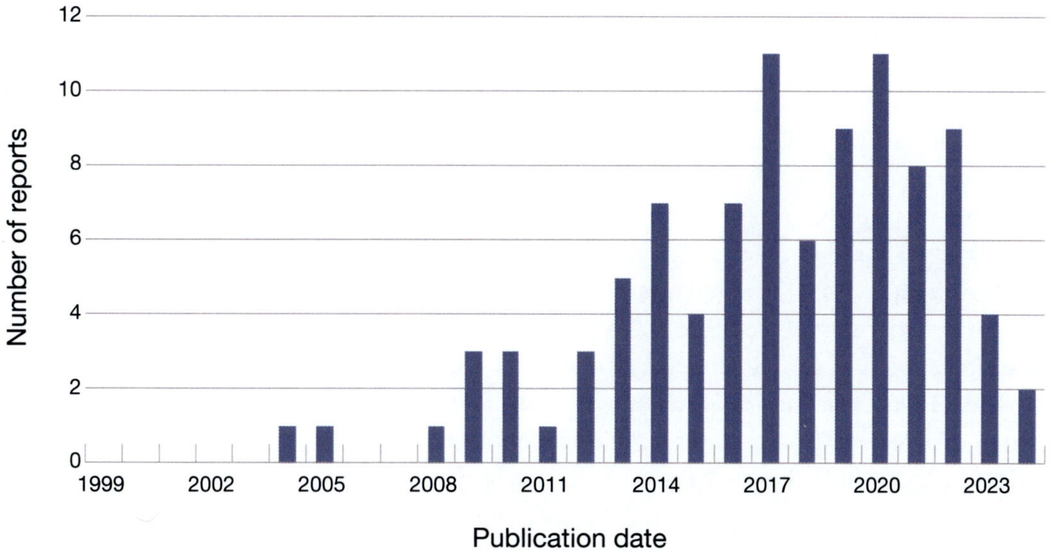

The Impact of Legal Marriage for Same-Sex Couples on Same-Sex Couples and LGBT Individuals

Same-sex couples and LGBT individuals are the populations most directly affected by laws and policies granting or withholding legal marriage for same-sex couples. Accordingly, most research on the consequences of these laws and policies has focused on the consequences for these populations. Of the 96 studies identified by our review, 66 of them (69 percent) addressed the experiences of same-sex couples or LGBT individuals. Because these studies assessed a wide variety of specific outcomes, we organized them into seven broad themes: psychological well-being, couple well-being, physical health, health insurance coverage, employment outcomes, financial well-being, and social connection. We summarize and evaluate the research on each of these themes in the subsections that follow.

Impacts on Psychological Well-Being

Key Points

- Marriage for same-sex couples is consistently associated with greater psychological well-being among LGBT individuals through heightened positive mood, lower stress, fewer depressive symptoms, and increased life satisfaction.
- When states banned or proposed bans on marriage between same-sex partners, LGBT residents of those states reported higher anxiety, stress, depression, and negative mood and experienced increased rates of multiple psychiatric disorders.
- Legal access to marriage for same-sex couples facilitates coming out and decreases identity concealment among LGBT individuals.

Theoretical Background

The dominant theoretical frameworks guiding research on the association between legal marriage and psychological well-being for LGBT individuals are minority stress theory and social stress theory. Minority stress theory posits that the stigma and discrimination experienced by members of minority groups negatively affect mental health, because the process of navigating a prejudicial environment produces internalized stigma, creates isolation, and demands taxing coping strategies (Meyer, 2003). Social stress theory makes the similar assertion that social disadvantage puts people at greater risk for experiencing stressful events even as it depletes their psychosocial coping resources to address stress (Aneshensel, Rutter, and Lachenbruch, 1991). LGBT individuals in the United States experience stigma and discrimination and are at increased risk for mental health disorders, including depression, anxiety, substance use, and suicide attempts (Plöderl and Tremblay, 2015).

From this perspective, the availability of legal marriage to same-sex couples has the potential to influence rates of mental health disorders and affect well-being and happiness among LGBT individuals. Whereas bans on marriage between same-sex partners are a prejudicial event that can heighten internalized homophobia and the need to conceal sexual identity, access to marriage creates a supportive policy environment that validates same-sex relationships. Our review identified 26 studies that examined policies toward marriage for same-sex couples and psychological well-being among LGBT individuals (see Table B.1). Most focused on legal marriage, civil unions, or domestic partnerships, but three studies also assessed how bans or proposed bans on marriage between same-sex partners relate to mental health. Jointly, these studies assessed the years 1997 to 2017; 15 reports collected data prior to the *Obergefell v. Hodges* decision, and the remaining ten include time points after the *Obergefell* decision.

Cross-Sectional Studies

Of the studies we identified, ten used cross-sectional designs to compare individuals in relationships with legal status with individuals who are unmarried or unpartnered. In general, these studies found that individuals in same-sex relationships with legal status experience greater psychological well-being than those in relationships without legal status. For example, individuals in same-sex relationships with any kind of legal status experienced fewer depressive symptoms than those in committed same-sex relationships without legal status even after controlling for other factors known to be associated with depression (Riggle, Rostosky, and Horne, 2010). Wight et al. (2012) replicated this result in a survey of sexual-minority men and found that both marriage and domestic partnership were associated with fewer depressive symptoms. In research on cognitive impairment among aging adults, individuals in same-sex couples typically experience greater rates of cognitive impairment than individuals in different-sex married couples, but this difference is nearly eliminated when same-sex couples are legally married (Liu et al., 2021).

Being in a relationship with legal status may lower internalized stigma and experienced discrimination by increasing social acceptance of the relationship and of LGBT identities. Individuals in same-sex relationships with any kind of legal status reported less internalized homophobia and lower stress levels than those in committed relationships without legal status (Riggle, Rostosky, and Horne, 2010; Wight et al., 2012). Analyses of a small sample assessed in 2010 and 2012 found similar results: Married individuals in same-sex relationships reported greater awareness of sexism and a higher likelihood of joining an LGBT movement (Swank, 2022).

Legal relationship status may also act as a buffer from the negative impacts of stress. Whereas increases in internalized stressors, such as shame and guilt about sexual identity, were associated with lower life satisfaction for individuals in same-sex couples with no legal status, increases in these stressors did not relate to life satisfaction for individuals in same-sex domestic partnerships (Fingerhut and Maisel, 2010). A more recent cross-sectional survey using data from 2013 to 2016 found that, because being married is associated with better mental health regardless of sexual orientation, mental health disparities between sexual-minority and heterosexual individuals could be partially explained by lower rates of marriage among LGBT individuals, although this mediation effect was true only for bisexual men, bisexual women, and lesbian women, and not for gay men (Hsieh, 2019).

Although any legal relationship status for same-sex couples is associated with better mental health, two cross-sectional studies suggest that marriage in particular is associated with benefits over and above other forms of legal status. In a survey conducted just after the *Obergefell v. Hodges* decision, married same-sex couples reported lower perceived unequal recognition, lower depressive symptoms, and lower psychological distress than same-sex couples in a domestic partnership or civil union (LeBlanc, Frost, and Bowen, 2018). Similarly, members of married same-sex couples in California in 2009 showed less psychological distress than lesbian, gay, and bisexual individuals not in relationships with legal status, while those in same-sex domestic partnerships did not differ from those not in relationships with legal status (Wight, LeBlanc, and Badgett, 2013).

Multiple studies found consistent evidence that legally partnered or married same-sex couples report higher levels of positive affect and well-being than those in relationships without legal status. Surveys comparing individuals in marriages or domestic partnerships with those in committed same-sex relationships without legal status show that individuals with legal relationship status reported greater positive affect, perceived more meaning in life, and had better quality of life (Goldsen et al., 2017; Riggle, Rostosky, and Horne, 2010; Wight et al., 2012). Sexual-minority women who were in relationships perceived more positive impacts of legal marriage than their single counterparts did, and women who identified as "lesbian" were more likely than those who identified as "queer" or "something else" to report positive impacts (Drabble et al., 2022).

Although the results of cross-sectional research have been consistent across studies, the well-known limits of cross-sectional comparisons prevent them from supporting strong conclusions. In particular, it is possible that the cross-sectional differences observed in these studies stem from a selection effect—that is, the fact that people with better mental health and greater psychosocial resources are more likely to marry and stay married (Mastekaasa, 1992; Stutzer and Frey, 2006). Stronger conclusions about the causal effects of legal recognition for same-sex couples require research that compares the well-being of LGBT individuals across policy environments, using repeated surveys or longitudinal studies that include assessments before and after changes in relationship recognition policy. We now turn to studies that use those designs.

Comparisons Across Policy Environments

Multiple studies have taken advantage of historical differences in states' relationship recognition policies to compare the well-being of LGBT residents in states with different policy environments. As a whole, these studies show that supportive policy environments benefit LGBT mental health, whereas bans on marriage for same-sex couples have a negative impact. Many of these studies focus on statewide bans on marriage between same-sex partners to identify associations between legal restrictions on same-sex couples and psychological outcomes among LGBT individuals. For example, in a cross-sectional survey conducted during the 2006 election season, LGBT individuals who resided in states with proposed marriage bans reported higher anxiety, negative affect, stress, and depressive symptoms than residents of states without bans or with prior enacted bans (Riggle, Rostosky, and Horne, 2009). However, proposed bans are likely highly correlated with the state policy environment; there may be related proposals or extant legislation that also contributes to negative affect. Nevertheless, in another pre-*Obergefell* study, LGBT residents of states with marriage bans for same-sex couples reported higher anxiety and lower life satisfaction than residents of states without bans even after controlling for other elements of the state political climate (Tatum, 2017).

In a survey of sexual-minority men across different state policy environments, Bauermeister (2014) found that state marriage bans moderated the association between fatherhood aspirations and well-being: For sexual-minority men in states with marriage bans, greater fatherhood aspirations were associated with lower self-esteem and higher depressive symptoms, while for their counterparts in states that granted legal statuses to same-sex couples, greater fatherhood aspirations were associated with higher self-esteem.

Before marriage between same-sex partners became legal nationwide, couples could cross state lines to obtain marriage licenses yet still reside in states in which their marriages were not recognized. This discrepancy in recognition negatively influenced well-being: Legally married same-sex couples residing in states that did not recognize their marriages reported greater negative affect than married couples who lived in states in which their marriages were recognized (Kennedy and Dalla, 2020). Residing in a state that recognized marriage between same-sex partners also prompted residents to conceal their identities less and be more "out" than residents of states without legal recognition (de Vries et al., 2009; Riggle et al., 2017). This decrease in identity concealment was also reflected in lower reported vigilance and perceived isolation for individuals in same-sex relationships in states with legal marriage compared with those in states without any form of legal relationship status (Riggle et al., 2017). Finally, among lesbian and gay baby boomers, one study found no relationship between state recognition policy and concerns about aging or end-of-life preparations (de Vries et al., 2009).

Results from Repeated Surveys

Two studies employed a repeated survey design to assess changes in psychological well-being over time as relationship recognition policies changed. An early repeated survey study conducted between 2002 and 2004 used clinic billing records to assess mental health care visits and costs before and after Massachusetts began issuing marriage licenses to same-sex couples (Hatzenbuehler et al., 2012). At a health clinic focused on serving sexual minorities, there was a 13-percent decrease in mental health care visits and a 14-percent decrease in mental health care costs for sexual-minority men in the 12 months following legalization compared with the 12 months before the policy, and these effects were similar across relationship statuses. In a study examining the *Obergefell* decision, a greater percentage of LGBT individuals who participated in a Gallup survey reported feeling happy and showed higher life satisfaction two weeks following the decision compared with two weeks before the decision (Flores, Mallory, and Conron, 2020). These gains in life satisfaction were highest for individuals who resided in states in which marriage was not previously legal.

By examining multiple years of state-level data, two studies examined whether changes in legal recognition for same-sex couples lead to changes in rates of suicide attempts and ideation among LGBT adolescents. The first study examined adolescent suicide attempts between 1999 and 2015 and found that legal marriage for same-sex couples was associated with a 7-percent reduction in the proportion of high school students who attempted suicide, even after controlling for state, age, and race and ethnicity (Raifman et al., 2017). This result was most concentrated among LGBT adolescents. A second study found no evidence that legalizing marriage for same-sex couples decreased the probability of suicide planning and suicidal ideation among LGBT youth (Anderson, Matsuzawa, and Sabia, 2021). Taken together, these studies suggest that the mechanisms behind the potential association between marriage for same-sex couples and youth suicidal ideation remain an open question. While Anderson, Matsuzawa, and Sabia speculate that the debate surrounding changes in policy created a heightened awareness of stigmatized identity, Raifman and colleagues provide strong evidence that legal marriage for same-sex couples reduced overall youth suicidal behavior (Anderson, Matsuzawa, and Sabia, 2021; Raifman et al., 2017).

Results from Longitudinal Analyses

The most rigorous way to assess the effect of legal recognition of same-sex couples is by assessing a sample of the same individuals at time points before and after changes in relationship recognition policy. One multi-wave longitudinal study using nationally representative data with time points encapsulating many of the passed state bans on marriage for same-sex couples (2001 to 2005) found that lesbian, gay, and bisexual individuals who resided in states that banned marriage experienced increases in generalized anxiety disorder, any mood disorder, any alcohol use disorder, and psychiatric comorbidity (Hatzenbuehler et al., 2010). These disorders did not increase for lesbian, gay, and bisexual residents of states without marriage bans. In a study assessing well-being of sexual-minority women between 2000 and 2012, legislation recognizing same-sex civil unions was associated with lower stigma consciousness, lower perceived discrimination, and lower depressive symptoms compared with pre-legislation levels (Everett, Hatzenbuehler, and Hughes, 2016). These well-being benefits were most concentrated among women who had lower levels of education or were racial or ethnic minorities.

Two 2019 longitudinal reports by Ogolsky and colleagues examined well-being and perceptions of stigma among individuals in same-sex relationships before and after the *Obergefell* decision. The change in life satisfaction before and after *Obergefell* among individuals in same-sex relationships differed depending on their levels of internalized homophobia. For individuals who reported high levels of internalized stigma, isolation, and vicarious trauma, life satisfaction increased after the decision, whereas those who already reported low levels of these negative measures of well-being did not experience much change in life satisfaction following the decision (Ogolsky et al., 2019b). A second study demonstrated that levels of felt stigma decreased over the year following the *Obergefell* decision for individuals in same-sex relationships (Ogolsky et al., 2019a).

Finally, two studies conducted over multiple years suggest that relationship recognition policies facilitate coming out as a sexual minority. Longitudinal data from the Nurses' Health Study II show that women who reported being heterosexual in 1995 were 30 percent more likely to report being bisexual or lesbian in 2009 if they lived in a state that enacted some form of legal relationship recognition (Charlton et al., 2016). A difference-in-differences analysis of enrollment in Catholic seminaries found that city-level enrollment decreased roughly 15 percent in states that adopted legal marriage for same-sex couples (Seror and Ticku, 2021). Because of the vow of celibacy associated with becoming a Catholic priest, gay men may select into seminary studies at higher rates than heterosexual men to avoid the potential pressures of adopting a heterosexual lifestyle. Thus, one possible explanation for these findings is that coming-out decisions are facilitated by policy on legal marriage for same-sex couples, thereby making gay men less motivated to enroll in priestly studies.

Conclusions

What happens to the mental health of LGBT individuals after legal marriage for same-sex couples becomes available? Research conducted over the past two decades reveals that LGBT individuals experienced a variety of beneficial effects on their mental health and emotional well-being, and these results were replicated across a variety of study designs, including cross-sectional comparisons, repeated surveys, and longitudinal studies. In contrast, actual and proposed legal bans on marriage for same-sex couples were associated with greater prevalence of multiple psychiatric disorders and heightened stress and anxiety among LGBT individuals. Through the lens of minority stress theory, these effects are consistent with the notion that bans on legal relationship statuses can further disadvantage LGBT individuals, whereas legal marriage contributes to a supportive environment that can buffer the effects of social stress. An important open question in this line of research is how long these benefits to mental health endure following a change in policy. The psychological benefits discussed in the literature may stem from the sudden impact of policy change rather than the more enduring effect of being in a relationship with legal status. There have been relatively few longitudinal studies or difference-in-differences analyses—the most-rigorous designs—to address this distinction, and the studies we reviewed do not include extended follow-up periods after policies were enacted.

Impacts on Couple Well-Being

Key Points

- The relationships of married same-sex couples are more stable than those of cohabiting same-sex couples.
- As a group, same-sex couples with any legal status dissolve their relationships at the same rate as married different-sex couples, but couples consisting of two women are more likely to dissolve than couples consisting of two men.
- Marriage increases investment in the relationship, and married same-sex couples report greater relationship satisfaction and commitment compared with unmarried same-sex couples.
- Couples consisting of two women take up marriage at higher rates than couples consisting of two men and are more likely to increase specialization of household and caregiving labor in response to relationship recognition policies.

Theoretical Background

Studies examining the impact of the availability of legal marriage on the well-being of same-sex intimate relationships have mostly been guided by the hypothesis that the benefits of marriage for different-sex couples generalize to same-sex couples. Among different-sex couples, marriage decreases the risk of relationship dissolution, incentivizes investment in the relationship, and is associated with higher relationship quality compared with cohabitation (Brown and Booth, 1996; Goodwin, Mosher, and Chandra, 2010). This literature suggests that when same-sex couples are given the opportunity to marry, their relationships should also become more stable. Furthermore, legal relationship status may help ameliorate the unique minority stressors that constrain same-sex couples' ability to build and sustain high-quality intimate relationships (Meyer, 2003; Rostosky and Riggle, 2017). Therefore, same-sex couples stand to benefit from legal marriage. It is also possible that merely living in an environment that acknowledges and supports same-sex relationships may benefit couple well-being in same-sex couples, regardless of whether those couples decide to marry.

Our review identified 13 studies that examined the effects of legal relationship recognition on the intimate relationships of LGBT individuals (see Table B.2). These studies used cross-sectional and longitudinal designs to examine how access to legal relationship statuses affected relationship stability, satisfaction, communication, and division of labor in same-sex couples. Four of these studies focused on civil unions or domestic partnerships, three of them examined the effects of any form of legal recognition (including marriage), and the other six focused exclusively on marriage or marriage bans.

Early Studies

The first series of studies in the United States to examine same-sex couples in relationships with legal status began shortly after Vermont became the first state to legalize civil unions in 2000. The members of this initial sample of same-sex couples with civil unions were recontacted multiple times and eventually provided data for four studies that used cross-sectional and longitudinal methods. In the first study in this series, same-sex couples who obtained civil unions in the first year they were available were contacted, and their relationships were compared with those of their friends in same-sex relationships without civil unions and their siblings in different-sex marriages (Solomon, Rothblum, and Balsam, 2004). In this study, men in same-sex relationships who did not have civil unions were more likely to report having considered or discussed ending the relationship compared with men in civil unions. Women with civil unions did not differ from those without civil unions on any of the relationship measures. A second report examining this sample focused on division of labor and negotiations about sex and conflict among these couples (Solomon, Rothblum, and Balsam, 2005). Men in civil unions reported being more egalitarian in bringing up issues within the relationship, including negotiating sex, than men not in civil unions and men married to women. Women in same-sex civil unions did not differ from those in same-sex relationships without civil unions on any variables, including conflict resolution practices, negotiations of sex, and other relationship maintenance behaviors.

In a three-year follow-up study with this sample, the same-sex couples without civil unions were more likely to have broken up than same-sex couples in civil unions and married different-sex couples, and there were no differences in dissolution rates between same-sex civil unions and different-sex marriages (Balsam et al., 2008). This study also found no differences in relationship quality between same-sex couples with civil unions and same-sex couples without civil unions. In 2013, the members of this sample were recontacted and combined with a sample of their LGBT friends: Married individuals in a same-sex couple reported higher support from their partner compared with unmarried individuals in same-sex relationships (Riggle et al., 2017). The results from these initial studies suggest that, as with different-sex marriage, legal relationship status for same-sex couples promotes relationship stability. However, because these studies used the same limited sample, we next review the other studies in this area to assess the generalizability of the results.

Cross-Sectional Studies

Five studies used a cross-sectional design to compare the well-being of same-sex couples with and without marital status or living in different policy environments. In an assessment of same-sex couples in California in 2007, those in domestic partnerships reported greater investment in their relationships compared with those without legal recognition (Fingerhut and Maisel, 2010). Domestic partnership status was not associated with relationship satisfaction, but couples who had some form of social recognition, such as a public ceremony, were more satisfied than those without social recognition. A pre-*Obergefell* analysis across policy environments found that married same-sex couples who lived in a state that recognized their marriages did not differ in relationship well-being from married same-sex couples who lived in a state that did not recognize their marriages. However, living in a state without legal marriage did negatively affect their individual psychological well-being (Kennedy and Dalla, 2020).

Two 2022 studies by Haas and Lannutti explored relationship maintenance behaviors, sex, and monogamy among married and unmarried same-sex couples. The first study demonstrated that married couples reported greater commitment, relationship satisfaction, and perceived closeness than unmarried couples, whereas unmarried couples reported greater sexual satisfaction (Haas and Lannutti, 2022a). Rates of nonmonogamy agreements did not depend on marital status. In the second study, partners in married same-sex couples reported more frequently exchanging advice with each other and were less likely than unmarried couples to rely on assurances about the relationship as a tool for strengthening the relationship (Haas and Lannutti, 2022b).

Although the results of these cross-sectional studies support the notion that married couples are more satisfied and committed than unmarried couples, it is possible that these conclusions are not a direct result of legal recognition but rather are due to a selection effect that has been previously described in the marriage literature: Couples who are more satisfied with and committed to their relationships are more likely to choose to marry (Stutzer and Frey, 2006). Longitudinal studies permit more-robust conclusions about the direct effects of relationship recognition. Next, we examine the studies that employed this design.

Longitudinal Studies

Two longitudinal studies analyzed data from the How Couples Meet and Stay Together survey and showed that rates of relationship dissolution for same-sex couples with any legal recognition do not differ from—or are lower than—dissolution rates for different-sex couples. In the first analysis, couples were assessed between 2009 and 2012. The rate of dissolution for same-sex couples was lower than that for different-sex couples after controlling for marriage and marriage-like unions. Controlling for relationship quality did not change the significant association between marriage and relationship stability (Rosenfeld, 2014). A second study analyzing these data from 2009 to 2015 replicated these results and found that receiving any form of legal status was associated with reduced risk of relationship dissolution in comparison with cohabitation. Dissolution rates of legal unions between two women were higher than those of unions between two men or between a man and a woman, but same-sex couples with legal status, as a group, did not differ from different-sex unions in risk for breakup (Ketcham and Bennett, 2019). These results suggest that sexual-minority women may have a lower threshold for formalizing a relationship than men. Both studies using these data found that couples consisting of two women formalize their relationships at significantly higher rates than couples consisting of two men or a man and a woman (Ketcham and Bennett, 2019; Rosenfeld, 2014). A third analysis using repeated survey data confirmed these results and found that couples consisting of two women were more likely to register for legal status than couples consisting of two men (Bernstein, Naples, and Harvey, 2016).

A 2019 difference-in-differences analysis of division of labor found that, in response to marriage legalization for same-sex couples, women in same-sex couples reduced their annual paid labor by 6 percent and redistributed those hours to household and caregiving labor (Hansen, Martell, and Roncolato, 2020). This effect was driven by secondary earners increasing their daily household labor and caregiving labor by roughly 60 minutes and 70 minutes, respectively. These results suggest that access to legal relationship status incentivizes further investment in the relationship, and the stability that marriage affords allows couples to specialize in either paid labor outside the home or child-rearing and household labor. These changes were not observed in couples consisting of two men. A third longitudinal study that examined the impact of banning marriage for same-sex couples on relationship stability between 2008 and 2013 reached a similar conclusion, finding that same-sex and different-sex cohabiting couples who lived in a state with such a ban were more likely to break up than those living in states without bans (Manning, Brown, and Stykes, 2016).

Conclusions

Does access to legal relationship recognition improve same-sex intimate relationships? These studies strongly support the hypothesis that the benefits of legal recognition identified in the different-sex marriage literature extend to same-sex couples. Dissolution rates for married same-sex couples are indistinguishable from those for different-sex couples, and couples with legal status reported greater relationship satisfaction and commitment. These studies also offer nuanced insights into how same-sex couples respond to relationship recognition based on couple gender composition. The early studies observed changes in relationship maintenance and communication among men in same-sex civil unions but not among women, and, following legalization of marriage for same-sex couples, couples consisting of two women were more likely to reallocate housework and caregiving labor to be more specialized. Therefore, the impact of marriage on division of labor and communication among couples with different gender and sexual orientation compositions may be a promising avenue for future research.

Impacts on Physical Health

Key Points

- Legal marriage for same-sex couples is associated with increases in health care use and improvements in patient-provider communication among LGBT individuals.
- Improvements in physical well-being following the availability of marriage are more robust for sexual-minority men than for sexual-minority women.
- STI rates decreased in states with legal marriage for same-sex couples and increased in states with bans on marriage for same-sex couples.
- Legal relationship recognition of same-sex couples is protective against problematic or disordered substance use.

Theoretical Background

LGBT individuals experience physical health disparities relative to heterosexual and cisgender individuals: They experience increased risk for cancer, cardiovascular disease, and other chronic conditions, such as diabetes (Lick, Durso, and Johnson, 2013). The minority stress literature explains these disparities as the result of stress caused by repeated experiences of stigma and prejudice (Frost, Lehavot, and Meyer, 2015). Sexual orientation has also been identified as a social determinant of health that constrains the resources and opportunities on which individuals are able to draw to maintain good health (Logie, 2012). Marriage, however, has been consistently linked to improved physical health and lower mortality (Johnson et al., 2000; Kiecolt-Glaser and Newton, 2001). A stable marriage can provide social support, improve financial stability, and reduce risky behaviors, all of which lead to downstream positive effects on physical well-being.

Taken together, the minority stress literature and the marriage literature suggest that the health disparities experienced by LGBT individuals could be partially alleviated by legal marriage for same-sex couples in two ways: through more-stable intimate relationships and through improved community and health care support. The increased relationship stability and validation provided by legal relationship status may reduce risky behavior, and changes in relationship recognition policy may improve LGBT individuals' interactions with the health care system. While health care coverage can improve directly, through eligibility for a spouse's employer-sponsored health insurance (see the "Impacts on Health Insurance Coverage" section, later in this chapter), the change in policy might also shift perceived community attitudes and motivate LGBT individuals to seek care that they previously would not have sought: That is, living in a supportive policy environment might encourage LGBT individuals to be more comfortable seeking health care and communicating openly with their providers. Our review identified 16 studies that examined the implications of legal relationship recognition on the physical well-being of LGBT individuals (see Table B.3). These studies report on four main clusters of outcomes: self-assessed general health, health care use, safe sex and STIs, and trends in substance use.

Self-Assessed General Health

Research on associations between legal status for same-sex relationships and self-reported health among LGBT individuals has been inconsistent, but the weight of the evidence indicates that legal status is associated with better self-reported health. Three cross-sectional studies that examine how LGBT individuals rate their own health provide preliminary evidence that access to marriage is associated with greater physical well-being. For example, in surveys conducted between 2010 and 2013, individuals in same-sex relationships who lived in states with legal marriage reported better health than those living in states with marriage bans, whereas individuals living in states with only civil unions or domestic partnerships available did not differ significantly from those living in states with bans (Kail, Acosta, and Wright, 2015). An analysis of older individuals between 2008 and 2019 found that in states in which marriage for same-sex couples had been legal for longer (at least five years), individuals in same-sex couples were less likely to report activity limitations—including difficulties with daily self-care, walking, or living independently—than those living in states in which marriage was not legal (Brodoff, Hiedemann, and Xue, 2024). In terms of marital status, this study found that married same-sex couples were less likely than their cohabiting counterparts to report activity limitations. Another survey of self-reported health found that married lesbian, gay, and bisexual individuals reported better health than their unmarried counterparts, but this marital advantage was no longer significant after adjusting for controls (Solazzo, Gorman, and Denney, 2020).

In three other studies, this association between legal relationship status and greater self-rated health was found to be more robust for sexual-minority men than for sexual-minority women. For example, a study comparing outcomes in varying policy environments found that only sexual-minority men who lived in states with "limited protections"—that is, states without legal marriage for same-sex couples; without hate crime protections; or without nondiscrimination laws regarding employment, housing, or public accommodations—were more likely than their heterosexual counterparts to report "poor" or "fair" health. In contrast, sexual-minority women overall were more likely than their heterosexual counterparts to report poor or fair health regardless of policy environment (Gonzales and Ehrenfeld, 2018). A cross-sectional survey of aging LGBT adults similarly found that married men reported better general health compared with unmarried partnered men and single men, whereas both married and unmarried partnered women reported better health and lower rates of physical disability than single women, suggesting no specific advantage of marriage over other committed relationships for these women (Goldsen et al., 2017). The third study found that lesbian women in relationships with any kind of legal status were less likely than married heterosexual women to report "good" or "excellent health" (Elwood et al., 2017), suggesting that women's health may not benefit as much from legal recognition of their relationships.

A final study on this association examined data spanning 2000 to 2017 and found no changes in self-reported health among individuals in same-sex households (Carpenter et al., 2021), despite the legalization of marriage for same-sex couples occurring during this period.

Together, these general assessments of health provide an initial picture of how legal marriage may improve well-being. The specific behaviors and mechanisms that may be driving these changes in reported general health are explored in the studies we review next.

Health Care Use

Four studies examined physical well-being through an analysis of LGBT individuals' use of health care and interactions with health care professionals. In a study conducted before and after Massachusetts began issuing marriage licenses to same-sex couples in 2004, a health care clinic focused on serving LGBT individuals experienced a decrease in medical health care visits and costs for sexual-minority men compared with the 12 months before the change in policy (Hatzenbuehler et al., 2012). This effect was not modified by relationship or marital status. In contrast, recent studies suggest that the availability of marriage for same-sex couples improves quality of care and encourages LGBT individuals to make regular visits to health care providers. Sexual-minority men who lived in states with legal marriage for same-sex couples reported better patient-doctor communication compared with men living in states without legal recognition: Men in states with legal marriage felt more comfortable discussing with their health care providers whether they had had sex with men and were more likely to have discussed unprotected sex with a man and HIV-prevention strategies with their providers (Skinner et al., 2023). In another survey, gay men in same-sex relationships with any kind of legal status were more likely to report visiting a doctor in the previous 12 months than gay men who were either unpartnered or in relationships without legal status, and gay men in relationships with legal status were more likely than their heterosexual counterparts to report a usual source of medical care (Elwood et al., 2017).

These clear improvements in health care use for sexual-minority men are not as robustly observed in samples of sexual-minority women. For instance, legal relationship status was not associated with visiting a doctor in the past year for lesbian women, and lesbian women in same-sex relationships with legal status continued to report delays in filling prescriptions, were less likely to have had a recent mammogram, and were less likely to report having a usual source of health care compared with heterosexual married women (Elwood et al., 2017). A difference-in-differences analysis using data spanning from 2000 to 2017 also did not find meaningful changes in health care use or outcomes for women in same-sex households following legal marriage for same-sex couples, but it found that men in same-sex households showed increases in reporting a usual source of care (a 3.9–percentage point increase) and seeing a provider in the past year (a 6.6–percentage point increase) (Carpenter et al., 2021).

Safe Sex and STIs

Studies analyzing STI rates support the hypothesis that legal relationship recognition policies decrease risky sex. A difference-in-differences analysis of STIs in 16 states between 2007 and 2015 found that marriage legalization for same-sex couples was associated with both an immediate and a longer-term (one-year post-policy) decrease in visits to emergency rooms for STIs (Aftab and Imanpour, 2022). The decrease in STI-related visits to emergency rooms was most concentrated among patients ages 18–24, who saw an 8.5-percent decrease. Nikolaou (2023) also observed a decrease in STIs following legal marriage for same-sex couples in an analysis of rates in the general population (see the "Impacts on Public Health" section in this chapter). A cross-sectional survey across different state policy environments found that sexual-minority men who lived in a state with legal marriage for same-sex couples reported greater awareness and use of pre-exposure prophylaxis (PrEP), a medicine that reduces risk of contracting HIV through sex, compared with those who lived in a state without recognition (Skinner et al., 2023). The difference in PrEP awareness between states with and without legal marriage for same-sex couples remained significant even after adjustments for race and ethnicity, age, education, income, and health insurance.

In contrast, in an analysis of CDC data across states between 2000 and 2012, bans on marriage and civil unions for same-sex couples were associated with an increase in syphilis, an STI concentrated among the LGBT population; there was no association between these bans and rates of gonorrhea, an infection concentrated among heterosexual individuals (Francis, Mialon, and Peng, 2012). In other words, marriage bans seemed to increase risky sexual behavior among LGBT individuals but seemed to have no effect on risky sexual behavior among heterosexual individuals. Although the association between these bans and syphilis infections is small, the results remained significant even after implementation of controls to address alternative hypotheses, such as state sex education programs, drug arrest rates, visibility of the LGBT community, and access to antiretroviral therapy to treat HIV.

Trends in Substance Use

Compared with heterosexual individuals, LGBT individuals are at increased risk for substance use (McCabe et al., 2009). Research on marriage among different-sex couples has repeatedly shown that marriage is protective against substance use (Duncan, Wilkerson, and England, 2006). Our review identified five studies that examined the link between the availability of marriage or other legal relationship statuses and substance use among LGBT individuals and same-sex couples. Individuals in marriages with same-sex partners reported lower alcohol consumption than their cohabiting counterparts, same-sex married couples reported similar levels of alcohol use as different-sex married couples (Reczek, Liu, and Spiker, 2014), and individuals in same-sex relationships without legal status reported higher rates of "problematic drinking" than those who were married (LeBlanc, Frost, and Bowen, 2018). For sexual-minority women assessed before and after the passage of civil union legislation in Illinois in 2011, "adverse drinking consequences" (including driving under the influence, drinking-related arguments, and drinking-related accidents) were lower after the legislation passed than before, although there were no changes in other drinking indicators, such as heavy drinking and frequency of intoxication (Everett, Hatzenbuehler, and Hughes, 2016). A longitudinal study of psychiatric disorders between 2001 and 2005 found that alcohol use disorders increased for lesbian, gay, and bisexual individuals living in states with marriage bans for same-sex couples. These disorders also increased for heterosexual residents of states with bans, but this increase (18 percent) was substantially smaller than the increase for lesbian, gay, and bisexual individuals (41.9 percent) (Hatzenbuehler et al., 2010).

One study did not find a protective effect of marriage on drinking behavior or marijuana use among LGBT individuals, and, for sexual-minority men, marriage was associated with increased odds of marijuana use (Trocki et al., 2020). Despite this, studies that measured problematic or disordered substance use show that marriage bans for same-sex partners increase substance use, whereas the availability of legal marriage decreases these adverse behaviors. The weight of the evidence suggests that marriage continues to be protective against substance use for LGBT individuals.

Conclusions

Does physical well-being of LGBT individuals improve following the availability of marriage? The 16 studies we reviewed indicate that the "marriage benefit" identified in the literature on different-sex marriages extends to sexual minorities: Legal relationship recognition was associated with improved self-reported general health, increased health care use and patient-provider communication, reduced STI rates, and reduced problematic substance use. These improvements may be attributed to two factors. First, improved relationship stability afforded by marriage can decrease risky behaviors, such as unprotected sex and problematic substance use. Second, alongside improvements in health insurance coverage, the supportive policy environment encourages LGBT individuals to seek health care and communicate openly with providers.

It is important to note that two of these studies focus solely on sexual-minority men, and many of the other studies emphasize the consistent improvements in physical health that legal relationship status affords men. This focus is unsurprising given the large body of literature addressing HIV awareness and prevention among sexual-minority men. However, the fact that research on the effects of legal marriage on physical well-being for sexual-minority women is still inconclusive points to a need for further research focusing on the nuances of the relationships between gender, sexual orientation, and health.

Impacts on Health Insurance Coverage

Key Points

- Legal marriage for same-sex couples improved their health insurance coverage, and this improvement was driven by an increase in same-sex spouses enrolling in employer-sponsored health insurance.
- Health insurance coverage changed and improved most for women in same-sex relationships following legal marriage.

Theoretical Background

Employers often offer health insurance plans that allow the spouse of an employee to be covered under a single employer-sponsored health insurance plan. Before marriage for same-sex couples became legal nationwide, individuals in same-sex relationships were significantly less likely than individuals in different-sex relationships to have health insurance coverage (Buchmueller and Carpenter, 2010). As states began to issue marriage licenses to same-sex couples, individuals married to same-sex partners gained the ability to enroll in a spouse's employer-sponsored insurance, potentially reducing the disparities in insurance coverage for LGBT individuals. These changes in health insurance coverage may also have downstream positive impacts on health and well-being outcomes (see "Impacts on Psychological Well-Being" and "Impacts on Physical Health").

Our review identified seven studies that examined the relationship between marriage for same-sex couples and health insurance coverage (see Table B.4). Jointly, these studies span the years 1996 to 2018, and four studies employed difference-in-differences analyses to investigate how the availability of legal marriage over time and across states affects health insurance type and coverage for same-sex couples.

Results from Cross-Sectional Studies

Cross-sectional studies show that same-sex couples in legally recognized relationships or who live in states with legal recognition are more likely to have health insurance. For instance, in a survey comparing health insurance coverage across relationship status, individuals in same-sex relationships with legal status were more likely than gay and lesbian individuals not in legal partnerships to have health insurance (Elwood et al., 2017). A second survey across policy environments that used data from 2008 to 2010 found that women in same-sex relationships who resided in states issuing marriage licenses for same-sex couples reported increased employer-sponsored health insurance compared with women in states without legal marriage (Gonzales and Blewett, 2014). For men in same-sex relationships, the disparities in employer-sponsored insurance were "negligible" between state policy environments. For both men and women in same-sex relationships in states without legal marriage or with marriage bans, the average rate of employer-sponsored coverage was 4 percent lower than in states granting marriage licenses.

Results from Repeated Surveys and Difference-in-Differences Analyses

Studies that assess health insurance type and coverage over multiple years in different policy environments provide insight into some of the mechanisms behind shifts in health insurance coverage for LGBT individuals. For example, a study examining labor force participation and health insurance between 1996 and 2011 found that the availability of legal relationship status changed health insurance sources for women in same-sex partnerships (Dillender, 2015). This was driven by women in same-sex couples shifting from both members of the couple working to an arrangement with only one member working. In this analysis, women in same-sex couples saw a 6.7–percentage point increase in employer-sponsored health insurance through a spouse's employer following the availability of legal relationship statuses. Neither the changes in insurance nor the shifts in labor arrangement were seen for men in same-sex couples. A difference-in-differences analysis of data from the 2008–2012 ACS found similar results: Legal marriage for same-sex couples in New York was associated with increases in employer-sponsored insurance and decreases in Medicaid coverage for individuals in same-sex relationships (Gonzales, 2015). These changes were more dramatic for women in same-sex relationships than for men when compared with their counterparts in different-sex relationships: Women in same-sex relationships saw an 8.9–percentage point increase in employer-sponsored insurance and a 3.9–percentage point decrease in Medicaid coverage, while men experienced a 6.3–percentage point increase in employer-sponsored insurance and a 2.2–percentage point decrease in Medicaid coverage.

An analysis using data from 2008 to 2017 found that legal marriage for same-sex couples led to a statistically significant increase (0.61 percentage point) in employer-sponsored insurance coverage in the general population but found no changes in rates of individuals being uninsured or having public insurance (Downing and Cha, 2020). In a study that focused specifically on the *Obergefell* decision, the number of same-sex couples in which both members had private insurance coverage increased from 79 percent to 88 percent after the decision, while there was no change for different-sex couples (90 percent) (Tumin and Kroeger, 2020). However, for unmarried same-sex couples in which both members had private insurance coverage, there was a 61-percent decrease in the odds of one partner being covered by the other's insurance following the *Obergefell* decision. The authors of the study note that this result could provide evidence that some employers withdrew coverage from other forms of legal relationship status, such as domestic partnerships. Finally, one difference-in-differences analysis of data from 2000 to 2017 found that legal marriage for same-sex couples increased the probability that men in same-sex households had health insurance by 4.1 percentage points, whereas the results for women in same-sex households were inconclusive (Carpenter et al., 2021).

Conclusions

The studies reviewed in this section employed rigorous research designs, and the majority used difference-in-differences approaches to analyze changes in insurance coverage over many years. The studies show a consistent increase in members of same-sex couples enrolling in employer-sponsored health insurance coverage following legal marriage for same-sex couples. Three studies found these effects to be especially pronounced for women in same-sex households, while one study found inconclusive results regarding women in same-sex households. Compared with couples consisting of two men, couples consisting of two women are more likely to be raising children (Goldberg and Conron, 2018) and more likely to specialize in either paid labor or household labor (Hansen, Martell, and Roncolato, 2020). Therefore, women in same-sex couples may be more likely to take advantage of employer-sponsored health insurance when it becomes available. Because these changes in insurance coverage are closely tied to decisions about labor force participation, newfound eligibility for employer-sponsored health insurance may have pushed same-sex couples to restructure their division of labor and employment decisions; the evidence for this is reviewed in the next section.

Impacts on Employment Outcomes

Key Points

- Marriage for same-sex couples increased the probability that individuals in such couples engaged in paid labor outside the home.
- Following policies allowing marriage for same-sex couples, women in same-sex couples were more likely than men in same-sex couples to specialize in either paid labor or household labor.

Theoretical Background

Marriage for same-sex couples can provide new eligibility for employer-sponsored health insurance coverage, improve financial and relationship stability, and change family formation decisions. Therefore, the life changes that come with legal marriage may have caused same-sex couples to reevaluate decisions about work and employment. The authors of the studies in this area hypothesized that legal marriage leads same-sex couples to specialize in either paid or household labor in response to the improved stability afforded by legal relationship status. Four of the studies used difference-in-differences analyses to investigate changes in members of same-sex households' employment in response to legal marriage for same-sex couples (see Table B.5).

Difference-in-Differences Analyses

Two studies that we reviewed specifically support the hypothesis that legal marriage encourages labor specialization in either paid labor or household labor. However, this effect was identified only among couples consisting of two women; couples consisting of two men did not show this effect. An analysis covering the years 1996 to 2011 found that when same-sex relationships gained legal status, women in same-sex couples were likely to shift from arrangements in which both members of the couple worked outside the home to arrangements in which only one member worked outside the home (Dillender, 2015). Couples consisting of two women who were raising children were especially likely to make this change. A second study reported similar results; it found that in couples consisting of two women, secondary earners reallocated paid work hours to caregiving and household labor (Hansen, Martell, and Roncolato, 2020). After legalization of marriage, women in same-sex relationships in this study reduced their annual labor supply by 6 percent.

In contrast to the hypothesis that marriage increases labor specialization and therefore decreases labor supply, an analysis spanning 2008 to 2016 found that legalization of marriage led to an increase in the likelihood that heads of same-sex households worked and an increase in the probability that both partners worked (Sansone, 2019). Furthermore, there were increases in time spent working weekly and in the probability that both partners worked full-time. These results were interpreted as a reflection of improved community climate toward LGBT individuals, and, although couples who marry may increase specialization and be more likely to have children, general trends reflect increased labor participation due to a more supportive policy environment. A study assessing the impact of the *Windsor* decision found similar effects: Members of same-sex couples were more likely to work and worked more hours following the ruling in 2013 (Isaac, 2024).

Conclusions

The findings of the studies reviewed in this section are inconsistent but not incompatible. While two studies found that legal marriage pushed women in same-sex couples to increase specialization and therefore decrease their labor supply, the other two studies found general increases in the probability that members of same-sex couples worked. Therefore, the mechanisms behind these results may be twofold: At a broader level, the supportive policy environment and shifting positive public opinion toward LGBT individuals may contribute to increases in employment, whereas at the relationship level, financial decisions and choosing to have children contribute to couples deciding to increase specialization. Further research should seek to understand the nuances behind these decisions, including understanding how family formation, health insurance, and financial well-being affect decisions about employment for same-sex couples.

Impacts on Financial Well-Being

Key Points

- Same-sex couples are generally better off financially when they are legally married than when they are not.
- While positive, the marriage premium is not as robust for same-sex couples as it is for different-sex couples.
- When married same-sex couples were unable to file their federal taxes jointly because of marriage bans, they experienced a tax penalty.

Theoretical Background

Marriage has a positive impact on wages and financial stability. This "marriage premium" has been identified in research on different-sex marriages and appears to operate through multiple mechanisms, including increased labor specialization and impacts on job choice (Reed and Harford, 1989). The marriage premium on wages has been identified most consistently in men married to women, and some have suggested that this result arises from gender-based divisions of labor (i.e., wives specializing in household labor and child care, allowing men to be more productive in their paid labor outside the home). However, evidence is stronger for a selection effect whereby higher earners are more likely to marry (Hersch and Stratton, 2000; McDonald, 2020). Marriage also affects taxes, as the ability to file jointly can lead to either a "marriage penalty" (in which the tax burden increases compared with two single filers) or a "marriage subsidy" (in which the tax burden decreases compared with two single filers) (Fisher, 2013).

Compared with heterosexual individuals, LGBT individuals experience a wage gap (Klawitter, 2015). This wage penalty is more often seen for gay and bisexual men, as sexual-minority women do not differ much from heterosexual women in their earnings, and some studies have even identified a "lesbian premium" (Badgett, 1995; Cushing-Daniels and Yeung, 2009). Furthermore, because family and economic life are intertwined, individuals in same-sex couples may face financial considerations that are different from those in different-sex relationships: They may choose to live in more–LGBT-friendly locales, differ in anticipated fertility, and exhibit less labor specialization because of the absence of gender roles in the relationship (Black et al., 2007). However, the increased stability and recognition provided by marriage may shift the role that these concerns play in the lives of same-sex couples. Legal marriage may therefore restructure the associations between sexual orientation, wages, taxes, and financial decisions. Our review identified 12 studies that examined whether the marriage premium extends to same-sex couples and how legal relationship status affects Social Security benefits, taxes, homeownership, and migration (see Table B.6). Of these 12 studies, 11 assessed the impact of marriage or marriage bans, and one examined civil unions.

Income and Financial Planning

The studies that examined the marriage wage premium and income surpluses for same-sex couples had inconsistent and complex results. In a comparison of the wages earned by individuals in same-sex versus different-sex relationships, both married and unmarried women in same-sex households earned significantly more than women in different-sex households (Schneebaum and Schubert, 2017). For men, however, unmarried men in same-sex households earned more than unmarried men in different-sex households, but married men in same-sex relationships earned less than married men in different-sex relationships. In other words, marriage negatively affected wages for men in same-sex couples. The authors describe a few possible explanations for this finding: (1) Married same-sex couples are more likely to be "out" as LGBT, which might lead to employment discrimination, or (2) the marriage premium in wages might apply only to men in different-sex couples because of gendered role expectations.

In a more recent study, married men and women in same-sex relationships were found to earn 3 percent and 6 percent more, respectively, than their cohabiting counterparts (Martell and Nash, 2020). This marriage premium was significant in states with and without legal marriage for same-sex couples but was larger in the former. The premium was larger for primary earners in same-sex couples, suggesting some effect of labor specialization following legal relationship recognition. A study focusing on poverty levels failed to find a marriage premium for same-sex couples using a counterfactual income distribution that controlled for race and ethnicity, education, age, policy environment, presence of children, and urbanicity (Alonso-Villar and del Río, 2023). This analysis found that poverty levels for same-sex couples did not depend on marital status and that levels of extreme poverty were highest for married couples consisting of two women. The authors interpret these results as suggesting that income does not influence the choice to get married for same-sex couples as much as it does for different-sex couples. In contrast to these results, however, another study that focused on poverty rates found that marriage was protective against poverty for same-sex couples, but this effect was stronger for couples consisting of two men than for couples consisting of two women (Badgett, 2018). The discrepancy in these results may be due to these studies' respective definitions of *poverty* and analytic approaches: Alonso-Villar and del Río (2023) concentrated on poverty intensity rather than incidence and used a counterfactual approach that controlled for a wide set of variables, whereas Badgett (2018) focused on certain variables (sexual orientation and family structure) that may combine with marital status to influence risk for poverty.

In terms of the income surplus that often accompanies marriage, an analysis using the ACS found differences in "excess income" based on legal relationship status and relationship duration (Delhommer and Hamermesh, 2021). For same-sex couples who did not have access to legal marriage, relationship duration did not predict excess income. However, same-sex couples who had spent a longer duration of their relationship in a legal marriage *did* experience a greater income surplus. In contrast, time spent in domestic partnerships and civil unions did not affect excess income, suggesting that marriage has unique effects on relationship investments and the resulting financial outcomes.

For financial planning outcomes, one study showed that older LGBT individuals who lived in a state without legal relationship recognition were more likely to have taken steps to prepare for end of life, including being more likely to have a will and designated durable power of attorney (de Vries et al., 2009). These results imply that LGBT individuals living in unsupportive policy environments had to go to greater lengths to arrange financial and caregiving plans in old age.

Taxes and Social Security Benefits

The impact of marriage on income tax can benefit some couples and penalize others. Before nationwide availability of marriage for same-sex couples, married same-sex couples were unable to file jointly for their federal taxes because of the Defense of Marriage Act, often resulting in an increase in taxes owed. For example, in 2008, married same-sex couples in Massachusetts experienced an average "tax penalty" of $2,495 (Psihountas, Dippel, and Slusarz, 2013). In other words, this was the difference between their actual tax liability and their predicted tax liability had they been able to file jointly. After the *Windsor* case struck down the Defense of Marriage Act and provided federal recognition to existing marriages, the subsequent changes in tax revenues due to federal marriage recognition resulted in an estimated loss of $56.9 million in tax revenue (Isaac, 2024). This deadweight loss was due not to the marriages themselves but to the shift from individual to joint taxation for same-sex married couples.

The legalization of marriage for same-sex couples increased rates of eligibility for claiming spousal Social Security benefits. One study examined the amounts that same-sex couples were eligible to claim and found that married same-sex couples were generally less likely to be eligible for spousal benefits because they had higher household incomes than different-sex couples (Pollard and Lopez-Garcia, 2022). However, when they *were* eligible, same-sex couples were able to claim more than different-sex couples were. Specifically, couples consisting of two men who qualified could claim $600 to $840 more per year than different-sex couples could.

Mortgages and Migration

The financial benefits that accompany marriage can affect how and where couples live. Some couples will be incentivized to enter homeownership, while others will migrate to locales with more-supportive policies. For instance, a difference-in-differences analysis spanning 2004 to 2014 found that states that issued marriage licenses to same-sex couples saw a 6-percent to 16-percent increase in mortgage applications from same-sex couples (Miller and Park, 2018). Similarly, longer relationship duration was associated with homeownership only when same-sex couples also had access to marriage (Delhommer and Hamermesh, 2021). However, same-sex couples continue to face a gap in having their mortgage applications denied compared with different-sex couples even after marriage legalization (Hagendorff, Nguyen, and

Sila, 2022). After the legalization of marriage for same-sex couples, the mortgage denial gap increased when loan officers were human but did not change when loans were run through Fintech, a lending company that relies more on technology-based approval. These results suggest that the attitudes toward sexual minorities held by financial officers or employers may play an important role in the financial well-being of same-sex couples, even after legalization of marriage.

In terms of migration, states issuing marriage licenses to same-sex couples experienced increased migration of men in same-sex households, but analyses of migration changes for women in same-sex households were inconclusive (Marcén and Morales, 2022). This effect for men was temporary, though, because the number of same-sex households per state did not significantly change because of migration.

Conclusions

How do financial well-being and financial decisions change for same-sex couples after marriage becomes available? The results from the 12 studies in our review are nuanced, but they generally point to financial gains for same-sex couples after they are granted legal status. The available evidence suggests that, following legal recognition, same-sex couples experienced income surpluses and wage premiums and were more likely to apply for a mortgage. The impact on wages for married same-sex couples was particularly complex: While an analysis published soon after the *Obergefell* decision found that gay men experienced a marriage penalty, more-recent studies identified either no change in wages or a marriage premium for same-sex couples, suggesting stronger evidence for neutral or positive impacts on wages.

There have been multiple analyses that have aimed to estimate the tax effects of legalizing marriage for same-sex couples (Alm, Badgett, and Whittington, 2000; Alm, Leguizamon, and Leguizamon, 2014), but there is little research investigating whether these predictions were realized following nationwide legalization. Furthermore, research should take into account the fact that income tax policy can affect who chooses to get married, further complicating the tax effects of legal marriage (Friedberg and Isaac, 2024). The evidence available suggests that same-sex couples missed out on tax benefits because of the Defense of Marriage Act. Further research should investigate the lasting financial and economic impacts of legal marriage for same-sex couples and disentangle the complex associations between wages, gender, and marriage.

Impacts on Social Connection

Key Points

- Same-sex couples perceived greater family support after legal marriage was enacted.
- Individuals in same-sex couples relied less on support from friends in response to legal marriage, as perceived stigma decreased.

Theoretical Background

Social connection and support are key components of well-being, and whether LGBT individuals conceal or disclose their identities to family and close others has significant downstream effects on mental health (Chang et al., 2021). Marriage for same-sex couples, by validating LGBT identities and legitimizing same-sex relationships, can affect these decisions and thereby may facilitate greater connections to friends and family. In contrast, the lack of a supportive policy environment may lead to overreliance on narrow social networks for support, thereby straining those relationships. Our review identified five studies that addressed these possibilities by examining the effects of marriage and civil unions on the social connections of LGBT individuals (see Table B.7). These studies addressed how the availability of legal status for same-sex relationships affects receipt of support from family and friends, feelings of social inclusion, and perceptions of community climate.

Social Support and Inclusion

The association between legal relationship status and social connection was first assessed in two seminal studies on civil unions in Vermont in the early 2000s. In the first study, men in same-sex civil unions reported greater closeness to their families of origin compared with their friends in same-sex relationships without civil unions, whereas there were no differences in familial closeness for women in same-sex relationships with or without civil unions (Solomon, Rothblum, and Balsam, 2004). This analysis found no differences in perceived social support from friends among these women or men with or without civil unions. In a three-year follow-up study with this sample, there were no differences in closeness with family, family inclusion, or perceived social support for women or men with or without civil unions (Balsam et al., 2008). Because LGBT individuals who have more support from family may be more likely to seek legal recognition for their relationships, it is difficult to determine the direct impact of legal relationship status from these early studies.

One longitudinal study assessed changes in social connection during the process of legalizing marriage for same-sex couples, and this study allows for stronger conclusions about the direct effects of access to marriage on social connection and support (Ogolsky et al., 2019a). It began three months before the *Obergefell* decision and ended one year after. Individuals in same-sex relationships reported increases in family support after the decision, and levels of family support were generally higher for individuals who lived in states that had already been issuing marriage licenses to same-sex couples before *Obergefell* than for individuals in other states. After marriage became legal for same-sex couples nationwide, individuals in same-sex couples reported lower levels of support from friends than before the *Obergefell* decision. This effect was interpreted as a reduction in the need for "exclusive reliance" on "internal mechanisms of support" as the community and political environments became more supportive for LGBT individuals (Ogolsky et al., 2019a, p. 428). The study found evidence for this interpretation in that levels of perceived stigma declined alongside support from friends.

Support from family members may also have effects on well-being. For instance, sexual-minority women who perceived high levels of family support for legal marriage for same-sex couples were more likely to report good health (Drabble et al., 2022). Finally, sexual-minority men reported greater social inclusion following legalization of marriage for same-sex couples in the United States, but these improvements were lower among individuals who reported high levels of internal or external stigma (Metheny and Stephenson, 2019). This study did not find any differences in perceived social inclusion based on political environment. Taken together, the studies in this area suggest that social support, particularly family support, improves following access to marriage and has impacts on well-being and perceived stigma.

Conclusions

How do the social networks and social connections of same-sex couples change after they gain access to legal marriage? While early studies focused on civil unions did not find many differences in social support in response to relationship recognition, later studies assessing marriage did show an increase in perceived family support. Legal marriage also resulted in a decrease in support from friends, potentially due to a decreased need for support in response to reduced stigma and a more supportive policy environment. Improvements in general community climate and feelings of inclusion may also have been reflected in decreased perceptions of stigma (see also "Impacts on Psychological Well-Being").

Compared with the extensive research literature on the social connections of different-sex couples (e.g., Haggerty, Bradbury, and Karney, 2022), the literature on the social connections of same-sex couples remains limited. For example, research on the marriages of different-sex couples has observed increases in the interdependence of couples' social networks after marriage (Haggerty et al., 2023; Kearns and Leonard, 2004). Similar changes have yet to be examined in same-sex couples. There remains an opportunity for future work to assess the generalizability of the different-sex marriage literature, as well as to investigate how social support can buffer the effects of minority stress on same-sex couples.

The Impact of Legal Marriage for Same-Sex Couples on the Children of Same-Sex Couples

Supporters and opponents of marriages for same-sex couples share an abiding concern for children's well-being. According to the U.S. Census Bureau, nearly 300,000 children in the United States were being raised by same-sex couples in 2019 (Taylor, 2020). Because same-sex couples underreport their status to the U.S. Census Bureau, this number is likely to be an underestimate. Supporters of marriage for same-sex couples believe that children in same-sex households benefit when the relationships between their parents are acknowledged and afforded the same rights and responsibilities as those of different-sex couples. Opponents believe that the gender composition of parents affects children's well-being and that different-sex parents provide the optimal environment for optimal emotional and developmental outcomes. In the arguments before the U.S. Supreme Court during the *Obergefell* case in 2015, opponents of legalizing marriage for same-sex couples made this argument explicitly, and Justices Alito and Thomas, in their dissenting opinions on that decision, echoed these views.

These debates raise two independent issues that are often conflated. One issue is whether—and, if so, how—the gender composition of parents (e.g., a man and a woman, two men, two women) affects children's outcomes. The other issue is whether the children of same-sex couples are affected by whether the relationship between their parents is legally recognized.

Because same-sex couples have been raising children for far longer than same-sex couples have been able to marry, the first of these issues has received far more scholarly attention. By the time the first legal marriages for same-sex couples were performed in 2004, there was already an extensive and well-developed body of research literature comparing the physical, emotional, educational, and developmental outcomes of children raised by same-sex and different-sex couples (Black, Sanders, and Taylor, 2007). In the intervening years, this literature has been the topic of a review sponsored by the American Psychological Association (American Psychological Association, 2005), a review sponsored by the American Academy of Pediatrics (Pawelski et al., 2006), a review sponsored by the American Sociological Association (Manning, Fettro, and Lamidi, 2014), a meta-analysis of 19 studies (Crowl, Ahn, and Baker, 2008), and numerous other narrative and meta-analytic reviews (e.g., Knight et al., 2017; Tasker, 2005; Tasker, 2010; Zhang et al., 2023).

Given the depth and range of this literature and the fact that the research has been conducted in multiple disciplines—including psychology, sociology, economics, medicine, and public health—it is striking to note that all of these reviews reached the same conclusions. The example below is typical:

> We conclude that there is a clear consensus in the social science literature indicating that American children living within same-sex parent households fare just . . . as well as those children residing within different-sex parent households over a wide array of well-being measures: academic performance, cognitive development, social development, psychological health, early sexual activity, and substance abuse. Our assessment of the literature is based on credible and methodologically sound studies that compare well-being outcomes of children residing within same-sex and different-sex parent families. Differences that exist in child well-being are largely due to socioeconomic circumstances and family stability. (Manning, Fettro, and Lamidi, 2014, p. 485)

Despite the consensus across scientific professional organizations, there have been vocal critiques of these conclusions (Allen, 2015; Marks, 2012; Schumm, 2016). The general argument in these critiques is that the existing research literature is not yet sufficient to support strong conclusions and that more research is needed before it is safe to offer equal legal status to same-sex and different-sex couples. None of these critiques, however, identifies reliable evidence of harms to children that can be attributed to the gender composition of their parents, as opposed to economic differences between same-sex and different-sex couples. One study that did find deficits in children of same-sex parents (Regnerus, 2012) has since been discredited for numerous specification errors; reanalyses of the same data using appropriate estimation strategies were unable to replicate the findings (Cheng and Powell, 2015). Testimony based on other studies, including by Allen and Marks, has been deemed to be "not credible" and to represent a "fringe viewpoint" (*DeBoer v. Snyder*, 2014, p. 768). Meanwhile, evidence that children of same-sex couples do as well as or better than children of different-sex couples on multiple dimensions of well-being continues to accumulate (Boertien and Härkönen, 2018; Bos et al., 2016; Mazrekaj, Fischer, and Bos, 2022; Zhang et al., 2023).

Given the existing and well-developed literature on the consequences of same-sex parenting for children, the goal of this review was to address the second issue in this debate: What are the implications for children when their same-sex parents are married or prevented from marrying by the state? This is a much narrower question, and, accordingly, it has received far less scholarly attention. Our review identified only four studies that directly examined whether and how legal recognition of same-sex couples is associated with outcomes for their children.

Key Points

- After controlling for socioeconomic variables, there are no reliable differences in the emotional and physical health of children in married versus cohabiting same-sex parents.
- Differences in rates of coverage by private health insurance between children of same-sex parents and children of married different-sex parents are greatly diminished or eliminated in states that have granted legal recognition to same-sex couples.
- Since 2010, studies have found no differences between the children of same-sex parents and the children of different-sex parents in their rates of progress through school. Prior to 2010, significant differences in rates of progress were observed only in states without legal recognition for same-sex couples.

Theoretical Background

Why would the presence or absence of legal recognition for same-sex couples make a difference to the children of those couples? In a theoretical review, Siegel and colleagues proposed that a distinguishing feature of families with same-sex parents is their exposure to *legal vulnerability*, which the researchers defined as "a heightened and stable risk for family members of expecting or experiencing adverse general and minority-specific outcomes related to health and family functioning due to (i) lacking legal recognition of family relationships, (ii) lacking protection against discrimination, or (iii) criminalization of the parents' sexual orientation" (Siegel et al., 2021, pp. 12–13). Drawing on minority stress theory and related frameworks (Frost and Meyer, 2023; Meyer, 2003), this perspective suggests that a legal environment that prohibits marriage for same-sex couples gives rise to insecurity and distress in the children of those couples. Extending legal recognition to same-sex couples reduces the experience of legal vulnerability in same-sex households, which should lead to reduced distress for all family members and, as a downstream consequence, improved developmental and educational outcomes for children in those households.

Findings

The four studies we identified examined three different domains of child well-being: parent-rated physical and mental health, health insurance coverage, and school progress (see Table B.8).

To examine the associations between legal marriage for same-sex couples and their children's health, two studies by the same research team drew on data from the annual NHIS. One of these studies (Reczek et al., 2016) pooled ten years of NHIS data (2004 through 2013) to compare children's parent-rated health and emotional well-being across different-sex and same-sex cohabiting and married households (i.e., four groups). Analyses revealed few differences between children of same-sex and different-sex couples, but there were significant differences between cohabiting parent and married parent households. Notably, the children of married same-sex parents experienced better health, fewer lost school days, and fewer emotional difficulties than the children of cohabiting same-sex parents. Even after controlling for socioeconomic differences between cohabiting and married couples, the effects on school days and emotional difficulties remained significant. However, in a second study drawing on data pooled from the 2008–2015 NHIS (Reczek et al., 2017), these differences were no longer significant: After socioeconomic variables were controlled for, the children of same-sex cohabiting parents and same-sex married parents did not differ significantly from each other on any of these variables.

Other research has examined the implications of legal status for same-sex couples on their children's access to health insurance (Gonzales and Blewett, 2013). Analyses of data from the 2008–2010 ACS indicated that, nationally, the children of same-sex couples (who were not distinguished by marital status) were less likely than the children of married different-sex couples to be covered by private health insurance (about 65 percent versus 78 percent) but were far more likely than the children of unmarried different-sex couples to be covered by private health insurance (38 percent). However, further analyses revealed that these differences depended on the legal environment in the state in which a family resided. In states that recognized marriages and civil unions between same-sex partners, the difference between children of two mothers and children of different-sex married parents disappeared and the difference between children of two fathers and children of married different-sex couples was reduced, although still significant. Notably, although unmarried different-sex couples had the highest rates of public health insurance, there were no differences between same-sex couples and married different-sex couples in access to public health insurance. This is likely the case because, unlike access to private insurance, a child's access to public insurance is determined solely by household income rather than the marital status of the parents.

The final study of child outcomes also drew on data from the ACS to evaluate whether the children of same-sex parents and different-sex parents differed in their rates of progfor marriage equality. In 1999, approximately two-thirds of Americans indicated in a Gallup poll that same-sex couples should not have the same legal recognition as different-sex couples (Newport, 1999).

Twenty years later, attitudes toward legal recognition for same-sex couples had shifted substantially. In a 2023 Gallup poll, only 29 percent of Americans indicated opposition to legal recognition of marriages between same-sex partners, whereas 71 percent indicated support, a level that had held stable for the past three years (McCarthy, 2023). Similar data from 2019 revealed that attitudes had shifted to a similar degree across a wide variety of demographic categories (Pew Research Center, 2019). Other attitudes (e.g., toward government, abortion, race, and religion) remained relatively stable during this period (Rosenfeld, 2017). What accounts for the relatively rapid, widespread, and dramatic swing in public sentiment toward legal marriage for same-sex couples?

Several distinct forces likely contributed to these changes in attitudes, including the increasing visibility of LGBT individuals and same-sex couples during these years (Walters, 2003). Another possible source of influence, and one that has received particular attention from researchers, is the spread of legal recognition for same-sex couples, in particular the Supreme Court's *Windsor* decision in 2013 and *Obergefell* decision in 2015 (Rosenfeld, 2017). Indeed, even as changes in public opinion often precede and motivate court decisions and legislative actions on controversial social issues, research has established that court decisions and legislative actions can also shape public opinion (Aksoy et al., 2020; Hetling, McDermott, and Mapps, 2008).

Changes in public policy can affect public opinion through several mechanisms, including direct experience with the policy; exposure to people affected by the policy; and, for groups with no direct or indirect experience with the policy, signaling (Gusmano, Schlesinger, and Thomas, 2002). *Direct experience* in this context might mean that people realized they knew more people who were in same-sex couples as more LGBT individuals and same-sex couples came out, or they saw or directly participated in the weddings or celebrations of same-sex couples. *Exposure to people affected by the policy* occurs when people who are not part of or directly related to a same-sex couple themselves nevertheless encounter (e.g., as coworkers or friends) people whose experiences have changed as a result of a change in policy. *Signaling* is the idea that changes in policy send clear messages about the groups that elites and authority figures (e.g., elected officials, judges, Justices) consider worthy of legal recognition and protection. When those authorities are recognized and trusted, changes in policies can predict rapid changes in perceived norms and subsequent changes in personal attitudes, especially for individuals whose opinions might have been undeveloped or ambivalent prior to the policy change (Stoutenborough, Haider-Markel, and Allen, 2006).

For individuals with entrenched opinions, however, an alternative possibility is that changes in policy may lead to backlash (Parker and Barreto, 2013). In particular, groups that are invested in maintaining the status quo may feel threatened when rights and privileges they enjoy are extended to members of stigmatized minorities (Sanbonmatsu, 2008). Perceptions of threat can be exacerbated by exposure to polarized information when new legislation or court decisions are being discussed in the media. The result can be *opinion backlash*, defined by Bishin et al. (2016) as "a large, negative, and enduring shift in opinion against a policy or group that occurs in response to some event that threatens the status quo" (p. 626). In the case of marriage for same-sex couples, opinion backlash would be demonstrated by more-negative public opinions toward marriage recognition and LGBT individuals, especially among people who were already inclined to disapprove of same-sex relationships, after policy changes extending legal status to same-sex couples.

Which of these possibilities best describes how public opinion actually responded to the legalization of marriage for same-sex couples? Our review identified 16 studies that directly evaluated this question (see Table B.9). These studies used repeated surveys, longitudinal assessments, and experiments to examine a wide variety of outcomes, including responses to public opinion polls, incidence of hate crimes and employment discrimination against members of sexual-minority groups, rates of online searches using homophobic prompts, and content of online comments. The findings of this work allow us to evaluate how extending or denying legal status to marriage for same-sex couples contributed to changes in public opinion over the past 20 years.

Analyses of Opinion Change Across Weeks and Months

Our review identified five studies that compared survey results collected immediately before and then shortly after major court decisions affecting legal marriage for same-sex couples. To the extent that elevated media attention surrounding major court decisions exposes members of the public to new information, such effects as polarization and backlash are most likely to be observed during the periods immediately before and after these decisions. Therefore, it is noteworthy that these studies found no evidence of backlash and little evidence of any short-term changes in public opinion after major court decisions affecting legal marriage for same-sex couples. For example, Bishin et al. (2016) drew on the National Annenberg Election Survey and online surveys to examine whether support for marriage for same-sex couples changed from the week before to the week after each of two major judicial decisions: the Massachusetts Supreme Judicial Court granting legal status to marriages between same-sex partners in that state in 2003 and the U.S. Supreme Court's *Windsor* decision in 2013. Although both decisions were accompanied by widespread media attention and debate, short-term changes in support for marriage for same-sex couples were negligible and did not reach statistical significance in either case. When the Iowa Supreme Court approved marriage for same-sex couples in 2009, a group of researchers collected opinion data from 503 state residents the week before the court's decision was announced and again the week after (Kreitzer, Hamilton, and Tolbert, 2014). Across these two assessments, 90 percent of respondents who opposed marriage for same-sex couples prior to the ruling continued to oppose it after the ruling, and 85 percent of respondents who supported marriage for same-sex couples prior to the ruling continued to support it after the ruling. Repeated surveys and longitudinal data collected in the months before and after the Court's *Obergefell* decision in 2015 revealed that, regardless of the research design, personal attitudes toward marriage for same-sex couples or toward LGBT individuals did not change in the weeks after the decision (Tankard and Paluck, 2017). What did change significantly in these studies was perceptions of social norms: Respondents believed that other Americans had grown more supportive of marriage legalization, even as their own opinions had remained stable.

Two studies did find evidence of significant short-term changes in public opinion, but neither of these studies supports strong conclusions. In the first study, content analyses of Twitter posts in the months before and after the *Obergefell* decision identified a slight increase in negative postings in states in which marriage for same-sex couples was not already legal, consistent with an opinion backlash, but this uptick disappeared within two months of the decision (Adams-Cohen, 2020). In the second study, researchers surveyed Nebraska residents in 2013 and then again during the three months after the *Obergefell* decision in 2015 (Kazyak and Stange, 2018). In contrast to predictions of opinion backlash, support for marriage recognition was significantly higher in 2015, even after controlling for demographic, political, and religious variables. However, without comparisons with national trends, these results cannot rule out the possibility that the difference across time reflects general changes in public opinion rather than a direct reaction to the Supreme Court's decision. Overall, then, research on the short-term effects of changes in legal recognition for same-sex couples has found no evidence of enduring negative backlash and very little evidence of any effects on public opinion at all.

Analyses of Opinion Change Across Years: Effects of Marriage Bans

Weeks and months might not be the most appropriate time intervals in which to examine how court decisions affect public opinion on controversial social issues, such as marriage for same-sex couples. By the time that major court cases are decided, support and opposition may already be hardened by repeated exposure to attitude-consistent information in the media. Across years, however, direct exposure and indirect exposure to the consequences of new policies have more time to take effect, suggesting that changes in public opinion toward marriage recognition may yet be observed over longer intervals.

Studies of the effects of banning marriage for same-sex couples on public opinion have taken this approach, testing the idea that signaling from courts that same-sex couples are less worthy of legal status might lead to more-negative views of marriage for same-sex couples and LGBT individuals in states where such bans were considered or passed. Our review identified three studies that evaluated this hypothesis, but none of them supported it. Donovan and Tolbert (2013), for example, evaluated how attitudes toward LGBT individuals changed between 2002 and 2004 in the 13 states in which voters approved bans on marriage for same-sex couples during those years, compared with states that did not vote on banning marriage. Across the two groups of states, there were, on average, no significant differences in how attitudes toward LGBT individuals changed, but there was evidence of polarization among those most inclined to disapprove of marriage recognition for same-sex couples. A separate study that examined statewide attitudes from 1982 to 2008 suggests that even polarization may be short-lived: Statewide attitudes predicted which states considered ballot measures banning marriage for same-sex couples, but the approval of such ballot measures was not significantly associated with subsequent changes in statewide attitudes two years later (Francis, Mialon, and Peng, 2012).

One possible explanation for these failures to observe effects of marriage bans on public opinion is that people may be reluctant to report on their attitudes honestly to survey researchers. To overcome this limitation, Levy and Levy (2017) examined sexual orientation–motivated hate crimes as a behavioral proxy for public opinion toward sexual minorities. Drawing on state-level hate crime data from 2000 to 2012, these authors found that hate crimes against LGBT individuals did rise in states that passed bans on marriage for same-sex couples, but this difference was entirely accounted for by demographic and political differences between states that did or did not consider such bans. In other words, states in which hate crimes against LGBT individuals were more common were also states that were more likely to pass bans on marriage for same-sex couples, but the passage of bans did not increase the rate of hate crimes.

Analyses of Opinion Change Across Years: Effects of Legal Marriage for Same-Sex Couples

With scant evidence that banning marriage for same-sex couples predicts long-term changes in public opinion, what about legalizing such marriages? Our review identified nine studies that addressed this question. Again, repeated surveys conducted over intervals of one year or longer found that attitudes toward legal marriage for same-sex couples and toward LGBT individuals are generally stable over time (Perrin et al., 2018). When people do change their opinions after a legal decision extending marriage rights to same-sex couples, they tend to move toward greater acceptance: Those who change their opinions most tend to be members of groups that are most inclined toward support for marriage for same-sex couples initially (e.g., registered Democrats, younger people). In contrast, those who oppose marriage for same-sex couples become more committed to their opposition (Flores and Barclay, 2016).

In perhaps the strongest study to date of the effects of legalizing marriage for same-sex couples on public opinion, researchers drew on hundreds of thousands of visitors to Project Implicit, a website that allows people to complete both standard assessments of their explicit attitudes and reaction-time assessments of implicit attitudes of which they might not be aware (Ofosu et al., 2019). By linking the timing and geolocations of these responses to the progress of marriage legislation across the country between 2005 and 2016, the researchers were able to examine how explicit and implicit attitudes changed in accordance with changes in the legal status of same-sex couples throughout those 11 years. Their analyses revealed that, although explicit and implicit attitudes toward LGBT individuals were already growing more favorable during this period, the rate of change toward acceptance accelerated after marriage for same-sex couples was legalized. This effect held true for explicit and implicit attitudes, as measured through the Project Implicit website, and was replicated in analyses of the repeated surveys in the American National Election Studies dataset. Distinguishing between states that legalized marriage for same-sex couples locally and states that were forced to recognize such marriage by the U.S. Supreme Court in 2015 complicates this picture somewhat. Although attitudes toward LGBT individuals grew more favorable in the states that passed their own legislation, consistent with a signaling effect, implicit and explicit attitudes grew more negative in states that were forced to recognize marriages between same-sex partners, consistent with the opinion backlash hypothesis. In all cases, the significant effects observed in this study were small, accounting for between 1 percent and 5 percent of the variance in attitudes within states.

Recognizing the limits of asking people to report on their attitudes, several scholars interested in the effects of legal marriage for same-sex couples on public opinion have examined specific behaviors as proxies for attitudes. For example, two studies examined changes in Google searches containing homophobic slurs after changes in marriage policy, and both found that state-level rates of such searches declined after states passed legislation legalizing marriages between same-sex partners (Nikolaou, 2022; Sansone, 2019). Analyses of news coverage of marriage recognition revealed that articles were more likely to frame the debate in terms of politics and legal issues prior to the *Obergefell* decision but were more likely to frame the discussion in terms of civil rights and equality afterward (Colistra and Johnson, 2021). One study examined the presence of LGBTQ student groups on the campuses of Christian colleges and universities, finding few changes between 2013 and 2019, despite the *Obergefell* decision in the middle of that interval (Coley, 2020). Another study analyzed data from the National Incident-Based Reporting System and found no differences in how police responded to same-sex intimate partner violence from the years before (2013–2014) to the years after (2016–2017) the *Obergefell* decision (Paintsil, 2024).

Two final studies examined how the spread of legal marriages for same-sex couples affected rates of sexual orientation–motivated hate crimes across states (Levy and Levy, 2017; Nikolaou, 2022). Levy and Levy (2017) found that states that legalized marriage for same-sex couples experienced an increase in hate crimes against LGBT individuals in the two years after the legislation passed, although the effect was very small (an additional one hate crime per 1.2 million people). The fact that the rise in hate crimes was observed after a delay rather than concurrent with the passage of the legislation led the authors to interpret it as a reporting effect—i.e., a greater willingness to report hate crimes following identity-affirming policy changes. Nikolaou (2022) extended the previous analyses with more-recent data over a longer interval and found that the passage of legislation granting legal status to marriages between same-sex partners predicted a 31-percent reduction in hate crimes against LGBT individuals and a 13-percent reduction in reports of employment discrimination against LGBT individuals, declines that were observed only after the legislation passed. Moreover, the observed declines associated with marriage legalization were greater than the declines associated with other forms of legal recognition for same-sex couples (e.g., civil unions), and the effects were especially strong for gay men.

Conclusion

In the United States, the legalization of marriage for same-sex couples began during a time when public opinion toward sexual minorities was already moving toward acceptance. Did legislative and judicial actions on marriage for same-sex couples during this period further influence public opinion? Although the results have been mixed across the 16 studies that addressed this question over the past decade, the weight of the evidence supports the idea that legal recognition for same-sex couples modestly accelerated the movement of public opinion toward acceptance of sexual minorities and same-sex relationships. While the studies found minimal short-term effects, over longer periods, a new status quo in which the marriages of same-sex couples and different-sex couples had the same legal status appeared to promote changes in public opinion toward acceptance of same-sex couples and LGBT individuals. These effects were small but significant and held true even after taking preexisting trends into account. More importantly, rates of sexual orientation–motivated hate crimes and employer discrimination declined when states recognized marriages between same-sex partners. To the extent that these behaviors reflect underlying attitudes toward sexual minorities, changes in these behaviors in the years following marriage recognition indicate lower levels of antipathy and disapproval.

Fears that court decisions allowing marriage for same-sex couples would inspire immediate negative opinion backlash proved to be unfounded. In the short term, the effects of legislative and judicial actions on public opinion about marriage for same-sex couples and LGBT individuals were either negligible or short-lived. The observed stability of public opinion in the weeks and months after major judicial decisions may be the result of the sustained media attention that tends to precede such decisions. By the time they are announced, broad swaths of the public may have already developed firm opinions that resist short-term changes. What do change are perceptions of other people's opinions; that is, people believe that judicial opinions reflect public opinion, even when those decisions do not reflect their own opinions.

Impacts on Public Health

Key Points

- When states vote on amendments to prohibit marriages between same-sex partners, the heterosexual family members of LGBT individuals report greater distress.
- When states legalize marriage for same-sex couples, state-level rates of syphilis, HIV, and AIDS fall significantly. These declines are driven primarily by declines for men who have sex with men but result in savings to the nation's health care system of $1 billion to $6 billion per year.

Theoretical Background

Because intimate relationships are so closely tied to partners' physical and emotional wellbeing (Robles et al., 2014), there are multiple reasons to predict that granting legal status to the marriages of same-sex couples should affect the health of those couples, as discussed earlier in this chapter. It is not as straightforward to explain how the legal status of same-sex couples might affect public health more generally. The most-obvious mechanisms are various forms of contagion. For example, the effects of policies that directly affect the mental health of LGBT individuals might be transmitted to their close friends and family through processes of emotional contagion (Herrando and Constantinides, 2021). The effects of policies that directly affect the physical health of LGBT individuals might be transmitted to the broader public by affecting the likelihood that viral and bacterial infections are transmitted to others. Our review identified only two studies (see Table B.10) that addressed the potential for state-level marriage policies to influence public health, and each of them focused on one of these routes of transmission.

Findings

The first of these studies examined the effects of states banning marriage for same-sex couples on the well-being of heterosexual family members of LGBT individuals in those states (Horne, Rostosky, and Riggle, 2011). When restrictions on same-sex couples are being debated and voted on, the family members of LGBT individuals may be likely to experience stress and negative affect for several reasons. First, family members can be the direct targets of discrimination because of their relationships to LGBT individuals: that is, stigma by association (Neuberg et al., 1994). Second, family members who feel especially close to LGBT individuals may experience attacks on those individuals as personally threatening (Aron et al., 1991). Third, family members may experience elevated stress due to concerns for the well-being of their stigmatized loved ones (Ben-Ari, 1995).

To evaluate these possibilities, the researchers assessed exposure to negative messages about LGBT individuals, perceived stress, and negative affect in an online survey of heterosexual family members of LGBT individuals. The survey was conducted shortly after the 2006 midterm elections, during which seven states voted on and passed amendments banning marriages between same-sex partners. Data from respondents in those states were compared with data from respondents in states that either had already passed bans on marriage recognition or had not considered banning marriage recognition. These comparisons revealed that family members in the two groups of states did not differ significantly in their perceived stress or general negative affect, but they did differ in their experiences directly related to marriage bans. Specifically, family members in the states that passed bans on marriage for same-sex couples reported greater exposure to negative messages about LGBT individuals and greater negative affect about the amendments compared with family members in the states that had not considered marriage bans during that election. These differences were small, as was the total sample size ($N = 198$), giving this study limited power to support strong conclusions about the effects of marriage bans on the health of the families of LGBT individuals.

Drawing on a much larger and more representative dataset, the second study examined the effects of legalizing marriage for same-sex couples on rates of STIs in the general population (Nikolaou, 2023). To understand why legislation related to same-sex couples might affect public health in this way, the study's author offered three possible mechanisms. First, to the extent that legalizing marriages between same-sex partners is associated with increasing acceptance for LGBT individuals, those individuals may be less likely to engage in risky sexual behavior (Francis and Mialon, 2010). Second, when legal marriage is available, LGBT individuals may be more motivated to protect themselves from STIs to improve their ability to find high-quality partners. Third, if the availability of legal marriage for same-sex couples increases partners' access to health insurance (as discussed earlier), LGBT individuals may receive better preventive care, better screening, earlier diagnoses, and better treatment for infections. All three of these mechanisms should have direct effects on rates of STIs among LGBT individuals, but because many LGBT individuals do not have sex with only other LGBT individuals (Dodge et al., 2016; Pathela et al., 2006), these effects should ripple outward, benefiting the general population as well.

To evaluate these possibilities, Nikolaou (2023) drew on 20 years of CDC data on state-level rates of six STIs—syphilis, gonorrhea, chlamydia, hepatitis, HIV, and AIDS—and used a difference-in-differences approach to relate changes in these rates to state-level changes in the legal status of marriage for same-sex couples during this period. Analyses revealed significant effects of granting legal status to the marriages of same-sex couples on three of these STIs. Specifically, when states legalized marriage for same-sex couples, syphilis rates fell by 33 percent, HIV rates fell by 55 percent, and AIDS rates fell by 9 percent. Moreover, the effects of the policies appear to accumulate over time, such that the effects on reducing these STIs grow larger the longer a state has had the new policy in place.

Although these analyses were conducted using state-level data representing the total population of each state, more than 50 percent of all cases of syphilis, HIV, and AIDS in the United States are found in men who have sex with men, a group likely to be directly affected by policies recognizing same-sex couples. To address whether the observed effects of these policies extended beyond men who have sex with men, detailed data on gender and sexual behaviors were available only for the AIDS cases. Analyses of effects on AIDS rates for men who have sex with men, men who have sex with women, and women revealed that legalizing marriage for same-sex couples primarily affected men who have sex with men. The primary mechanisms for this effect were increased social acceptance of LGBT individuals and prevalence of same-sex couples (which presumably decrease the motivation to engage in risky sexual behavior) and increased access to and reimbursement for protective pharmaceuticals, such as PrEP.

AIDS rates among women and among men who have sex with women were generally not affected by changes in legal status for same-sex couples, suggesting that the direct public health impact of these policies is mostly confined to men who have sex with men. However, in terms of health care costs, this effect has general implications for public health after all. Because the annual costs of preventing and treating HIV and AIDS are high, reductions in infections observed after changes in marriage recognition policies represent a savings of $1 billion to $6 billion per year for the health care system (Nikolaou, 2023).

Conclusions

To date, only two studies have explored the ripple effects that improving the well-being of LGBT individuals may have on public health generally, and neither found strong evidence that the significant health benefits of granting legal recognition to same-sex couples extend beyond LGBT individuals (although neither found any evidence of adverse effects on public health). A priority for future research is to examine how changes in policies regarding same-sex couples affect trends in a broader variety of emotional and physical public health outcomes. What is already clear, however, is that directly improving the health of LGBT individuals (e.g., through reductions in STIs) leads to substantial savings across the entire health care system. These savings are likely to be even greater when other marriage-related health benefits for LGBT individuals are considered, another priority for future research.

Impacts on Economic Outcomes

Key Points

- In the years leading up to the *Obergefell* decision, male-headed same-sex households and female-headed different-sex households were more likely to move out of states that prevented same-sex couples from marrying, controlling for other economic and demographic differences between states.
- States that legalized marriage for same-sex couples experienced a rise in the number and impact of patents issued in those states.
- When states legalized marriage for same-sex couples, the market value of companies headquartered in those states rose immediately and significantly.

Theoretical Background

Prior to the *Obergefell* decision, business leaders were among the most prominent voices in favor of legalizing marriage for same-sex couples. In a brief filed in support of the petitioners in that case, many of the most high-profile employers in the United States (Amazon, Apple, Disney, Goldman-Sachs, Google, Morgan-Stanley, Office Depot, Target, and many others) argued that granting same-sex couples access to legal marriage would promote economic growth for several reasons (*Obergefell v. Hodges*, Brief of 379 Employers and Organizations Representing Employers as Amici Curiae, 2015). First, LGBT individuals are likely to gravitate toward states with policies friendly to same-sex couples but move away from states with policies unfriendly to same-sex couples, increasing or restricting the pool of talented potential employees in those states. Second, to the extent that policies friendly to LGBT individuals increase the diversity of the pool of potential employees, the mingling of diverse perspectives within companies should increase innovation and enhance performance. Third, protections offered to employees who are members of sexual-minority groups should reduce their stress and increase their productivity, benefiting the companies where they work.

A growing body of research literature supports these arguments, showing that companies that enact policies friendly to LGBT individuals and same-sex couples go on to experience improved value and productivity on average (Li and Nagar, 2013; Pichler et al., 2018). Yet this literature does not address the question of whether the economies of states are similarly affected by state-level changes in the legal status of same-sex couples. Our review identified only three studies that examined this issue (see Table B.11). Each of these studies drew on large, representative datasets collected over 12 to 14 years, offering strong bases for conclusions about the economic impacts of legalizing marriage for same-sex couples.

Findings

The first study we identified used data from the 15 years prior to the *Obergefell* decision to examine the effects of state-level policies toward same-sex couples on migration between states (Beaudin, 2017). Earlier in this chapter, we reviewed research showing that states recognizing marriages between same-sex couples experienced an increase in same-sex households (Miller and Park, 2018). Beaudin (2017) examined whether changes in a state's marriage laws affect decisions to leave or remain in that state by the heads of same-sex or different-sex cohabiting households. Reporting being in a same-sex household is not a perfect measure of being in a same-sex romantic relationship, but it has generally been considered a reasonable proxy (Black et al., 2007). Results indicated that, in a given year, the heads of same-sex households and the heads of different-sex households were both more likely to move out of states that withheld legal status for the marriages of same-sex couples, even after controlling for demographic and economic differences between states. Although the effect was significant at the population level, more–fine-grained analyses revealed that the effect was significant only for male-headed same-sex households and female-headed different-sex households. In female-headed same-sex households and male-headed different sex households, the effect of marriage equality laws on migration was not significant. This pattern is consistent with broader patterns of discrimination experienced in workplace settings; sexual-minority men and heterosexual women are the most likely to experience wage discrimination (Drydakis, 2019). Therefore, the results suggest that marriage equality laws in a state are a sign of a broader system of gender- and sexual-minority–related protections that motivate members of the most-disadvantaged groups (i.e., sexual-minority men and heterosexual women) to leave states that do not have those protections.

The second study examined whether legalizing civil unions and domestic partnerships between same-sex couples affected rates of innovation within a state (Vakili and Zhang, 2018). Level of innovation was measured by the number of patents issued to a state in a given year. Using data on all the patents granted by the U.S. Patent and Trademark Office between 1994 and 2006, this difference-in-differences analysis estimated that about three years after states granted legal recognition to same-sex couples through civil unions or domestic partnerships, the number of patents awarded within those states rose by an average of 6 percent, even after controlling for dynamic state-level factors, such as economic conditions and political orientation. The authors used a variety of creative operationalizations to show that policies favorable to same-sex couples increase the number and diversity of collaborations among inventors in a state, which in turn increases the speed and rate at which new patents are cited in subsequent patent applications.

The final study examined the immediate effects of state-level changes in marriage policies on the market valuation of companies headquartered in each state (Zhu and Smieliauskas, 2022). To address this question, the researchers drew on several short-term indicators of a company's value (e.g., the cumulative abnormal returns in the two-day window following a change in policy). Across several of these measures, the analyses revealed that state-level actions to grant legal status to the marriages of same-sex couples predicted immediate increases in the market value of companies headquartered in those states. The effects were largest for states that extended legal recognition voluntarily (i.e., before the *Windsor* and *Obergefell* decisions). Older and more-profitable companies experienced the greatest benefits, whereas companies headquartered in states that did not change their policies experienced no benefits.

Conclusions

To date, research on the state-level economic impacts of granting legal status to same-sex couples has been limited to a narrow set of indicators: migration across states, number of patents issued in a state, and the market value of companies headquartered in a state. Yet analyses of each of these indicators have revealed consistent results. When states gave legal status to same-sex couples, families were less likely to leave the state; innovators within the state were more productive and more successful; and companies headquartered within the state saw their market values rise. As industry leaders predicted in their amicus brief in 2015, extending legal status to same-sex couples appears to be good business. To the extent that the limited existing literature leaves many other economic indicators still to be studied (e.g., unemployment rates, state-level gross domestic product, household earnings), additional findings consistent with those described here would suggest that the total economic impact of changes in these policies could be much greater than has so far been documented.

Impacts on Trends in Family Formation

Key Points

- Although opponents of legalizing marriage for same-sex couples were concerned that doing so would hasten a decline in marriage for different-sex couples, multiple studies have found no evidence that legal marriage for same-sex couples has any negative impact on marriage rates for different-sex couples.
- Legal marriage for same-sex couples also has no effects on state-level divorce rates, abortion rates, the proportion of children born to single women, the percentage of children in female-headed households, or rates of child poverty.
- Extending legal recognition to same-sex couples does affect state-level adoption rates, which rise by between 4 percent and 6 percent after marriage between same-sex partners becomes legal.

Theoretical Background

During the debates over legalizing marriage for same-sex couples, opponents argued that treating same-sex and different-sex marriage equally would have negative implications for different-sex marriages and households. Central to this perspective is the observation that marriage rates in the United States have been declining over the past several decades (Fry and Parker, 2021), even as alternative family forms (e.g., living alone, cohabitation, single-parent households) have been on the rise (e.g., Manning and Carlson, 2021). Opponents of legal marriage for same-sex couples argued that granting legal status to same-sex couples would further accelerate the "deinstitutionalization of marriage" (Cherlin, 2004; Cherlin, 2020) by lowering the perceived value of marriage for different-sex couples. As a consequence, legalizing marriage for same-sex couples should lead to fewer different-sex couples seeking marriage and, subsequently, other adverse downstream consequences, such as a rise in divorce, higher rates of extramarital births, and higher rates of child poverty. In the opinion of the state governments of 15 states that jointly urged the U.S. Supreme Court not to recognize marriages between same-sex partners in the *Obergefell* case, the damage to American families if same-sex couples were allowed to marry legally would be "severe, unavoidable, and irreversible" (*Obergefell v. Hodges*, Brief of Louisiana, et al. as Amici Curiae, 2015, p. 13).

Because indices of family formation change over time for many reasons, evaluating whether these predictions came to pass requires analyses that directly assess whether preexisting state-level trends in family formation for different-sex couples (e.g., marriage and divorce rates) changed after states legalized or banned marriage for same-sex couples (i.e., a difference-in-differences analysis). Our review identified eight studies that adopted a version of this analysis to evaluate how legal marriage for same-sex couples affected trends in family formation in the general population (see Table B.12). Although the majority of this work has focused on the effects on marriage rates, research has also examined the possibility of effects on rates of divorce, abortion, child poverty, birth of children to single parents, and adoption. All of these outcomes, to the extent that they are negatively affected by legalizing marriages between same-sex partners, would give rise to even broader negative effects (e.g., on child welfare) than opponents of marriage for same-sex couples predicted would come to pass.

Effects on Marriage Rates

Of the eight studies we identified, seven examined the implications of legalizing marriage for same-sex couples on marriage rates among different-sex couples. None of these analyses found any evidence that legalizing marriage for same-sex couples negatively affected marriage rates for different-sex couples.

The first study to address this question compared state-level data on marriage rates from 1990 with data from 2000 and 2004 and compared states that allowed any form of legal recognition for same-sex couples (i.e., marriage or civil unions) with states that allowed no form of legal status (Langbein and Yost, 2009). In contrast to the fears of opponents of marriage equality, these analyses found that states that granted legal status to same-sex couples experienced a slight but significant *increase* in marriage rates compared with states that did not grant such status. In a critique of this study, Allen and Price (2015) questioned the earlier researchers' estimation procedures and decisions about coding variables. They obtained the same data and conducted their own version of the analyses, addressing their critiques of the earlier analyses. Yet their reanalyses also found no significant evidence of any adverse effects on marriage rates, as the authors of the original paper noted in their rebuttal (Langbein and Yost, 2015).

Subsequent analyses used more data (Dinno and Whitney, 2013), more-recent data (Carpenter, 2020), multiple approaches to analyzing the data (Langbein, Ranallo-Benavidez, and Palmer, 2021), and a wide variety of statistical controls and robustness checks (Dillender, 2014). All reached the same conclusion: Extending legal status to same-sex couples did not lead to declines in marriage rates for different-sex couples. One of these analyses focused specifically on data from Massachusetts, where marriage for same-sex couples was legalized the earliest and where any adverse effects on different-sex marriage have therefore had the longest time to manifest (Carpenter, 2020). This analysis found that, as many as nine years after the Massachusetts Supreme Judicial Court legalized marriage between same-sex partners in 2004, the probability that men and women in that state reported being married was unchanged from what it had been before the ruling. The study that used the most-recent data compared states that legalized marriage for same-sex couples prior to the *Windsor* ruling (early adopters) with states that legalized it only after the ruling (reluctant adopters), using three different strategies for estimating effects (Langbein, Ranallo-Benavidez, and Palmer, 2021). Regardless of the estimation strategy, these analyses found no evidence of any negative effect of legalizing marriage for same-sex couples on rates of marriage for different-sex couples.

If recognizing the marriages of same-sex couples did not harm different-sex couples, did banning marriage for same-sex couples protect different-sex couples? Three of these studies examined this question, and none found any evidence that laws banning marriage for same-sex couples affected the marriage rates of different-sex couples (Allen and Price, 2015; Bowen, 2014; Langbein and Yost, 2009).

Effects on Other Outcomes

Because the most-vocal opponents of marriage for same-sex couples expressed explicit concerns about marriage for different-sex couples, that is the topic on which most scholarship has been focused. However, some of these studies also examined the implications of legalizing marriage for same-sex couples on a broader set of outcomes. Langbein and her colleagues cast the widest net in this regard: In the earlier of their two studies on this topic, they drew on data from the U.S. Census Bureau to examine, in addition to the effect of legal status for same-sex relationships on marriage, the effects on divorce, abortion rates, the proportion of children born to single women, and the percentage of children in female-headed households (Langbein and Yost, 2009). Extending legal status to same-sex couples had no effects on any of these outcomes. Although these analyses were the subject of a published critique (Allen and Price, 2015), a reanalysis of the dataset using improved methods also failed to obtain any significant effects (Langbein and Yost, 2015). A subsequent study by the Langbein team drew on more-recent census data to examine, in addition to effects on marriage, the effects of legalizing marriage for same-sex couples on rates of child poverty, divorce, and children living in single-parent households (Langbein, Ranallo-Benavidez, and Palmer, 2021). Again, across three different strategies for modeling their data, they found no evidence that changes in marriage policies had any significant effect on any of these variables. A separate study that examined divorce rates also found no significant effects from these policies (Bowen, 2014).

Are any family outcomes affected when legal recognition is extended to same-sex couples? Our review of the literature identified one: adoptions. Analyses of data on adoptions and foster care from 1995 to 2020 revealed that legalizing marriages between same-sex partners raised adoption rates by between 4 percent and 6 percent, which translates to between 10,000 and 17,500 additional adoptions nationally in the four years after a change in law (Martin and Rodriguez, 2022). Driving this increase was a shift in the structure of families adopting: fewer unmarried couples and single parents and greater numbers of married couples. Martin and Rodriguez speculate that being in a legally recognized marriage increases the demand for children within same-sex couples at the same time that it removes barriers to adoption that same-sex couples would otherwise face (see also Kimberly and Moore, 2015).

Conclusions

In the debates preceding the *Obergefell* decision in 2015, opponents of legalizing marriage for same-sex couples predicted that doing so would have severe negative implications for different-sex couples and their families, hastening a decline in the motivation to marry and stay married. To date, those dire predictions have not come to pass. The available literature is strikingly consistent: Across different sources of data, disparate estimation strategies, and a variety of dependent variables (e.g., marriage rates, divorce rates, rates of child poverty), no study has identified any adverse impact of legalizing marriage for same-sex couples on the outcomes of different-sex couples. On the contrary, the single significant effect has been a rise in the number of adoptions, arguably a positive effect for children. The failure to find adverse effects of marriage equality on different-sex couples in the United States echoes very similar results obtained in analyses of the effects of legal recognition for same-sex couples in other countries (Trandafir, 2014a; Trandafir, 2014b; Trandafir, 2015).

Numerous studies have identified other state-level policies that do have measurable effects on family formation in the general population. For example, after states raise their minimum wages, lower-income earners delay marriage and are less likely to divorce (Karney et al., 2022). After states expanded Medicaid coverage through the Affordable Care Act, residents in those states married at slightly lower rates and divorced at slightly higher rates, presumably because partners were less reliant on each other for health insurance (Hampton and Lenhart, 2022). The way in which states implemented welfare reform after the Personal Responsibility and Work Opportunity Reconciliation Act of 1996 was passed had measurable (and unintended) negative effects on rates of marriage and divorce for women receiving benefits (Bitler et al., 2004; Pub. L. 104-193, 1996). Given that a variety of state-level policies can affect decisions about marriage and divorce in the general population, it is all the more noteworthy that state-level policies toward same-sex couples did not.

General Conclusions

Prior to the *Obergefell* decision in 2015, when the prospect of legalizing marriage for same-sex couples was being hotly debated, both supporters and opponents agreed that the proposed changes in policy would be historic and consequential. The research community concurred (Herek, 2006). As states gradually extended the privileges and responsibilities of marriage to same-sex couples, researchers from a wide variety of disciplines evaluated the effects of these changes on a wide variety of outcomes. After 20 years of these efforts, our review identified 96 studies that examined what happened when same-sex couples and different-sex couples were granted the same legal status.

Summary of Results

What were the consequences of the policy change that swept across the United States between 1999 and 2015? Our review answered this question with respect to three different populations.

For LGBT individuals and same-sex couples, the populations most directly affected by legal recognition of their relationships and, therefore, the focus of more than two-thirds of this research, the consequences were unambiguously positive. Compared with LGBT individuals living in states that took no action prior to the *Obergefell* decision, those living in states that issued marriage licenses to same-sex couples experienced improved psychological well-being (i.e., more positive affect, less stress, greater life satisfaction) and those living in states that enacted bans on marriage for same-sex couples experienced declines in psychological well-being (i.e., more depression, higher rates of psychopathology). When states allowed same-sex couples to marry, the physical health of LGBT individuals in those states also improved, as demonstrated by higher levels of health care use, higher levels of health insurance coverage, and declining rates of STIs. Same-sex households in those states experienced more-stable relationships, higher earnings, higher rates of homeownership, and better preparation for retirement and end-of-life care. All of these effects are consistent with minority stress theory (Frost and Meyer, 2023), which proposes that LGBT individuals generally experience worse health outcomes due to greater exposure to stigmatization and discrimination. By legitimizing same-sex relationships, states reduced the stigma experienced by same-sex couples and by LGBT individuals more generally. The downstream effects of being validated in this way should have been positive, and, across 66 independent studies and a variety of outcomes, they were.

There has been far less research on the effects of legal marriage on the children of same-sex couples, as most of the scholarly attention has been focused on the comparability of children's outcomes in same-sex and different-sex households, regardless of legal status. Because that well-populated literature has already been reviewed multiple times (see, for example,

Manning et al., 2014; American Psychological Association, 2005; and Pawelski et al., 2006), this review focused more narrowly on the direct consequences of legal marriage for same-sex relationships on the children of same-sex couples. There were only four of these studies, but all four suggest that children benefit when their parents have the option of marrying. Specifically, in states that prohibit marriage for same-sex couples, the children of same-sex parents are less likely than the children of different-sex parents to have access to health insurance and more likely to experience delayed progress through school; these differences are greatly reduced or even disappear when states grant same-sex couples the right to marry.

Do the benefits associated with legalizing marriage for same-sex couples stem from the fact that same-sex couples gain legal status, or are there unique benefits associated with granting same-sex couples access to the institution of marriage specifically? Most of the research reviewed in this chapter compared married households with unmarried households, or it compared outcomes in states that allowed marriage for same-sex couples with outcomes in states that prohibited it. Very few studies directly compared outcomes associated with different forms of legal status for same-sex couples (i.e., marriage, civil unions, and domestic partnerships), but those that did found that granting same-sex couples access to marriage offered unique benefits that other forms of legal recognition did not provide. For example, two studies found that married same-sex couples report less psychological distress than same-sex couples in civil unions or domestic partnerships (LeBlanc, Frost, and Bowen, 2018; Wight, LeBlanc, and Badgett, 2013). Compared with LGBT individuals living in states that banned marriage for same-sex couples, those living in states that granted same-sex couples access to marriage prior to *Obergefell* reported better physical health, but those living in states that recognized only civil unions or domestic partnerships did not (Kail, Acosta, and Wright, 2015). Same-sex couples earn more income the longer they are in a legal marriage but do not earn more the longer they are in a civil union or domestic partnership (Delhommer and Hamermesh, 2021). Finally, legalizing marriage predicts steeper declines in hate crimes against LGBT individuals than recognizing civil unions (Nikolaou, 2022). Clearly, more research comparing the effects of marriage with the effects of other forms of legal status for same-sex couples is warranted, but the direction of the limited research to date suggests that marriage offers benefits to LGBT individuals and same-sex couples that are not associated with other forms of legal status.

And what of the rest of the country? Did heterosexual individuals and different-sex couples pay a cost for the benefits accrued by LGBT individuals, same-sex couples, and their children? They did not. In fact, the reverse seems to be true: The general public also appears to have benefited. Although some feared that judicial and legislative actions to extend recognition to same-sex couples would provoke a backlash in public opinion, there have been no lasting negative changes in public opinion toward LGBT individuals. On the contrary, in nationally representative polls of public opinion, more than two-thirds of the U.S. population now approve of marriage for same-sex couples (McCarthy, 2023). Moreover, when states recognized same-sex couples, sexual orientation–motivated hate crimes and employment discrimination both declined. The economies of states that recognized same-sex relationships also improved by some measures, including higher rates of patents awarded in those states and higher market values for corporations headquartered in those states.

Evaluating Specific Predictions About Harms to U.S. Families

In light of the uniformly beneficial effects observed in 20 years of research on the consequences of granting legal status to same-sex couples, it is also worth noting the effects that were not observed. Despite strong predictions from opponents of granting legal status to the marriages of same-sex couples that doing so would inflict severe adverse effects on different-sex families, those predictions did not come to pass. After 20 years and multiple studies using national datasets and the most-sophisticated methods for inferring causal relationships (e.g., difference-in-differences approaches), research on these issues consistently fails to find any effects of changes in the legal status of same-sex couples on marriage rates, divorce rates, abortion rates, rates of single-parent fertility, or rates of child poverty in the general population. These results echo similar results obtained in research on the consequences of legal recognition for same-sex couples in European countries (Trandafir, 2014a; Trandafir, 2015). It appears that, when making decisions about their own families, different-sex households do not attend closely to the legal status of same-sex couples.

Priorities for Future Research

Despite the breadth of the outcomes considered in the 96 studies identified in this review, some topics remain understudied, and others have been neglected entirely. Foremost among the understudied topics is the role of gender in moderating the consequences of legalizing marriage for same-sex couples. As our review has made clear, although many of the consequences of legal marriage are the same for couples consisting of two men and couples consisting of two women (e.g., improved mental health, greater social connection), some are not (e.g., marriage penalty on wages, interactions with health care providers). Scholarship in this area awaits an explicit model that addresses how gender interacts with legal marriage to shape its consequences for same-sex couples.

Also understudied is how same-sex couples negotiate the effects of changes in their legal status. As noted in our review, prior research has found that, when their commitment to each other has legal status, same-sex couples alter their household division of labor toward more specialization, which has downstream consequences for couples' labor-market participation. What remains unknown is how couples negotiate these choices and allocate tasks in the absence of the clearly defined gender roles that guide these decisions for different-sex couples. To date, research on these issues has lacked assessments of couple interactions that could shed light on these questions.

Several other outcome categories identified in this review were clearly underpopulated. For example, although there have been studies of how legalization affected health insurance coverage and school progress for children of same-sex couples, there have been no studies of how legalization affects other important child outcomes, such as social, emotional, and cognitive development. Similarly, although there has been research documenting the improved health and lower rates of STIs for LGBT individuals after legalization, the broader effects of legal marriage for same-sex couples on the health care system itself have so far received only cursory analyses. Finally, although research has estimated the effects of extending legal status to same-sex couples on a few economic indicators (e.g., patents, market values of state-based companies), the broader effects of legalization on state economies have yet to be documented.

There are also at least two important issues related to understanding the consequences of legal recognition for same-sex couples that have yet to be studied at all. First, although we have referred to "LGBT individuals" as a general category throughout this review, we identified very few studies that examined the consequences of legal marriage for bisexual, nonbinary, or trans individuals.[1] Second, as the United States enters its second 20 years of legal marriage for same-sex couples, it will be possible to explore differences between LGBT individuals who grew up without access to legal marriage and then obtained it and those born a generation later who have never known a world in which same-sex and different-sex couples had unequal status before the law. The decisions and experiences of people who had adjusted to prohibitions on marriage that were later lifted may be different from the decisions and experiences of those raised with the option to marry from birth.

[1] Carpenter (2020), which directly addressed people identifying as bisexual, is a notable exception.

CHAPTER 3

New Analytic Evidence

A central argument made by those who oppose legal status for the marriages of same-sex couples has been that doing so would harm different-sex couples and their families. In the previous chapter, we identified eight studies that directly evaluated the evidence for such effects (seven of which specifically examined effects on rates of marriage). None of the eight found any evidence that extending legal status to same-sex couples had adverse consequences on marriages among different-sex couples.

However, before accepting this evidence as the final word, we acknowledge that these existing studies have been limited in several ways. First, the methods used by the more-rigorous, causal studies have become somewhat outdated. Econometricians have pointed out that the traditional difference-in-differences approach (stacking up states' policy changes and aggregating) to modeling state-initiated policy changes can lead to inaccurate (and even wrong-signed) estimates of policy impacts when (1) early-adopting states are different from late adopting states in a way that may affect outcomes and (2) effects vary over time since the policy change (e.g., grow stronger or weaker; see Baker, Larcker, and Wang, 2022, for discussion). If a retreat from marriage is more likely in later-adopting states (which are likely more politically conservative), older methods may understate the magnitude of this effect. Fortunately, econometricians have developed new estimation approaches to address these concerns (discussed further in the "Generalized Approach" section).

Second, the policy landscape has evolved. Several of the studies focused on a period in which only a handful of very early-acting states permitted marriage between same-sex couples. In the years since, same-sex couples gained the right to marry in a total of 37 states (although local implementation varied in some states prior to *Obergefell*). The remaining states were required by the *Obergefell* decision to license marriages to same-sex couples. Effects from the early-adopting states (such as Massachusetts) might not readily generalize to the later-adopting states (such as Arizona), nor to those compelled under *Obergefell* (such as Texas).

Third, the existing literature may conflate potentially offsetting effects, finding no effect instead of two opposed effects. Many of the studies focused on the U.S. population overall, assuming that the number of LGBT individuals in the data is slight enough to not affect estimates. But we might anticipate a short-term increase in overall marriages driven by new access to marriage for same-sex couples, which could obscure any retreat from marriage among different-sex couples (see the box on the next page).

Language Note: *Same-Sex Couple*

The data used in this chapter do not contain any measure of sexual orientation or detailed gender identity measures. For the purposes of this chapter, we use the term *same-sex couple* to describe a couple observed in a formalized cohabitation or marriage. We note that this does not include all same-sex couples (e.g., those in noncohabiting relationships), nor does *same-sex couple* fully align with the definition of *LGBT individuals* offered in the prior chapter: Some LGBT individuals form different-sex couples, and some members of same-sex couples do not identify as LGBT.

Supporting strong conclusions about the consequences of legal marriage for same-sex couples on family formation among different-sex couples requires research that employs recently developed estimation approaches and narrows the focal population to current or potential different-sex couples. The goal of this chapter is to present new analyses that overcome the limitations of the existing literature in evaluating the effects of legal marriage status. Using the latest advances in difference-in-differences methodology, we estimate the effects of state-level policy changes in the legal status of marriage for same-sex couples across policy eras, constrain our analyses to exclude same-sex couples where possible, replicate our analyses across a variety of data sources with different sampling structures, and test sensitivity across a variety of parameterizations of each outcome of interest.

The rest of this chapter is organized as follows. We outline our approach in several steps, discussing the selection of outcomes for analysis, the data sources from which they are drawn, and the empirical strategy for estimation. We then discuss the results by outcome, unifying the discussion across data sources. The final sections detail the limitations of our analyses and summarize findings and implications of our analyses for future policy. Additional discussion of identifying assumptions and econometric specifications can be found in Appendix C. Additional results, including event study plots for each specification, can be found in Appendix D.

Selection of Outcomes

A central argument raised by the opposition in *Obergefell v. Hodges* focused on the perceived potential consequences of granting same-sex couples access to legal marriage (see Table 3.1 for examples). These included (1) an undermining of the "traditional family" resulting in decreased incentives for different-sex couples to marry, (2) a subsequent increase in divorce, (3) a decline in marital fertility, and (4) a possible increase in nonmarital fertility (i.e., among single mothers). These concerns center not on the population newly granted legal marriage but on the population seeking to form different-sex partnered households. To reflect this focus, where possible, our analyses exclude individuals observed in same-sex (cohabiting or married) relationships.

TABLE 3.1
Alignment of Arguments and Analysis

Topic	Argument	Our Evaluation Approach
Protecting children	"The State has an interest in the biological father-child bond" (Bursch, *Obergefell v. Hodges*, 576 U.S. 644, 2015). Children need both a mother and a father (e.g., as proffered by the Alliance Defending Freedom, undated; the U.S. Conference of Catholic Bishops [Brief Amicus Curiae of United States Conference of Catholic Bishops in Support of Respondents and Supporting Affirmance, 2015]; Justice Thomas dissenting in *Obergefell v. Hodges*, 576 U.S. 644, 2015; and the Republican National Committee, 2020).	Literature review
Devaluing of marriage and erosion of traditional family	"[If couples believe] that marriage is more about their emotional commitment to each other, and if that commitment fades, then they may not stay together" (Bursch, *Obergefell v. Hodges*, 576 U.S. 644, 2015). Legal marriage for same-sex couples will devalue marriage and dissuade couples from marrying and/or increase divorce (e.g., as proffered by the Catholic Diocese of Honolulu reprinting TFP Student Action, 2013; Justice Alito dissenting in *Obergefell v. Hodges*, 576 U.S. 644, 2015; and the Family Research Council, undated).	Literature review; analyses of marriage, divorce, and cohabitation rates; marriage attitudes

The opposition and Justice Thomas's dissent also suggested that children benefit from having a female parent and a male parent (i.e., from the gender difference, not just from having two parents) and argued that there may be negative effects on children raised by same-sex couples. Because national survey data do not capture a sufficient number of same-sex couples raising children, we were unable to examine the outcomes of such children in our analyses. We were similarly unable to examine the impacts on the fertility of different-sex couples, discussed later in this chapter.

We set up our analyses to evaluate each of these concerns in turn. A decline in marriage could be detected by a reduction in the *stock* of marriages (i.e., the number of people married at any given time) or by reduced *flow* of marriages (i.e., the number of people getting married in a given year). We first examined stocks through shifts in marital status: Does issuing marriage licenses to same-sex couples change the share of individuals reporting that they are currently married? Next, we turned to the flows. In survey data, flows are best measured by new marriages; we analyzed individuals declared to have married in the past year. We also used state marriage records: specifically, a count of marriage licenses issued.[1] Marriage rates in the United States had been declining prior to Massachusetts' granting of legal status to marriages between same-sex couples in 2004 (see Figure 3.1); therefore, a retreat from marriage induced by policy changes would require an acceleration in the rate of decline. Conversely, a continuation of the existing downward trend in marriage rates does not by itself imply a negative effect of policy changes.

[1] Note that some couples ultimately might not wed even if a license was issued.

FIGURE 3.1
Share of Adults Who Are Married, United States

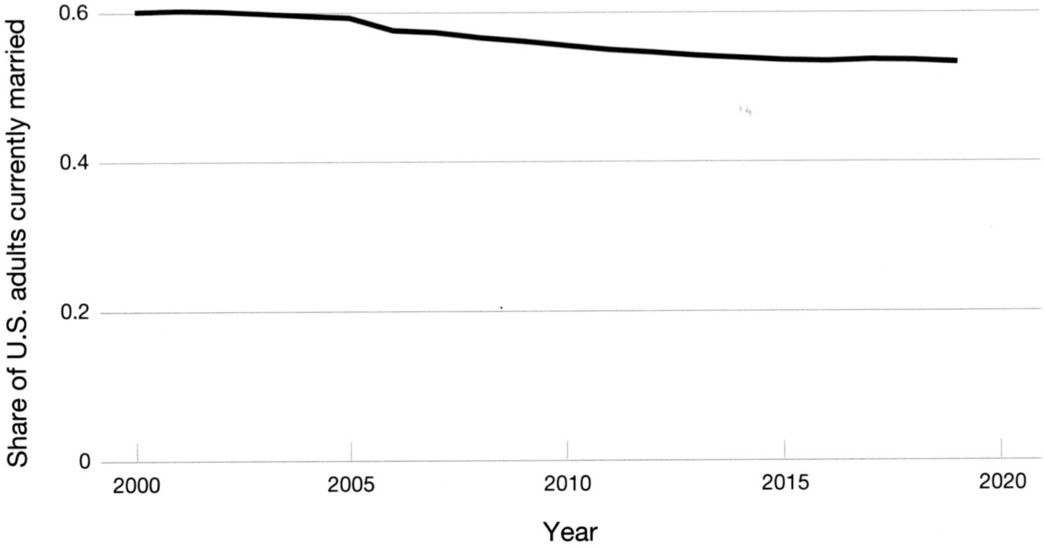

SOURCE: Features data from the authors' analyses of the ACS, 2000 to 2019 (Ruggles et al., 2023).

A retreat from marriage does not necessarily imply a retreat from coupling. We also examined cohabitation (living with an unmarried partner), alone and jointly with marriage, to determine whether individuals substitute away from marriage to cohabitation. Before and during the analysis period, cohabitation rates generally were rising in the United States (see Figure 3.2). An increase in cohabitation as a result of marriage policy changes would take the form of a sharper rise in cohabitation; a slight increase common across states may just be a continuation of the preexisting trend.

The share of currently married individuals can change because of reduced entry into marriage but can also be influenced by changes in divorce (and widowhood, which we expect would be unaffected by changes in marriage policies). Moreover, changes in the image of marriage as an institution may induce some already-married couples to divorce.[2] Therefore, we looked at the rate of divorce among married individuals and the incidence of divorce in the population to ensure that our analyses could separate out changes due to compositional shifts in who gets married and changes potentially due to shifts in attitudes toward marriage.

Family formation processes can be difficult to influence, particularly in the short term. We considered up to five years post–policy change for each state. But divorce is likely pre-

2 We did not include separation in our analyses for two reasons. First, the definition (and required duration) of *legal separation* varies by state, and the term is not explicitly defined in the survey datasets that assess it. Second, separation is a sufficiently noisy outcome, even on a national scale, that we find the conditional parallel trends assumption implausible.

FIGURE 3.2
Cohabitation Rates over Time, United States

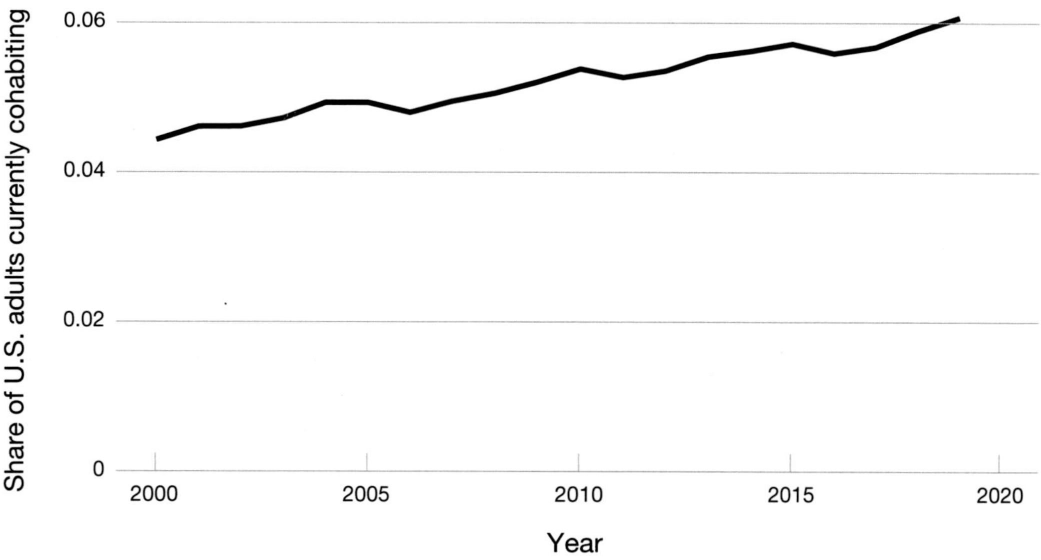

SOURCE: Features data from the authors' analyses of the ACS, 2000 to 2019 (Ruggles et al., 2023).

ceded by marital strain and arguments, which we cannot measure in most national data sources. The decision to forgo marriage may be influenced by changes in relationship satisfaction, which is, again, largely invisible in secondary data sources. Finally, changes in attitudes toward marriage may be most likely to affect family formation among those who have not yet started forming families. Therefore, in a final analysis, we considered a more interim outcome—young adults' attitudes toward marriage and premarital cohabitation—to assess the impacts of legal marriage for same-sex couples on attitudes likely indicative of future family formation decisions.

Our analyses omit another possible dimension of effect: fertility. The arguments raised in *Obergefell* forecasted an inability to incentivize marital procreation and marriage more generally. In particular, John Bursch argued that "there's harm if you change the definition because, in people's minds, if marriage and creating children don't have anything do with each other, then what do you expect? You expect more children outside of marriage" (Bursch, *Obergefell v. Hodges*, 576 U.S. 644 (2015)). Therefore, any analysis of fertility would need to distinguish between marital and nonmarital fertility, since the forecasted effects trend in different directions.

Policy changes that affect marriage mean that the composition of the married and nonmarried populations is changing over time. In particular, we found some evidence that marriage rates among different-sex couples increased around the time states started issuing marriage licenses to same-sex couples. Any examination of the direct effects of marriage recognition policies on fertility among different-sex couples needs to account for possible changes in the composition of the married and nonmarried populations, an endeavor out of the scope of this current work. Prior international work has identified a reduction in extramarital births as a consequence of legalizing marriage for same-sex couples (Trandafir, 2015). However, despite finding a modest increase in marriage, this work does not address the potential for compositional effects influencing who could have nonmarital births, so the effect of marriage licenses for same-sex couples on fertility is, as yet, unknown.

Further analysis of this policy change could elucidate effects on other dimensions of family formation. Because of the estimated positive marriage effect for different-sex couples, concerns about changing composition precluded marital and nonmarital fertility analyses with our approach.[3] In addition, our approach was intended to maximize variation and the likelihood of detecting any possible effect. Those who are explicitly interested in detecting the "one true effect" need to be mindful of contemporaneous policy changes and demographic factors that might influence fertility.

Selection of Data Sources

To examine the impact of state policies legalizing marriage for same-sex couples on different-sex couples, we drew on multiple data sources: the ACS, the CPS, National Vital Statistics Data from the CDC, the Panel Study of Income Dynamics (PSID), and the Monitoring the Future (MTF) main study.[4]

The ACS is a nationally representative household survey conducted by the U.S. Census Bureau. The survey is conducted annually to collect data on demographic, social, and economic characteristics of the American population. We used data from the 2000–2014 waves of the ACS to construct marriage rates, divorce rates, and cohabitation rates at the state level as outcomes of interest. We also examined the impact of extending legal status to the marriages of same-sex couples on these outcomes at the individual level to be able to account for individual heterogeneity in age, race, education, labor force participation, earnings, and foreign birthplace. In addition, data from the ACS were used to construct marriage market characteristics at the state level, including sex ratios, sex-specific shares of race and ethnicity groups, sex-specific shares of education groups, female labor force participation, and share

[3] One could condition on the already-married population, looking at changes in fertility within that subpopulation of married households. This sample would have limited generalizability (in particular, it could not speak to any changes in *nonmarital* fertility) but would not be vulnerable to compositional changes.

[4] Other datasets considered for this analysis include the Survey of Income and Program Participation (which is not representative beyond the census region), National Survey of Family Growth (which has limited data before 2006 and is not intended for annual analysis), National Longitudinal Survey of Youth 1997 (which consists of a single cohort), National Longitudinal Study of Adolescent to Adult Health (which consists of a single cohort and has limited geographic information), and General Social Survey (which has a small sample for a given question and questions that are inconsistent over time).

of foreign-born residents.[5] These control variables were used to account for marriage market conditions in all the analyses we conducted.

We also analyzed data from the CPS, a monthly nationally representative household survey conducted by the Census Bureau and Bureau of Labor Statistics. Similar to the ACS analyses, we use data from the 2000 to 2014 CPS Annual Social and Economic Supplements to examine marriage, cohabitation, and divorce at the state and individual levels. We intentionally built these redundancies into our analysis plan to ensure that the results we found were not an artifact of a specific data source or sampling procedure.

While data from the ACS and CPS are well suited to examine the stock of marriages (the number of people married at any given time), our ability to examine the flow of marriages (the number of people getting married in a given year) was limited because of data availability across sample years. To examine the impact of issuing marriage licenses to same-sex couples on a flow measure of marriage, we obtained data on annual marriage rates by state from the CDC. These marriage rates are calculated as the number of marriages per 1,000 adults in the state using the full census of marriage licenses issued in a given year. It is important to note that the CDC-provided marriage rates include marriages of both same-sex couples and different-sex couples.

Additionally, we used data from the PSID, a longitudinal household survey that started in 1968 with a nationally representative sample of households, making it the longest-running longitudinal household survey in the world. It began as an annual survey but has been conducted biennially since 1997. We used the panel structure of the PSID to examine changes in marriage and divorce for a fixed panel of individuals over time and to account for unobserved individual-level heterogeneity, neither of which are possible with cross-sectional surveys, such as the ACS and the CPS.

To examine the impact of issuing marriage licenses to same-sex couples on attitudes toward marriage and family formation, we used data from the MTF study. The MTF study is an annual survey of U.S. high school students that collects data on a variety of health and social behaviors, including substance use, sexual behavior, and attitudes toward marriage and family. We used MTF data on the responses of high school seniors to examine changes in attitudes toward marriage among young people before and after their states started issuing marriage licenses to same-sex couples.

Data on state legal recognition policies—including legal marriage, civil unions, and domestic partnerships—were obtained from the Williams Institute and primary data collection. Finally, we obtained state-level annual unemployment data from the Bureau of Labor

[5] Prior empirical work has shown that sex ratios affect the search for a spouse and marriage entry (Becker, 2009; Guzzo, 2006), as well as racial differences in rates of marriage and divorce (Bennett, Bloom, and Craig, 1989).

Statistics and used these data in all our analyses to control for economic conditions of the state marriage market.[6]

Generalized Approach

To assess the causal effect of issuing marriage licenses to same-sex couples on the outcomes discussed above, one would ideally implement a randomized control trial: the gold standard for causal analyses, in which experimental subjects are randomly assigned to treatment and control conditions. The random assignment means that any differences arising at the end of the experiment can generally be attributed to the treatment. In our context, this would be akin to putting all 50 states' names in a hat and selecting a subset of states to start issuing marriage licenses to same-sex couples.

However, state-initiated changes to eligibility for marriage licenses and states' introduction of most policies more generally are inherently nonrandom processes. In such situations, social scientists often use quasi-experimental approaches, such as the difference-in-differences methods we employ and describe below, to identify the causal effect of policies on outcomes of interest.

One might think that it is possible to compare outcomes after the policy to outcomes before the policy and attribute any difference to the effect of the policy. However, outcomes are rarely unchanging over time, and, without further assumptions and modeling, this before-and-after comparison would attribute all changes in the outcome to the policy, including those changes driven by the march of time. Difference-in-differences methods exploit the fact that policies are sometimes introduced in some states and not in others and compare how an outcome changes in states that introduce a policy, compared with states that do not introduce the same policy (difference number one), before and after the implementation of the policy (difference number two). By comparing outcomes from treated states (those states that introduced a policy) and control states (those states that had not yet introduced a policy), before and after the policy, one can disentangle the effect of policy implementation (treatment) from other changes in the outcome that occur at the same time.

In our setting, the policy of interest is the legalization of marriage for same-sex couples, which, while eventually in place in all states, was legalized in different states at different times. This means that for each legalization year, there were some states that legalized marriage for same-sex couples and other states that did not. Consider the outcome of marriage stock (currently married individuals), described previously. As we show in Figure 3.1, the stock of marriages generally declined between 2000 and 2019.

---

[6] Prior work has connected marriageability, marriage timing, and marriage stability to local labor market conditions; see Blau, Kahn, and Waldfogel, 2000; Karney et al., 2022; Kearney and Wilson, 2018; and Schaller, 2013.

This decline has implications for our analytic approach. For example (simplifying to policy changes in 2008), if we simply compared the stock of marriages before 2008 with the stock of marriages since 2008 and attributed the difference to legalization, we would conclude that legalization of marriage for same-sex couples led to a decline in marriage. But this analysis would not account for the fact that marriage was generally declining in all states around 2008. The difference-in-differences methodology compares the change in marriage stock around 2008 in the states that legalized marriage for same-sex couples in 2008 with the change in marriage stock around 2008 in the states that did not legalize marriage for same-sex couples in that time. The change in marriage stock around 2008 for states that did not legalize marriage in that time frame is used to account for the overall time trends in marriage stock around that time, a general decrease in this case. A change in the marriage stock around 2008 for the states that legalized marriage for same-sex couples in 2008 is attributed to legalization only if that change is different from the change in marriage stock in the nonlegalizing states. Analysis results are summarized in this chapter and formally presented in event study figures in Appendix D. A detailed discussion of how to interpret event study graphs is included in the "Interpreting Event Study Figures" section in Appendix D.

Although the above example used one legalization year, the method can be generalized to cover multiple periods and multiple states. In our models, we generalized the above example to the rollout of legalized marriage for same-sex couples across the United States over the period from 2000 to 2014, given that in 2015 all remaining states became treated because of the *Obergefell* ruling and there was no longer any untreated control group for comparison. We used the final treated states (those that became treated in 2015) as our control states and compared these control states with states that started issuing marriage licenses to same-sex couples in each year prior to 2015.

The difference-in-differences approach specified above relies on three key assumptions, discussed in more detail in Appendix C. First is the parallel trends assumption, which requires that the control and treatment states—those without and with policy changes—(1) must have similar trends (but, importantly, not necessarily similar values) in the outcome studied *before* the policy change (which we can observe) and (2) would have *continued* to have similar trends if there had not been a policy change (which we cannot observe). If trends are diverging before the policy, then it is plausible that post-policy differences are driven by these preexisting trends rather than by the policy change itself. We employed a variant of this assumption, requiring *conditional* parallel trends after accounting for a slate of economic and demographic characteristics at the state level.[7] We also further adapted this assumption in some specifications by incorporating cohort-specific linear trends (along the lines of the

[7] There are a nearly infinite number of possible policy, economic, and demographic controls that correlate with family formation. To maximize the usable variation (and maximize our ability to detect an effect), we employed a subset of controls that was sufficient to establish conditional parallel trends. Unless other state policy changes were substantially correlated with the granting of marriage licenses to same-sex couples, their omission does not pose a risk to our analyses.

"parallel paths" approach of Mora and Reggio [2019]). This allowed us to analyze outcomes in which the treatment and control states were less similar pre-policy (e.g., marriage trends). The various versions of the parallel trends assumption can be visually assessed using event study graphs, provided in Appendix D.

Second, the stable unit treatment values assumption (SUTVA) requires that there is no contamination of the policy—that is, that extending legal status to the marriages of same-sex couples in Iowa does not affect family formation in Missouri.[8] This assumption is untestable, but our sample restriction to those not in or formalizing same-sex partnerships makes it more plausible, as these residents are presumably unaffected by the policy toward a different population in a different state.

Finally, our approach requires strict exogeneity—that is, that policies were adopted or not adopted without concern for or relation to the family formation outcomes we study. The strict exogeneity assumption is likely violated if states legalized marriage in response to changing family formation patterns among different-sex couples—for example, if states granted marriage licenses to same-sex couples to offset a decline in marriage.

A correlation between state willingness to change marriage policy and particular family formation trends would also violate strict exogeneity. In this context, it is worth remembering that, as pointed out by Sansone (2019), some of the states most perceived as liberal, such as New York and California, were *not* among the first to start issuing marriage licenses to same-sex couples. Iowa, a politically moderate state, was the third state to do so. Sansone (2019) highlights that the passage of marriage legalization for same-sex couples was largely driven by court decisions, and many of the early-legalizing states legalized prior to public opinion being in favor of marriage legalization for same-sex couples. Citing evidence from Europe, Aksoy and colleagues indicate that marriage legalization for same-sex couples likely changed public opinion rather than marriage legalization for same-sex couples being an endogenous response to public opinion (Aksoy et al., 2020; see Chapter 2 for details). Broadly, these facts increase the likelihood that the exact timing of legal marriage for same-sex couples was unknown and therefore increase the likelihood that strict exogeneity is satisfied.

Sample size and modeling choices can reduce statistical power, thereby increasing the likelihood that a given approach—regardless of the true effect—finds no significant effects. We made few modeling restrictions that limited statistical power in order to intentionally favor finding a significant effect. In other words, we made modeling choices that would make it easier to detect (positive or negative) effects. For example, we estimated treatment effects

[8] One possible violation of SUTVA in our context would be that treatment (marriage recognition for same-sex couples) resulted in people migrating out of states that legalized marriage for same-sex couples because of their *distaste* for the policy. Note that the temporary or permanent migration of same-sex couples seeking marriage recognition is not an issue in most of our sample. As noted in Chapter 2, prior work suggests that the interstate migration spurred by marriage laws was concentrated among gay men (Marcén and Morales, 2022) and female heads of household (Beaudin, 2017), and migration came only in the form of leaving states that did not recognize the marriages of same-sex couples. We also conducted a composition balance test and determined that population demographics were not changing within a state.

using both state-level and individual-level data, we estimated models without (and with) controls, and we declined to adjust for multiple hypothesis testing in order to use the full variation of the data.[9]

Results

Marriage

As shown in Table 3.1, opponents of extending legal status to the marriages of same-sex couples hypothesized that doing so would result in a retreat from marriage among different-sex couples. We investigated the weight of evidence for this hypothesis using four of our five data sources, looking at both marriage stock (the number of people who are currently married) and marriage flow (the number of new marriages and/or people newly married). Because the primary concerns about a retreat from marriage centered on heterosexual individuals, and the extension of marriage rights to same-sex couples was likely to cause a (potentially offsetting) increase in marriage among LGBT individuals, we attempted to limit our analysis to individuals not in a formalized (cohabiting or married) same-sex couple.[10]

Using the difference-in-differences approach discussed in the prior section, we estimated the effect of legalization of marriage between same-sex partners on marriage formation among people potentially entering a different-sex marriage (see Appendix C for details). If the hypothesis that issuing marriage licenses to same-sex couples would result in an overall retreat from marriage were correct, we would expect our event studies to find a decrease in both the stock and flow of marriage.

[9] Statistical significance is usually defined in relation to the likelihood of Type I errors: rejecting a true null hypothesis, which in our case would be saying that marriage license eligibility had an effect on marriage rates when it did not. With a typical α (threshold for the likelihood of Type I error) of 0.05, running 12 hypothesis tests would generate at least one significant result by chance 46 percent of the time. Multiple hypothesis testing correction reduces α to control this likelihood across tests, classifying more results as statistically indistinguishable from 0. Because we wanted to preserve statistical power to detect any possible effects, we did not adjust α.

[10] The two exceptions to this limitation are the CDC and PSID data. Prior studies have leveraged the underlying records that state health agencies provide to the CDC, some of which appear to distinguish partner gender. However, there were sufficient data inconsistencies—exact matches between total marriages of same-sex couples and total civil unions of same-sex couples, recorded marriages between same-sex couples in years prior to states granting formal legal status to such relationships—that we elected to use the more reliable CDC aggregate data. The PSID did not track partner gender until 2015, and not systematically until 2017; same-sex couples were categorized as other nonfamilial relationships. Backdating those in same-sex couples in 2017 to our analysis period, we found that there are 159 same-sex partnerships among the 10,094 respondents in our analytic sample. We do not exclude them.

Marriage Stock

Table 3.2 summarizes results for both marriage stock and marriage flow across four data sources. Each cell generally represents 12 individual specifications: two levels of analysis (state versus individual) × two estimation methods (two-way fixed effects [TWFE] versus an interaction-weighted estimator; Sun and Abraham [2021]) × three controls specifications (no controls, state-specific economic and marriage market conditions, and controls plus a cohort-specific linear time trend). CDC analyses include only state-level analysis, and PSID analyses include only individual-level analysis. Each specification yields event study coefficient estimates for six periods (years 0–5); up to 72 data post-policy points are summarized in each cell.

Both data sources that allow analysis of marriage stock (*share married*) at the state level indicate that there was no significant change in the stock of people reporting that they were currently married during the period studied. This finding of no statistically significant effect held with and without controlling for state-specific economic and marriage market conditions and cohort-specific linear time trends. Event study coefficients suggest that effects in a given year were generally less than 2 percent (an increase of 1.2 percentage points from a base of approximately 60 percent). The consistently small and not statistically significant treatment effects found across model specifications and data sources provide a strong indication that there was no discernible change in the stock of married different-sex couples that could be attributed to the legalization of marriage between same-sex partners.

At the individual level, both model specifications across three data sources indicate that there was broadly no change in marriage stock after legalization even when controlling for state-specific economic and marriage market conditions, cohort-specific linear time trends, and individual demographics. Two specification-data combinations (TWFE in the CPS and the interaction-weighted estimator in the ACS) suggest a small but statistically significant increase in the likelihood that the average American adult is married, on the order of 0.5 to

TABLE 3.2

Marriage Legalization Either Did Not Affect or Increased Marriage

Data Source	Change in Share Married	Change in Rate of New Marriages
ACS	11/72 stat. sig. increase	22/72 stat. sig. increase
CPS	1/72 stat. sig. increase	N/A
PSID[a]	0/36 stat. sig.	1/36 stat. sig. decrease
CDC[a]	N/A	32/36 stat. sig. increase

SOURCE: Features data from Ruggles et al., 2023; Flood et al., 2023; Institute for Social Research, 2023; CDC, undated.

NOTE: ACS = American Community Survey; CDC = Centers for Disease Control and Prevention; CPS = Current Population Survey; N/A = not applicable; PSID = Panel Study of Income Dynamics. *Stat. sig.* refers to statistical significance at the *a* < 0.05 level. The analytic period is 2000 to 2014. The table summarizes findings from difference-in-differences regression models of each outcome. The rows for PSID and CDC have half the number of coefficients summarized because PSID analysis is conducted only at the individual level and CDC analysis is conducted only at the state level. See Appendix D for details.

[a] All marriages are included, regardless of partner sex.

1 percentage points in a given year (approximately 60 percent of the sample is currently married). As shown in Figure 3.1, marriage stock had been declining in the United States since 2000. Taken together, our analyses of marriage stock suggest that if issuing marriage licenses to same-sex couples had any effect on the marital patterns of different-sex couples,[11] it was to spur a very modest increase in marriage, although this result for marriage stock is not robust across datasets and specifications. Event study figures for the models summarized above are available in Appendix D.

Marriage Flow

The ACS and the PSID, as well as the data obtained from the CDC, also allow investigation of marriage flow. Because this outcome does not include the history of previously married individuals, as marriage stock does, one might expect it to be more responsive to policy. As with marriage stock, the cells in Table 3.2 summarize up to 12 underlying regressions across six time points. In the ACS, we excluded same-sex couples from our analysis, so any detected effects in these data are driven by new marriages between different-sex partners. In both the ACS and the CDC data (note that the CDC data include marriages between same-sex partners), we identify a small but statistically significant *increase* in entry into marriage.

In the ACS state-level analysis, we identify a slight increase in new marriages of different-sex couples immediately after marriage legalization for same-sex couples (about a 1.25-percent increase in year 0), a return to baseline for the next several years, and then a slight increase again around four years post-legalization. At the individual level, all model specifications in the ACS indicated a small but statistically significant average treatment effect of marriage legalization on individuals' likelihood of entering into different-sex marriages, centering on a 0.10–percentage point increase (from a base of 5 percent) in the first three years after marriage legalization. These results, though small (about a 2-percent change), were statistically significantly different from 0.[12]

Unsurprisingly, we found larger increases using the CDC data, which include *all* marriages, including those between same-sex partners. Results using the CDC data suggest a persistent increased flow into marriage on the order of 10 percent in each post-legalization year (with a maximum estimated effect over 25 percent), significant in the first year for all specifications and through five years for five out of six specifications. That increase is likely partially driven by the known increase in marriages among same-sex couples. In 2000, there were 9.8 new marriage licenses per 1,000 residents in the average state captured in the CDC data. A 10-percent increase would mean approximately one additional license per 1,000 residents. When aggregated to 330 million U.S. residents, this equates to almost 330,000 additional marriage licenses per year.

[11] The PSID results include both different-sex and same-sex couples, as same-sex couples are inconsistently identified in this data source and could not be excluded from the analysis.

[12] The negative point estimates in the ACS were not statistically significant and had a maximum estimated effect of a decrease of 1.25 percentage points from a base of 5 percent.

In contrast, analyses of the PSID data, which also include same-sex couples, found an overall downward trend in the first four years after marriage legalization before a return to baseline in year 5 or later. These treatment effect estimates, which range from an increase of 1 percent to a decrease of 4 percent, are imprecise and are not statistically different from 0, with the exception of one year of one event study that was not robust to controls. With a base of 2 percent of the sample newly marrying in a given year, the largest negative point estimate of 4 percent (which is not statistically distinguishable from 0) translates to a drop in the newly married rate from 2 percent to 1.92 percent.

Overall, we found strong evidence of an increase in marriage license issuance, and we note again that the data we used include same-sex couples. In datasets that exclude formalized same-sex couples, we found mixed evidence of an increase in marriage among different-sex couples. Across our 324 point estimates, one is negative and statistically significant, 57 are positive and statistically significant, and most are not statistically distinguishable from 0.

To assure readers that treatment effects are (1) unaffected by the shifting composition of states across post-policy years and (2) relatively homogeneous, we show that our marriage results are robust to restricting to a balanced panel of states and that early adopters and later adopters have similar effects immediately after policy change (see Appendix D). This suggests that our effects may generalize to the states compelled by *Obergefell*, not just early actors.

Cohabitation

Opponents of issuing marriage licenses to same-sex couples hypothesized that it would devalue marriage overall and lead to more nonmarital cohabitation. We investigated the evidence for this hypothesis in two of our data sources.[13] As with the analysis described above, we attempted to limit this analysis to individuals not in a formalized (cohabiting or married) same-sex couple. If the hypothesis were correct, we would expect to find an increase in the number of different-sex couples cohabiting without entering into marriage.

TABLE 3.3

Marriage Legalization Did Not Affect Cohabitation

Data Source	Change in Share Cohabiting
ACS	8/72 stat. sig. decrease, 1/72 stat. sig. increase
CPS	6/72 stat. sig. decrease

SOURCE: Features data from Ruggles et al., 2023; Flood et al., 2023.

NOTE: ACS = American Community Survey; CPS = Current Population Survey. *Stat. sig.* refers to statistical significance at the *a* < 0.05 level. The analytic period is 2000 to 2014. The table summarizes findings from difference-in-differences regression models of each outcome. See Appendix D for details.

[13] Although cohabitation is possible to assess in the PSID using the household roster, only current cohabitations, rather than full cohabitation history, are tracked. With a biennial survey, we are unable to determine cohabitation transitions precisely enough to align with our definition of treatment timing. Therefore, we did not analyze cohabitation in the PSID.

Table 3.3 summarizes results for changes in cohabitation in the available data sources. We examined change in cohabitation at the individual level (whether a person is currently cohabiting with an unmarried partner) and at the state level (the share of residents currently cohabiting). As with marriage analyses, we used two different model specifications to study cohabitation, and we controlled for state-specific economic and marriage market conditions and cohort-specific time trends. These 12 specifications yielded six event study coefficients; the cells in Table 3.3 summarize 72 point estimates. Across all specifications and datasets, one out of 144 estimates indicated a statistically significant increase in cohabitation, 14 indicated a statistically significant decrease in cohabitation, and the rest indicated that there were no statistically significant changes in cohabitation rates among different-sex couples as a result of issuing marriage licenses to same-sex couples.

At the state level, event study coefficients suggest a decline of 5 percent to 10 percent (from a baseline of 4 percent, a 10-percent decline is equivalent to going from 4 percent of adults in a cohabiting couple to 3.6 percent of adults). These effects were small in magnitude in both the ACS and CPS and were not statistically different from 0. Similarly, we generally found no statistically significant change in the likelihood of being in a cohabiting nonmarital relationship at the individual level. However, the interaction-weighted estimator suggests a modest decline (0.002 percentage points, approximately 5 percent) in the first few years after marriage licenses could be issued to same-sex couples. These results are robust to the inclusion of market and individual-level controls and cohort-specific time trends.

Our point estimates for cohabitation generally span 0 and range from an estimated decrease of 25 percent to an increase of 5 percent. With a baseline cohabitation rate of 4 percent, this corresponds to an estimated decrease to 3 percent and an estimated increase to 4.2 percent. Overall, we found no evidence of an increase in cohabitation (e.g., as an alternative to marriage). We found some evidence of a decrease in cohabitation, although this is sensitive to dataset and specification.

Divorce

We were able to investigate evidence for the hypothesis that issuing marriage licenses to same-sex couples would increase divorce in three of our five data sources. We examined both the proportion of people who are currently divorced and the incidence of new divorces. Because the primary concerns about a retreat from or devaluing of marriage centered on heterosexual individuals, we again limited our analysis to individuals not in a formalized (cohabiting or married) same-sex couple. Table 3.4 summarizes results for both the share of people currently divorced and the incidence of new divorces for the ACS, CPS, and PSID. As with prior analyses, we used two different model specifications to study divorce, and we controlled for state-specific economic and marriage market conditions and cohort-specific time trends. Because the identified increase in marriage can shift the population eligible for divorce, we constructed both conditional and unconditional models of divorce. The difference between these two measures is the denominator: Conditional divorce considers only those who have with the traditional TWFE estimator but is mirrored five years after policy changes with the interaction-weighted estimator.

Respondents are also asked about the wisdom of premarital cohabitation, which we interpret as a negative sentiment toward marriage. We found a modest increase in disagreement with both estimators, consistent across specifications and concentrated two to four years after policy changes.

Taken together, these results suggest that issuing marriage licenses to same-sex couples had, if anything, a small positive impact on marriage attitudes among high school seniors.

Limitations

Our analyses are subject to several limitations. Because we sought to increase the trustworthiness of a finding of no effect, we made several modeling choices to maximize precision (and the odds of a statistically significant effect). By using individual-level data to analyze a state policy change, we overstate the level of precision of our estimated treatment effect. This was an intentional choice to over-detect a nonzero treatment effect. For this reason, identified effects should be interpreted with caution relative to their magnitude and their robustness to aggregation to the state level.

Several of the assumptions underlying our analyses are untestable. Although visual inspection of the graphs in Appendix D along with the results from joint significance tests for the TWFE specifications suggest that we meet conditional parallel trends in the pre-policy periods, we cannot discern whether earlier- and later-treated states' family formation would have continued to evolve in tandem in the absence of policy changes.

SUTVA would be violated if there were selective migration by those not in same-sex couples seeking to leave states making policy changes. Prior work finds no evidence for such flight (see Beaudin, 2017; Marcén and Morales, 2022). Finally, we cannot rule out states' endogenous adoption of marriage policies, although media reports and prior literature provide some evidence to the contrary.

Mechanically, our estimates for several years of post-policy change are driven primarily by states that were early adopters. This means that the states compelled by *Obergefell* do not contribute to our identified effects (they remain in the control group until the analysis period ends in 2014). An analysis contrasting early- and later-adopting states suggests that the effects are similar.

The MTF data pose some additional limitations. These are cross-sectional data, so the student body (always high school seniors) is changing over time. There have been notable increases in youth identifying as LGBT over the past two decades (Jones, 2022), and, because

leading to fuller lives, consistent across specifications. We also found a statistically significant decline in the share of respondents rating a good marriage as "not very important," isolated to the interaction-weighted estimator. (TWFE shows a decline but lacks precision.)

we cannot ascertain sexual orientation or gender identity in the data, such youth are respondents in the survey (whereas in our ACS and CPS analyses, we were able to exclude changes driven by couples in formalized same-sex households). Marriage policy changes might be particularly salient for these youth, and their attitudes might not be generalizable to other cohorts.

Finally, all reduced-form specifications are approximations of real-world relationships and involve researcher choices. The interaction-weighted estimator overcomes several known issues with TWFE estimation (Sun and Abraham, 2021), but it still uses regression as a basis, which places some limitations on how covariates influence treatment effects and trends (Callaway and Sant'Anna, 2021).

Summary and Conclusions

To evaluate the impact of policies legalizing marriage for same-sex couples on different-sex couples and the general population, we leveraged advances in research methodology and multiple data sources to assess the causal effect of granting legal status to marriages between same-sex couples. We examined the effects of such state-level policy changes between 2000 and 2014 on different-sex couples' marriage rates, cohabitation rates, and divorce rates.

Our results are broadly consistent with prior research on the effects of extending legal marriage to same-sex couples. The previously prevailing approach, TWFE, is generally quite similar to what we found using an interaction-weighted estimator approach (Sun and Abraham, 2021): Point estimates are more sensitive to the set of controls rather than the underlying specification.

Yet this was not just an academic exercise. Previous work tends to focus on a subset of outcomes or a subset of data sources. Our broad selection with a consistent approach across outcomes allowed us to assess evidence jointly. In doing so, we found no evidence for a retreat from marriage; in fact, the only evidence of change we found is of a possible *increase* in marriage resulting from legalization of marriage between same-sex partners. Importantly, we can identify that this is not driven solely by newly marrying same-sex couples. Alternate explanations include (1) renewed salience of the value of marriage among the country more generally created by the prolonged national discussion of marriage; (2) heterosexual individuals perceiving themselves as allies waiting to marry until same-sex couples could; and (3) bisexual individuals waiting for states to license marriages between same-sex couples before forming different-sex marriages, as an acknowledgment of their underlying identity (Carpenter, 2020).

We extended these analyses to additional years of data and a more politically diverse set of states, meaning that we can see whether early-adopting states have effects from marriage legalization that differ from those of later-adopting states. We found no difference between later-adopting states' and early-adopting states' effects in the early years (zero years and one year after policy change, the maximum number of years that can be observed with an adequate control group pre-*Obergefell*).

We were unable to examine cohabitation in detail because of specification challenges, but we generally found no evidence of statistically significant effects of changes in cohabitation rates due to states issuing marriage licenses to same-sex couples. We found no consistent evidence of effects on divorce, even when accounting for compositional shifts in the married population. Finally, we examined marriage attitudes across a variety of questions asked of high school seniors. We found no evidence of a decline in attitudes toward marriage and some evidence of improved status, such as a declining belief in the value of premarital cohabitation.

CHAPTER 4

Conclusions and Policy Implications

When the Massachusetts Supreme Judicial Court considered the case of *Goodridge v. Department of Public Health* in 2003, the justices were confronted with competing visions of the likely consequences of granting same-sex couples and different-sex couples the same legal status. For supporters referencing the equal protection clause of the Fourteenth Amendment, the central issues in the case revolved around equity for LGBT individuals. From this perspective, lifting restrictions on marriage for same-sex couples should relieve LGBT individuals of the burden of legal discrimination, presumably benefiting their relationships and their families. For opponents, the prospect of granting equal status to the marriages of same-sex couples represented a grave threat to marriage itself. In their view, allowing same-sex couples to marry would diminish the value of marriage for different-sex couples, leading to lower rates of marriage, higher rates of divorce, and poorer outcomes for children.

May 17, 2024, marks 20 years since the first marriage licenses were issued to same-sex couples in the United States. Since then, and since the U.S. Supreme Court's *Obergefell* decision lifted restrictions on marriage for same-sex couples nationwide in 2015, hundreds of thousands of same-sex couples have embraced the opportunity to marry (Scherer, 2022). In that time, the consequences of issuing marriage licenses to same-sex couples have been studied extensively by a diverse set of independent scholars, informed by multiple academic disciplines, with respect to a wide variety of populations and outcomes. There is no need to speculate about what the consequences of granting equal status to same-sex and different-sex marriage might be. It is now possible to go beyond speculation and evaluate what the impacts of issuing marriage licenses to same-sex couples have been.

The overarching goal of this report was to conduct such an evaluation. We pursued this goal in two ways. First, we assembled and reviewed the existing research literature on the consequences of legalizing marriage for same-sex couples. Second, we drew on multiple national datasets to conduct new analyses to estimate how state-level changes in marriage policies toward same-sex couples affected state- and individual-level rates of marriage, divorce, and cohabitation, as well as individual attitudes toward marriage.

Summary of Results

Our literature search identified 96 studies that assessed some form of legal status for same-sex couples (usually legal marriage, but also civil unions and domestic partnerships) and examined its association with an outcome. The outcomes examined by these studies ranged widely, from the emotional, physical, and financial health of LGBT individuals, same-sex couples, and their children to nationwide changes in public opinion, STIs, and rates of marriage, divorce, and fertility. Yet despite the diversity of the methods and topics in the research we reviewed, the conclusions of these 96 studies are remarkably consistent. Granting same-sex couples access to marriage offered substantial benefits to LGBT individuals, same-sex couples, children raised by same-sex couples, and the states that made these changes. Across 20 years of research and 96 studies, we found no reliable evidence that legalizing marriage for same-sex couples produced any lasting negative effects on any outcomes.

Given the arguments made in marriage cases from the Massachusetts Supreme Judicial Court's *Goodridge* case to the U.S. Supreme Court's *Obergefell* case, we paid particular attention to research that bears on the specific predictions offered by opponents of legalizing marriage for same-sex couples: the idea that legalizing marriage for same-sex couples would diminish the institution of marriage for different-sex couples. We identified seven studies that addressed this possibility directly. None found any evidence that marriage rates for different-sex couples are adversely affected by changes in the legal status of same-sex couples. Several of those studies also examined additional outcomes, such as divorce rates, abortion rates, and rates of child poverty. None of those outcomes were affected by changes in the legal status of same-sex couples.

To address limitations in those studies, we conducted our own analyses, using multiple national datasets that included assessments of marriage, divorce, and cohabitation across states in the years before the *Obergefell* decision. Differences in the timing of the legalization of marriage for same-sex couples across states allowed us to estimate how changes in marriage policies affected state-level changes in these family formation outcomes, over and above the preexisting family formation trends within each state. Despite employing analytic approaches designed to maximize the chances of observing a significant effect, our analyses reached the same conclusions as the other studies of this issue: Granting same-sex couples access to legal marriage had no adverse effects on marriage, divorce, or cohabitation among different-sex couples. Far from the diminishment predicted by opponents of legal marriage for same-sex couples, the few significant effects observed in our analyses suggest a slight increase in marriage rates after same-sex couples were granted access to legal marriage by a state. Overall, the fears of opponents of marriage for same-sex couples simply have not come to pass.

Strengths and Limitations of This Work

There are several reasons for confidence in these conclusions. First, we made every effort to make our review of existing research comprehensive, including searching through four separate databases, imposing no restrictions on the outcomes addressed, and scouring the reference lists of those studies to identify studies that our other searches may have missed. The 96 studies that we reviewed represent, at the very least, most of the existing research on the effects of legal marriage for same-sex couples. Second, the sheer consistency of the findings of these studies supports the idea that there are no unmeasured moderators to complicate our general conclusion of no adverse effects. Third, our new quantitative analyses support this conclusion as well, replicating the same patterns of results across multiple national datasets. Fourth, our new analyses employed estimation strategies biased in favor of finding effects; the fact that we still found none strongly supports the conclusion that there are no effects on different-sex couples to be found.

Yet despite these noteworthy strengths, the analyses in this report were also limited in several ways. First, although we made every attempt to conduct a comprehensive review of existing research on the consequences of legal marriage for same-sex couples, it is likely that there are studies that escaped detection. Nevertheless, it is very unlikely that studies that we may have missed would change the overall conclusions of this report. Such a study would have to identify a major and widespread harm arising from legalizing the marriages of same-sex couples to outweigh the numerous and well-documented benefits of legalization identified in our review. If there were such a notable contradictory finding, we believe that it would have been cited in one of the 96 studies that we did find.

Second, our new quantitative analyses, and the majority of the prior studies evaluating the effects of extending access to legal marriage to same-sex couples, examined data only before 2015, when variability in policies across states allowed for a quasi-experimental analysis that supports causal inferences. After 2015, the *Obergefell* decision lifted all remaining restrictions on marriage for same-sex couples, eliminating the variability across states used to support causal inferences. Using states that were already issuing marriage licenses to same-sex couples as controls for states compelled by *Obergefell* would bias estimates of the effect of marriage legalization if we suspected that already-issuing states might still be experiencing the effects of legalization. Because we found some significant effect estimates as far as four and five years out, we believe that this is a valid concern. Nevertheless, if the *Obergefell* decision led to changes in family formation that differed from the effects of state-level policy changes prior to *Obergefell*, our analyses could not detect them. However, we believe that the likelihood of effects differing between states compelled by Obergefell and state-initiated legalization is quite low, in light of the consistent effects of the state-level policy changes prior to *Obergefell* and the uniformly positive effects of issuing marriage licenses to same-sex couples on other outcomes that were measured after *Obergefell*. If the Supreme Court's decision in 2015 led to adverse effects on any outcome, we would have found them in the existing literature, but we found none.

Third, the period of these analyses limits the duration of effects we are able to detect. If family formation outcomes or the social status of marriage takes a long time to influence, we might not observe all of the relevant changes. However, our event study estimates for years 4 and 5 generally mirror what we see in earlier years, suggesting that our horizon is sufficient.[1]

Fourth, throughout this report, we exclusively focus on studies that empirically evaluated the effects of legalizing marriage for same-sex couples in the United States, and our new analyses are also constrained to the United States. The United States was not the first country to issue marriage licenses to same-sex couples, nor is it the last. Therefore, the conclusions of the evidence review and empirical analysis might not extend to other countries.

Fifth, as noted earlier, most of the datasets available to address issues related to the effects of legalizing marriage for same-sex couples do not include direct measures of sexual orientation, leaving researchers to infer sexual orientation from whether or not respondents are in same-sex or different-sex relationships. This is imprecise, preventing the existing research and data from addressing the potential impact of legalizing marriage for same-sex couples on single individuals, bisexual people, and transgender people. Executive Order 14075 required an exploration of expanding data collection on sexual orientation and gender identity in federal statistics (Biden, 2022), and, in late 2023, the Census Bureau invited public comment on its proposed sexual orientation and gender identity questions for the ACS (U.S. Census Bureau, 2023). In 2016, the Department of Labor explored adding sexual orientation and gender identity questions to the CPS (Ellis et al., 2018). These efforts may facilitate more-precise investigation in the future.

Policy Implications

Given all that we have learned about the consequences of extending legal status to the marriages of same-sex couples, we can extrapolate about what might happen were the U.S. Supreme Court to revisit the *Obergefell* decision.

First, the arguments available to opponents of legal marriage for same-sex couples today are narrower than they were in 2015. Where once it was possible to speculate about the consequences of extending legal status to same-sex couples in the United States, now the consequences are known. There is no empirical basis for concerns that allowing same-sex couples to marry will negatively affect the intentions and choices of different-sex couples and families. The only empirical evidence of changes suggests a potential renewed salience of marriage among the broader public. Although opponents of legalizing marriage for same-sex couples may bring other legal arguments before the court, fears for the fate of U.S. families should not be among them.

[1] One exception is cohabitation; we see a somewhat sudden drop in cohabitation five years after the first issuing of marriage licenses to same-sex couples. If anything, this result is suggestive of a *strengthening* of the institution of marriage.

Second, if *Obergefell* were to be overturned, this report offers a basis for predicting that the consequences would be negative. Marriage bans that are currently dormant in 34 states would suddenly be activated. Because of the passage of the Respect for Marriage Act in 2022, current marriages and marriages enacted in states that continue to issue marriage licenses to same-sex couples would still be recognized in all 50 states. New marriages for same-sex couples, however, could be banned in parts of the country. Same-sex couples without the means to travel to another state would be prevented from marrying. The past research reviewed in this report found consistent evidence that enacting bans on marriage for same-sex couples harms the mental health and well-being of LGBT individuals living under those bans, even if marriage for same-sex couples is legal elsewhere. Separate from the negative impact of reimposed bans, the existing research review indicates that LGBT individuals, same-sex couples, and their children would suffer from the loss of the social, physical, and economic benefits that we now know are the consequences of legalizing marriage for same-sex couples.

APPENDIX A

Studies Included in Evidence Review

Table A.1 presents details on the 96 studies we reviewed, listed in alphabetical order.

TABLE A.1
Studies Used in the Evidence Review

Author	Year	Design	Legal Status Examined	Population Studied	Outcome Category
Adams-Cohen	2020	Cross-sectional survey	Civil union	LGBT individuals	Couple well-being
Aftab and Imanpour	2022	Cross-sectional survey	Civil union	LGBT individuals	Psychological well-being, financial well-being
Allen and Price	2015	Cross-sectional survey	Marriage, domestic partnership, civil union, marriage ban	LGBT individuals	Psychological well-being
Alonso-Villar and del Río	2023	Cross-sectional survey	Marriage	LGBT individuals	Psychological well-being
Anderson, Matsuzawa, and Sabia	2021	Cross-sectional survey	Marriage	LGBT individuals	Physical health
Badgett	2018	Cross-sectional survey	Marriage	LGBT individuals	Couple well-being
Balsam et al.	2008	Difference-in-differences	Any legal status, marriage bans	General population	Public opinion
Bauermeister	2014	Difference-in-differences	Marriage	LGBT individuals	Financial well-being
Beaudin	2017	Difference-in-differences	Marriage	LGBT individuals, general population	Employment, public opinion
Bernstein, Naples, and Harvey	2016	Difference-in-differences	Marriage	General population	Public health

Table A.1—Continued

Author	Year	Design	Legal Status Examined	Population Studied	Outcome Category
Bishin et al.	2016	Repeated survey	Marriage	LGBT individuals, general population	Trends in family formation
Boertien and Bernardi	2019	Repeated survey	Marriage	LGBT individuals	Financial well-being
Bowen	2014	Repeated survey	Marriage	LGBT individuals	Physical health
Brodoff, Hiedemann, and Xue	2024	Repeated survey	Marriage	LGBT individuals	Health insurance
Carpenter	2020	Repeated survey	Marriage	LGBT individuals	Financial well-being
Carpenter et al.	2021	Repeated survey (pooled)	Marriage	LGBT individuals	Psychological well-being
Charlton et al.	2016	Repeated survey	Marriage	LGBT individuals	Financial well-being
Coley	2020	Cross-sectional survey	Civil union	LGBT individuals	Couple well-being, social connection
Colistra and Johnson	2021	Cross-sectional survey	Marriage bans	LGBT individuals	Psychological well-being
de Vries et al.	2009	Cross-sectional survey	Marriage bans	General population	Public health
Delhommer and Hamermesh	2021	Cross-sectional survey	Marriage, marriage bans	LGBT individuals	Financial well-being
Dillender	2014	Cross-sectional survey	Marriage, civil union, domestic partnership	LGBT individuals	Health insurance
Dillender	2015	Cross-sectional survey	Marriage, civil union	LGBT individuals	Psychological well-being
Dinno and Whitney	2013	Cross-sectional survey	Marriage	LGBT individuals	Psychological well-being
Donovan and Tolbert	2013	Cross-sectional survey	Marriage, domestic partnership, civil union, marriage ban	LGBT individuals	Psychological well-being, physical health
Downing and Cha	2020	Difference-in-differences	Marriage, civil union, domestic partnership	General population	Trends in family formation

Table A.1—Continued

Author	Year	Design	Legal Status Examined	Population Studied	Outcome Category
Drabble et al.	2022	Difference-in-differences	Marriage	LGBT individuals	Psychological well-being
Elwood et al.	2017	Difference-in-differences	Marriage	LGBT individuals	Psychological well-being
Everett, Hatzenbuehler, and Hughes	2016	Experiment, repeated survey	Marriage	General population	Public opinion
Fingerhut and Maisel	2010	Longitudinal study	Marriage bans	LGBT individuals	Psychological well-being, physical health
Flores and Barclay	2016	Longitudinal study	Marriage	LGBT individuals	Psychological well-being, social connection
Flores, Mallory, and Conron	2020	Repeated survey	Marriage	General population	Public opinion
Francis, Mialon, and Peng	2012	Repeated survey	Marriage	LGBT individuals	Financial well-being
Goldsen et al.	2017	Cross-sectional survey	Domestic partnership	LGBT individuals	Psychological well-being, couple well-being
Gonzales	2015	Cross-sectional survey	Marriage, domestic partnership	LGBT individuals	Psychological well-being
Gonzales and Blewett	2013	Cross-sectional survey	Marriage, civil union, domestic partnership	Children	Children of same-sex parents
Gonzales and Blewett	2014	Cross-sectional survey	Marriage, marriage bans	LGBT individuals	Psychological well-being
Gonzales and Ehrenfeld	2018	Cross-sectional survey	Marriage	LGBT individuals	Psychological well-being, physical health
Haas and Lannutti	2022a	Cross-sectional survey	Marriage	LGBT individuals	Psychological well-being, couple well-being
Haas and Lannutti	2022b	Cross-sectional survey	Marriage	LGBT individuals	Financial well-being
Hagendorff, Nguyen, and Sila	2022	Cross-sectional survey	Marriage	LGBT individuals	Social connection

Table A.1—Continued

Author	Year	Design	Legal Status Examined	Population Studied	Outcome Category
Hansen, Martell, and Roncolato	2020	Cross-sectional survey	Marriage	LGBT individuals	Financial well-being
Hatzenbuehler et al.	2010	Cross-sectional survey	Marriage	LGBT individuals	Psychological well-being, couple well-being
Hatzenbuehler et al.	2012	Cross-sectional survey	Marriage	LGBT individuals	Physical health
Horne, Rostosky, and Riggle	2011	Cross-sectional survey	Marriage	LGBT individuals	Couple well-being
Hsieh	2019	Difference-in-differences	Any legal status, marriage bans	General population	Trends in family formation
Isaac	2024	Difference-in-differences	Marriage bans	General population	Trends in family formation
Kail, Acosta, and Wright	2015	Difference-in-differences	Marriage, civil union, domestic partnership	LGBT individuals	Employment, health insurance
Kazyak and Stange	2018	Difference-in-differences	Marriage	General population	Trends in family formation
Kennedy and Dalla	2020	Difference-in-differences	Marriage	LGBT individuals	Health insurance
Ketcham and Bennett	2019	Difference-in-differences	Marriage	General population	Public opinion
Kreitzer, Hamilton, and Tolbert	2014	Difference-in-differences	Marriage	General population	Public opinion
Langbein, Ranallo-Benavidez, and Palmer	2021	Difference-in-differences	Marriage	LGBT individuals	Physical health, health insurance
Langbein and Yost	2009	Difference-in-differences	Marriage	LGBT individuals	Health insurance
LeBlanc, Frost, and Bowen	2018	Difference-in-differences	Marriage	General population	Public opinion
Levy and Levy	2017	Difference-in-differences	Marriage	LGBT individuals	Physical health
Liu et al.	2021	Difference-in-differences	Marriage	General population	Trends in family formation

Table A.1—Continued

Author	Year	Design	Legal Status Examined	Population Studied	Outcome Category
Manning, Brown, and Stykes	2016	Difference-in-differences	Marriage	LGBT individuals	Employment, financial well-being
Marcén and Morales	2022	Longitudinal study	Civil union	LGBT individuals	Couple well-being, social connection
Martell and Nash	2020	Longitudinal study	Civil union	LGBT individuals	Psychological well-being, physical health
Martin and Rodriguez	2022	Longitudinal study	Any legal status	LGBT individuals	Psychological well-being
Metheny and Stephenson	2019	Longitudinal study	Marriage	General population	Public opinion
Miller and Park	2018	Longitudinal study	Any legal status	LGBT individuals	Couple well-being
Nikolaou	2022	Repeated state comparison	Marriage, civil union, domestic partnership	LGBT individuals	Couple well-being
Nikolaou	2023	Longitudinal study	Marriage	LGBT individuals	Psychological well-being
Ofosu et al.	2019	Repeated survey	Marriage, civil union, marriage and civil union bans	LGBT individuals	Physical health, public opinion
Ogolsky et al.	2019a	Repeated survey	Marriage, domestic partnership, civil union, marriage ban	LGBT individuals	Physical health
Ogolsky et al.	2019b	Repeated survey	Marriage bans	General population	Public opinion
Paintsil	2024	Repeated survey	Marriage	General population	Public opinion
Perrin et al.	2018	Repeated survey	Marriage	General population	Economic trends
Pollard and Lopez-Garcia	2022	Repeated survey	Marriage	General population	Public opinion
Psihountas, Dippel, and Slusarz	2013	Repeated survey	Marriage	LGBT individuals	Financial well-being

Table A.1—Continued

Author	Year	Design	Legal Status Examined	Population Studied	Outcome Category
Raifman et al.	2017	Repeated survey	Marriage	LGBT individuals	Physical health
Reczek, Liu, and Spiker	2014	Repeated survey	Marriage	General population	Public opinion
Reczek et al.	2016	Repeated survey	Marriage	Children	Children of same-sex parents
Reczek et al.	2017	Repeated survey	Marriage	General population	Public opinion
Riggle, Rostosky, and Horne	2009	Repeated survey	Marriage	General population	Public opinion
Riggle, Rostosky, and Horne	2010	Repeated survey (pooled)	Marriage	Children	Children of same-sex parents
Riggle et al.	2017	Repeated survey (subset longitudinal study)	Marriage	LGBT individuals	Psychological well-being, physical health
Rosenfeld	2014	Cross-sectional survey	Marriage	LGBT individuals	Psychological well-being
Sansone	2019	Cross-sectional survey	Marriage	LGBT individuals	Psychological well-being, social connection
Schneebaum and Schubert	2017	Difference-in-differences	Civil union, domestic partnership	General population	Economic trends
Seror and Ticku	2021	Difference-in-differences	Marriage	LGBT individuals	Psychological well-being
Skinner et al.	2023	Event-history analysis	Marriage	General population	Economic trends
Solazzo, Gorman, and Denney	2020	Longitudinal study	Marriage	General population	Public opinion
Solomon, Rothblum, and Balsam	2004	Cross-sectional survey	Any legal recognition	LGBT individuals	Physical health, health insurance
Solomon, Rothblum, and Balsam	2005	Longitudinal study	Marriage bans	LGBT individuals	Couple well-being
Swank	2022	Cross-sectional survey	Marriage	LGBT individuals	Psychological well-being

Table A.1—Continued

Author	Year	Design	Legal Status Examined	Population Studied	Outcome Category
Tankard and Paluck	2017	Difference-in-differences	Marriage, domestic partnership	General population	Trends in family formation
Tatum	2017	Difference-in-differences	Marriage	LGBT individuals	Employment, couple well-being
Trocki et al.	2020	Difference-in-differences	Marriage	General population	Trends in family formation
Tumin and Kroeger	2020	Longitudinal study	Marriage, domestic partnership	LGBT individuals	Couple well-being
Vakili and Zhang	2018	Repeated survey	Marriage	Children	Children of same-sex parents
Wight, LeBlanc, and Badgett	2013	Repeated survey	Marriage	LGBT individuals	Psychological well-being
Wight et al.	2012	Repeated survey	Marriage	LGBT individuals	Financial well-being
Zhu and Smieliauskas	2022	Repeated survey	Marriage	LGBT individuals	Physical health

APPENDIX B

Evidence Review Approach and Included Studies

Search Strategy and Terms

Our search strategy and terms were guided by preliminary informal literature searches and consultation with a research librarian. To ensure that our search captured research conducted across the widest possible variety of disciplines (including economics, psychology, demography, sociology, and medicine), we conducted our search using four independent databases: Web of Science, Scopus, Social Sciences Abstracts, and Policy File Index. The same search terms were submitted to each database, and the results across databases were compared to identify articles that emerged from more than one search.

The database search was conducted in August 2023 using the following general strategy: *[effect] AND [type of policy] AND [same-sex] AND [form of legal recognition] AND [United States]*. For each term in brackets, multiple synonyms and truncated versions of each term were submitted using the Boolean command "OR." Thus, the search submitted to each dataset was

- (effect* OR impact* OR consequen* OR benefit* OR risk* OR implication* OR outcome* OR change* OR associat* OR affect* OR compar* OR signif* OR aftermath OR result* OR propos* OR valid* OR suggest*) AND
- (legal* OR recogn* OR formal* OR law* OR ratif* OR enact* OR vote* OR acknowledg*) AND
- ("same-sex" OR "same sex" OR "same-gender*" OR "same gender*" OR gay* OR lesbian* OR homosexual* OR queer* OR bisexual*) AND
- (marriage OR "civil union" OR "domestic partnership" OR "civil partnership" OR cohabit* OR divorc* OR "liv* together") AND
- ("United States" OR "U.S." OR America*).

Across the four separate databases, submitting these searches retrieved a total of 944 records. Deleting results that emerged from more than one database left 636 unique records to be screened.

Eligibility and Screening

Articles were eligible to be included if their content was within the scope of the search described earlier. Additional eligibility criteria were as follows:

- Included reports had to be quantitative studies that assessed a defined group of participants, treated some form of legal recognition of same-sex couples as an independent variable, and treated some outcome as a dependent variable.
- Purely descriptive studies describing trends for same-sex couples were excluded.
- Qualitative research (e.g., ethnographies, interviews, focus groups) was excluded.
- Peer-reviewed papers, reports, and working papers being prepared for submission to peer-reviewed journals were retained, but dissertations were excluded.
- Original analyses were included, but reviews, essays, editorials, and legal analyses that did not report new data analyses were excluded.

Two reviewers screened the title and abstract of each record retrieved from the database search. During the screening process, disagreements between reviewers about the eligibility of particular studies were discussed and resolved. This preliminary screening stage excluded 549 reports, leaving 87 remaining studies to consider. All 87 remaining reports were further evaluated for eligibility by one reviewer. Ambiguous cases were discussed and agreed on by both reviewers. After this second stage of screening, 67 reports remained eligible to be included in the review.

Identification of Additional Studies

Following the database search, existing review articles and the reference lists of the reports retrieved from our search were further reviewed to identify additional articles for inclusion. We also consulted literature compilations from experts in the field of LGBT law and policy. This process yielded an additional 29 eligible articles, bringing the final number of studies included in our review to 96.

The process for study identification, screening, and inclusion is shown in Figure B.1. Details on the 96 studies we reviewed are presented in Tables B.1 through B.12.

FIGURE B.1
PRISMA Flow Diagram

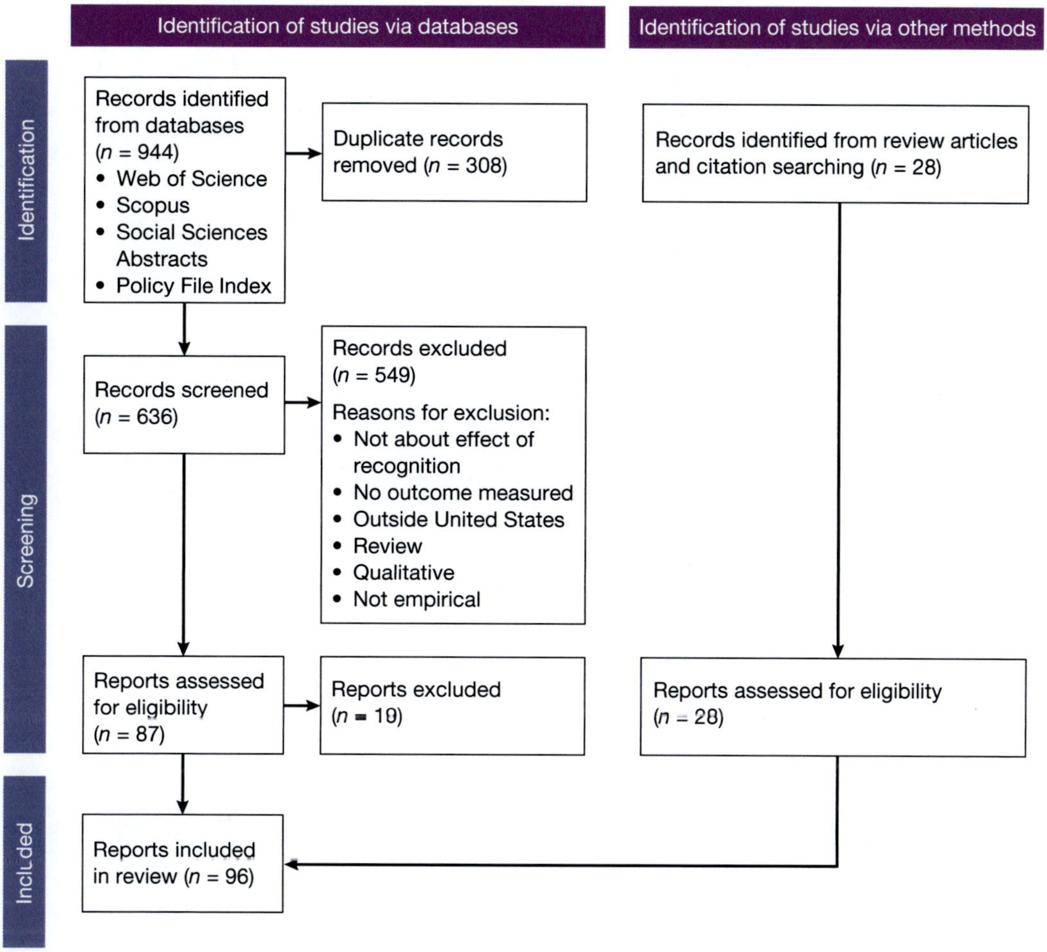

TABLE B.1

Research on Effects of Legal Relationship Status on Psychological Well-Being in LGBT Individuals

Author (date)	Sample Source	Year of Assessment	Design	Legal Status Examined	Outcome
Anderson, Matsuzawa, and Sabia (2021)	State Youth Risk Behavior Survey	1999–2017	Difference-in-differences	Marriage	Suicide attempts, suicide planning, suicidal ideation, depression
Bauermeister (2014)	Online convenience sample	2012–2013	Cross-sectional survey	Marriage, marriage ban	Depressive symptoms, self-esteem, fatherhood aspirations
Charlton et al. (2016)	Nurses' Health Study II	1995–2009	Longitudinal study	Any type of legal recognition	Reported sexual orientation
de Vries et al. (2009)	Online convenience sample	2006	Cross-sectional survey	Civil union	Aging concerns, outness
Drabble et al. (2022)	Online convenience sample	2020	Cross-sectional survey	Marriage	Stigma concerns, perceived personal impact of legal marriage
Everett, Hatzenbuehler, and Hughes (2016)	Chicago Health and Life Experiences of Women Study	2000–2001, 2003–2004, 2010–2012	Longitudinal study	Civil union	Stigma consciousness, perceived discrimination, depression, hazardous drinking
Fingerhut and Maisel (2010)	Online convenience sample	2007	Cross-sectional survey	Domestic partnership	External gay-related stress and discrimination, internal gay-related stress, life satisfaction
Flores, Mallory, and Conron (2020)	Gallup Daily Tracking Well-Being Index Survey	2015	Repeated survey	Marriage	Happiness, life satisfaction
Goldsen et al. (2017)	Aging with Pride: National Health, Aging, and Sexuality/Gender Study	2014	Cross-sectional survey	Marriage	Quality of life, perceived discrimination, outness

Table B.1—Continued

Author (date)	Sample Source	Year of Assessment	Design	Legal Status Examined	Outcome
Hatzenbuehler et al. (2010)	National Epidemiologic Survey on Alcohol and Related Conditions	2001–2002, 2004–2005	Longitudinal study	Marriage ban	Psychiatric disorders: mood disorders, generalized anxiety disorder, alcohol use disorder, psychiatric comorbidity
Hatzenbuehler et al. (2012)	Clinic outpatient billing records	2002–2004	Repeated survey and longitudinal study	Marriage	Mental health care visits and costs
Hsieh (2019)	NHIS	2013–2016	Cross-sectional survey	Marriage	Psychological distress, life interference from distress
Kennedy and Dalla (2020)	Online convenience sample	2014	Cross-sectional survey	Marriage	Negative and positive affect, life satisfaction, sexual identity distress
LeBlanc, Frost, and Bowen (2018)	Online convenience sample	2015–2016	Cross-sectional survey	Marriage, domestic partnership, civil union	Psychological distress, perceived unequal recognition, depression symptoms
Liu et al. (2021)	Health and Retirement Study	2000–2016	Cross-sectional survey	Marriage	Cognitive impairment, depressive symptoms
Ogolsky et al. (2019a)	Online convenience sample	2015–2016	Longitudinal study	Marriage	Psychological distress, felt stigma, stress, life satisfaction
Ogolsky et al. (2019b)	Online convenience sample	2015–2016	Longitudinal study	Marriage	Psychological distress, life satisfaction, felt stigma, internalized homonegativity
Raifman et al. (2017)	Youth Risk Behavior Surveillance System	1999–2015	Difference-in-differences	Marriage	Suicide attempts

Table B.1—Continued

Author (date)	Sample Source	Year of Assessment	Design	Legal Status Examined	Outcome
Riggle et al. (2017)	Online convenience sample	2013	Cross-sectional survey	Marriage	Identity centrality and concealment, vigilance, isolation, daily discrimination
Riggle, Rostosky, and Horne (2009)	Online convenience sample	2006	Cross-sectional survey	Marriage ban	Perceived stress, depressive symptoms, positive and negative affect
Riggle, Rostosky, and Horne (2010)	Online convenience sample	Not reported	Cross-sectional survey	Marriage, domestic partnership, civil union	Perceived stress, depressive symptoms, internalized homophobia, meaning of life
Seror and Ticku (2021)	Center for Applied Research in the Apostolate	2000–2015	Difference-in-differences	Marriage	Enrollment in Catholic seminaries
Swank (2022)	American National Election Survey	2010–2012	Cross-sectional survey	Marriage	Pro-LGBT and feminist attitudes, activism
Tatum (2017)	Online convenience sample	Not reported (pre-*Obergefell*)	Cross-sectional survey	Marriage	Internalized homonegativity, depression, anxiety, subjective well-being
Wight, LeBlanc, and Badgett (2013)	California Health Interview Survey	2009	Cross-sectional survey	Marriage, domestic partnership	Psychological distress
Wight et al. (2012)	Multicenter AIDS Cohort Study	2009–2010	Cross-sectional survey	Marriage	Positive affect, depressive symptoms, perceived gay-related stigma

TABLE B.2

Research on Effects of Legal Relationship Status on Couple Well-Being in Same-Sex Couples

Author (date)	Sample Source	Year of Assessment	Design	Legal Status Examined	Outcome
Balsam et al. (2008)	Vermont Civil Union Registry	2002–2005	Longitudinal study	Civil union	Frequency of sex, sex outside the relationship, considering or discussing ending the relationship, relationship duration and termination, relationship quality
Bernstein, Naples, and Harvey (2016)	Census data, surveys, government reports	Not reported	Repeated survey	Marriage, civil union, domestic partnership	Rates of formalization
Fingerhut and Maisel (2010)	Online convenience sample, California Domestic Partnership Registry	2007	Cross-sectional survey	Domestic partnership	Relationship satisfaction, relationship investments
Haas and Lannutti (2022a)	Online convenience sample	2017	Cross-sectional survey	Marriage	Relationship maintenance behaviors, relationship quality
Haas and Lannutti (2022b)	Online convenience sample	2017–2018	Cross-sectional survey	Marriage	Relationship quality, monogamy agreement
Hansen, Martell, and Roncolato (2020)	CPS, ACS	2003–2015	Difference-in-differences	Marriage	Division of labor
Kennedy and Dalla (2020)	Convenience sample (from Iowa and states bordering it)	2014	Cross-sectional survey	Marriage	Relationship satisfaction
Ketcham and Bennett (2019)	How Couples Meet and Stay Together	2009–2015	Longitudinal study	Any type of legal recognition	Relationship dissolution rates
Manning, Brown, and Stykes (2016)	Survey of Income and Program Participation	2008–2013	Longitudinal study	Marriage ban	Relationship dissolution rates

Table B.2—Continued

Author (date)	Sample Source	Year of Assessment	Design	Legal Status Examined	Outcome
Riggle et al. (2017)	Recontacted Solomon, Rothblum, and Balsam (2004) sample	2013	Cross-sectional survey	Marriage	Support from partner
Rosenfeld (2014)	How Couples Meet and Stay Together	2009–2012	Longitudinal study	Marriage, domestic partnership	Relationship duration, dissolution rates, relationship quality
Solomon, Rothblum, and Balsam (2004)	Vermont Civil Union Registry	2002–2003	Cross-sectional survey	Civil union	Division of labor, leisure activities together, considering or discussing ending the relationship
Solomon, Rothblum, and Balsam (2005)	Vermont Civil Union Registry	2002–2003	Cross-sectional survey	Civil union	Division of household tasks and finances, relationship maintenance behaviors, frequency of sex, monogamy, relationship quality

TABLE B.3

Research on Effects of Legal Relationship Status on Physical Health in LGBT Individuals

Author (date)	Sample Source	Year of Assessment	Design	Legal Status Examined	Outcome
Aftab and Imanpour (2022)	State Emergency Department Database, State Inpatient Database	2007–2015	Difference-in-differences	Marriage	STI-related emergency department visits
Brodoff, Hiedemann, and Xue (2024)	ACS	2008–2019	Repeated survey	Marriage	Activity limitations
Carpenter et al. (2021)	Behavioral Risk Factor Surveillance System	2000–2016	Difference-in-differences	Marriage	Health care utilization, general physical health
Elwood et al. (2017)	California Health Interview Survey	2009–2013	Cross-sectional survey	Any type of legal recognition	Self-reported health, health care use and visits

Table B.3—Continued

Author (date)	Sample Source	Year of Assessment	Design	Legal Status Examined	Outcome
Everett, Hatzenbuehler, and Hughes (2016)	Chicago Health and Life Experiences of Women Study	2000–2001, 2003–2004, 2010–2012	Longitudinal study	Civil union	Hazardous drinking, adverse drinking consequences
Francis, Mialon, and Peng (2012)	CDC, General Social Survey, health care provider records, state health department data	1981–2008	Repeated survey	Marriage, marriage and civil union bans	Gonorrhea rates, syphilis rates
Goldsen et al. (2017)	Aging with Pride: National Health, Aging, and Sexuality/ Gender Study	2014	Cross-sectional survey	Marriage	Self-reported health, physical disability
Gonzales and Ehrenfeld (2018)	Behavioral Risk Factor Surveillance System	2014–2016	Repeated survey	Marriage	Self-reported health
Hatzenbuehler et al. (2010)	National Epidemiologic Survey on Alcohol and Related Conditions	2001–2002, 2004–2005	Longitudinal study	Marriage ban	Alcohol use disorder
Hatzenbuehler et al. (2012)	Clinic outpatient billing records	2002–2004	Repeated survey and longitudinal study	Marriage	Clinic visits and health care costs
Kail, Acosta, and Wright (2015)	CPS, Freedom to Marry Inc.	2010–2013	Repeated survey	Marriage, domestic partnership, civil union, marriage ban	Self-reported health
LeBlanc, Frost, and Bowen (2018)	Online convenience sample	2015–2016	Cross-sectional survey	Marriage, domestic partnership, civil union	Alcohol use, problematic drinking
Reczek, Liu, and Spiker (2014)	NHIS	1997–2011	Cross-sectional survey	Marriage, civil union	Alcohol consumption
Skinner et al. (2023)	Fenway Institute MSM Internet Survey	2013	Cross-sectional survey	Marriage	Patient-provider communication, PrEP awareness and use

Table B.3—Continued

Author (date)	Sample Source	Year of Assessment	Design	Legal Status Examined	Outcome
Solazzo, Gorman, and Denney (2020)	Behavioral Risk Factor Surveillance System	2011–2015	Cross-sectional survey	Marriage	Self-reported health, cardiovascular disease
Trocki et al. (2020)	U.S. National Alcohol Survey	2000, 2005, 2010, 2015	Repeated survey	Marriage	High-intensity drinking, alcohol use disorder, marijuana use

TABLE B.4

Research on Effects of Legal Relationship Status on Access to Health Insurance in LGBT Individuals

Author (date)	Sample Source	Year of Assessment	Design	Legal Status Examined	Outcome
Carpenter et al. (2021)	Behavioral Risk Factor Surveillance System	2000–2017	Difference-in-differences	Marriage	Health insurance coverage
Dillender (2015)	CPS	1996–2011	Difference-in-differences	Marriage, civil union, domestic partnership	Health insurance coverage and type
Downing and Cha (2020)	ACS	2008–2017	Difference-in-differences	Marriage	Employer-sponsored health insurance coverage
Elwood et al. (2017)	California Health Interview Survey	2009–2013	Cross-sectional survey	Any type of legal recognition	Health insurance coverage
Gonzales (2015)	ACS	2008–2012	Difference-in-differences	Marriage	Health insurance coverage and type
Gonzales and Blewett (2014)	ACS	2008–2010	Cross-sectional survey	Marriage, civil union, domestic partnership	Health insurance coverage and type
Tumin and Kroeger (2020)	NHIS	2012–2014, 2016–2018	Repeated survey	Marriage	Health insurance coverage and type

TABLE B.5

Research on Effects of Legal Relationship Status on Employment in LGBT Individuals

Author (date)	Sample Source	Year of Assessment	Design	Legal Status Examined	Outcome
Dillender (2015)	CPS	1996–2011	Difference-in-differences	Marriage, civil union, domestic partnership	Labor force participation
Hansen, Martell, and Roncolato (2020)	CPS, ACS	2003–2015	Difference-in-differences	Marriage	Annual hours of work, minutes of daily paid work, wages
Isaac (2024)	ACS	2012–2015	Difference-in-differences	Marriage	Annual hours of work, labor force participation, predicted earnings
Sansone (2019)	ACS	2008–2016	Difference-in-differences	Marriage	Labor force participation, weekly work hours

TABLE B.6

Research on Effects of Legal Relationship Status on Financial Well-Being in LGBT Individuals

Author (date)	Sample Source	Year of Assessment	Design	Legal Status Examined	Outcome
Alonso-Villar and del Río (2023)	ACS	2015–2019	Repeated survey	Marriage	Poverty incidence and intensity
Badgett (2018)	NHIS	2013–2016	Cross-sectional survey	Marriage	Poverty
de Vries et al. (2009)	Online convenience sample	2006	Cross-sectional survey	Civil union	End-of-life plans
Delhommer and Hamermesh (2021)	ACS	2013–2017	Repeated survey	Marriage	Household income, homeownership
Hagendorff, Nguyen, and Sila (2022)	Home Mortgage Disclosure Act Loan Application Registry	2004–2017	Repeated survey	Marriage	Mortgage applications, mortgage applications denied
Isaac (2024)	ACS	2012–2015	Difference-in-differences	Marriage	Predicted earnings
Marcén and Morales (2022)	ACS	2001–2015	Repeated survey	Marriage	Migration

Table B.6—Continued

Author (date)	Sample Source	Year of Assessment	Design	Legal Status Examined	Outcome
Martell and Nash (2020)	ACS, NHIS	2013–2017	Repeated survey	Marriage	Yearly earnings, hourly earnings
Miller and Park (2018)	Federal Financial Institutions Examination Council Mortgage Applications	2004–2014	Difference-in-differences	Marriage	Mortgage applications
Pollard and Lopez-Garcia (2022)	ACS, National Longitudinal Study of Adolescent to Adult Health, Health and Retirement Study, RAND American Life Panel	2011–2015	Cross-sectional survey	Marriage	Social Security benefits, benefit amounts
Psihountas, Dippel, and Slusarz (2013)	Mailed survey to married same-sex couples	2008	Cross-sectional survey	Marriage ban	Tax liability and filing status
Schneebaum and Schubert (2017)	ACS	2013–2015	Repeated survey	Marriage	Wages

TABLE B.7

Research on Effects of Legal Relationship Status on Social Connections of LGBT Individuals

Author (date)	Sample Source	Year of Assessment	Design	Legal Status Examined	Outcome
Balsam et al. (2008)	Vermont Civil Union Registry	2002–2005	Longitudinal study	Civil union	Family support, friend support, contact and closeness with parents
Drabble et al. (2022)	Online convenience sample	2020	Cross-sectional survey	Marriage	Family support, local social climate
Metheny and Stephenson (2019)	Project Nexus, online convenience sample	2016–2017	Cross-sectional survey	Marriage	Perceived social inclusion

Table B.7—Continued

Author (date)	Sample Source	Year of Assessment	Design	Legal Status Examined	Outcome
Ogolsky et al. (2019a)	Online convenience sample	2015–2016	Longitudinal study	Marriage	Family support, friend support, community climate
Solomon, Rothblum, and Balsam (2004)	Vermont Civil Union Registry	2002–2003	Cross-sectional survey	Civil union	Family support, friend support, contact and closeness with parents

TABLE B.8

Research on Effects of Legal Relationship Status on the Children of Same-Sex Couples

Author (date)	Sample Source	Year of Assessment	Design	Recognition Type	Outcome
Boertien and Bernardi (2019)	ACS	2008–2015	Repeated survey	Legal marriage for same-sex couples	School progress
Gonzales and Blewett (2013)	ACS	2008–2010	Repeated survey, pooled	Legal marriage, civil unions, and domestic partnerships for same-sex couples	Child's type of health insurance (private, public, uninsured)
Reczek et al. (2016)	NHIS	2004–2013	Repeated survey, pooled	Legal marriage for same-sex couples	Children's health: overall physical health, activity level, lost school days, behavioral problems, emotional problems
Reczek et al. (2017)	NHIS	2008–2015	Repeated survey, pooled	Legal marriage for same-sex couples	Children's health: overall physical health, activity level, lost school days, behavioral problems, emotional problems

TABLE B.9

Research on Effects of Legal Relationship Status for Same-Sex Couples on Public Opinion Toward LGBT Individuals and Marriage for Same-Sex Couples

Author (date)	Sample Source	Year of Assessment	Design	Recognition Type	Outcome
Adams-Cohen (2020)	Twitter	2015	Difference-in-differences	Legal marriage for same-sex couples	Attitudes toward marriage for same-sex couples
Bishin et al. (2016)	Online survey experiment using Amazon Mechanical Turk; National Annenberg Election Survey	2004, 2013	Experiment; repeated survey	Legal marriage for same-sex couples	Attitudes toward marriage for same-sex couples, attitudes toward LGBT individuals
Coley (2020)	U.S. Department of Education data on four-year Christian colleges and universities	2013, 2019	Repeated survey	Legal marriage for same-sex couples	Presence of LGBT+ student groups
Colistra and Johnson (2021)	Newspaper articles	2014–2016	Repeated survey	Legal marriage for same-sex couples	Framing of newspaper articles
Donovan and Tolbert (2013)	American National Election Studies	2002, 2004	Repeated survey	Ban on marriage for same-sex couples	Attitudes toward gay and lesbian individuals
Flores and Barclay (2016)	American National Election Studies	2012, 2013	Repeated survey	Legal marriage for same-sex couples	Attitudes toward marriage for same-sex couples
Francis, Mialon, and Peng (2012)	General Social Survey	1982–2008	Repeated survey	Ban on marriage for same-sex couples, bans on civil unions for same-sex couples, legal marriage for same-sex couples, civil unions for same-sex couples	Tolerance for same-sex sex

Table B.9—Continued

Author (date)	Sample Source	Year of Assessment	Design	Recognition Type	Outcome
Kazyak and Stange (2018)	Mail survey of Nebraskans	2013, 2015	Repeated survey	Legal marriage for same-sex couples	Attitudes toward marriage for same-sex couples
Kreitzer, Hamilton, and Tolbert (2014)	Random statewide telephone survey	2009	Longitudinal survey	Legal marriage for same-sex couples	Attitudes toward marriage for same-sex couples
Levy and Levy (2017)	State-level data on sexual orientation–motivated hate crimes	2000–2012, annually	Difference-in-differences	Bans on marriage for same-sex couples; any legal recognition for same-sex partners	Sexual orientation–motivated hate crimes
Nikolaou (2022)	National Incident-Based Reporting System of the FBI's Uniform Crime Reporting program	1998–2019, 2010–2020	Difference-in-differences	Legal marriage for same-sex couples	Sexual orientation–motivated hate crimes, sexual orientation–motivated employment discrimination charges
Ofosu et al. (2019)	American National Election Studies; visitors to the Project Implicit website	2005–2016, annually	Difference-in-differences	Legal marriage for same-sex couples	Explicit and implicit antigay bias
Paintsil (2024)	National Incident-Based Reporting System	2013–2014 and 2016–2017	Repeated survey	Marriage	Intimate partner violence clearance by law enforcement
Perrin et al. (2018)	Amazon Mechanical Turk	2015, 2016	Repeated survey	Legal marriage for same-sex couples	Attitudes toward marriage for same-sex couples; attitudes toward LGBT individuals
Sansone (2019)	Google Trends	2004–2016	Difference-in-differences	Legal marriage for same-sex couples	Homophobic Google searches

Table B.9—Continued

Author (date)	Sample Source	Year of Assessment	Design	Recognition Type	Outcome
Tankard and Paluck (2017)	Amazon Mechanical Turk	2015	Longitudinal survey	Legal marriage for same-sex couples	Attitudes toward marriage for same-sex couples, attitudes toward LGBT individuals, perceived social norms

TABLE B.10

Research on Effects of Legal Relationship Status for Same-Sex Couples on Public Health Outcomes

Author (date)	Sample Source	Year of Assessment	Design	Recognition Type	Outcome
Horne, Rostosky, and Riggle (2011)	Online survey	2006	Cross-sectional survey	Bans on marriage for same-sex couples	Perceived stress, negative affect/ emotional distress
Nikolaou (2023)	CDC data from health clinics	2000–2019	Difference-in-differences	Legal marriage for same-sex couples	STIs

TABLE B.11

Research on Effects of Legal Relationship Status for Same-Sex Couples on State-Level Economic Outcomes

Author (date)	Sample Source	Year of Assessment	Design	Recognition Type	Outcome
Beaudin (2017)	ACS	2001–2014	Repeated survey	Legal marriage for same-sex couples	Interstate migration
Vakili and Zhang (2018)	All the patents granted by the U.S. Patent and Trademark Office between 1975 and 2010	1994–2006	Difference-in-differences	Civil unions, domestic partnerships for same-sex couples	State-level patenting
Zhu and Smieliauskas (2022)	Compustat and Center for Research in Security Prices	2003–2015	Event-history analysis	Legal marriage for same-sex couples	Daily stock returns, firm size, leverage, book-to-market ratio, return on assets, daily illiquidity

TABLE B.12

Research on Effects of Legal Relationship Status for Same-Sex Couples on State-Level Trends in Family Formation

Author (date)	Sample Source	Year of Assessment	Design	Recognition Type	Outcome
Allen and Price (2015)	U.S. Census Bureau	1990–2004	Difference-in-differences	Any legal recognition of same-sex couples; bans on marriage for same-sex couples	Marriage, divorce, abortion rates, percentage of children born to single women, and percentage of children in female-headed households
Bowen (2014)	Not stated	1999–2010	Difference-in-differences	Bans on marriage for same-sex couples	Marriage rates, divorce rates
Carpenter (2020)	Massachusetts Behavioral Risk Factor Surveillance System	2001–2013	Difference-in-differences	Legal marriage for same-sex couples	Marriage rates
Dillender (2014)	CDC	1995–2010	Difference-in-differences	Legal marriage, domestic partnerships for same-sex couples	Marriage rates
Dinno and Whitney (2013)	National Center for Health Statistics	1988–2009	Difference-in-differences	Legal marriage for same-sex couples, any legal recognition of same-sex couples	Marriage rates
Langbein, Ranallo-Benavidez, and Palmer (2021)	Public data from the U.S. Census Bureau and CDC	2011–2016	Difference-in-differences	Legal marriage for same-sex couples	Rates of child poverty, divorce, marriage, and children living in single-parent households

Table B.12—Continued

Author (date)	Sample Source	Year of Assessment	Design	Recognition Type	Outcome
Langbein and Yost (2009)	U.S. Census Bureau	1990, 2000, 2004	Difference-in-differences	Any legal recognition of same-sex couples; bans on marriage for same-sex couples	Marriage, divorce, abortion rates, percentage of children born to single women, and percentage of children in female-headed households
Martin and Rodriguez (2022)	Adoption and Foster Care Analysis and Reporting System	1995–2020	Difference-in-differences	Legal marriage for same-sex couples	Adoption rates

APPENDIX C

Analytic Approach

Identification Strategy and Econometric Approach

The first crucial assumption underpinning the identification of causal effects in difference-in-differences approaches is the so-called parallel trends assumption. In the context of our Chapter 3 example (evaluating the effects on marriage in states that changed their marriage policies in 2008), this assumption requires that the change in marriage stock in the states that did not legalize marriage for same-sex couples in 2008 accurately reflects what the change in marriage stock would have looked like for the states that did legalize in 2008 had they not legalized. It is this assumption that allows any difference in the change in marriage stock between the two groups of states (those that legalized and those that did not) around 2008 to be attributed to legalization. A strength of difference-in-differences methods is that it is not required that the stock of marriages is the same in the different states, only that the changes in the stock of marriages are the same. Generally, the parallel trends assumption states that the evolution of the outcomes in the control states (the states that legalized in 2015 in our case) accurately reflects how those same outcomes would have evolved in treated states (the states that legalized before 2015) had those states not been treated (not legalized marriage for same-sex couples).

Economic theory and past literature indicate numerous factors that influence outcomes like marriage and divorce, such as economic conditions. If states that legalized in 2015 had different economic landscapes from those of states that legalized before 2015, we might suspect that the evolution of the marriage stock, for example, would differ across those states. That would be a failure of the parallel trends assumption. To account for such factors, we adopted a so-called conditional parallel trends assumption, in which we conditioned on economic and demographic characteristics.[1] The conditional parallel trends assumption assumes that states with the same economic and demographic characteristics would experience the same evolution of outcomes in the absence of treatment. We also employed a further variant of this assumption by accounting for cohort-specific linear trends; this variant allows for differential trends in outcomes between treated and control cohorts and assumes that the change in those

[1] Prior work (e.g., Blau, Kahn, and Waldfogel [2000]; Karney et al. [2022]; Kearney and Wilson [2018]) has connected both the likelihood and the timing of marriage to local employment opportunities. Therefore, we controlled for state-level economic factors, such as earnings and unemployment.

trends would have been similar absent treatment. Again, this assumption allows the level of the outcome to differ across states with the same economic and demographic characteristics; the inclusion of cohort-specific linear trends merely requires parallel changes in paths (Mora and Reggio, 2019).

The second assumption is SUTVA. SUTVA assumes that no interference exists and that no hidden variations of treatment exist. No interference means that the outcomes of one unit should not be affected by the treatment of others. In our case, that means that the outcomes of people in control states should not be directly affected by the passage of legal marriage recognition for same-sex couples in other states—or, more simply, that there are no spillovers. The most likely case in which SUTVA is violated in our example is that treatment (the passage of legal marriage recognition for same-sex couples) resulted in people migrating out of states that passed legal marriage recognition for same-sex couples because of their distaste for the policy. Note that the temporary or permanent migration of same-sex couples seeking marriage recognition is not an issue in most of our sample. As noted in Chapter 2, prior work suggests that the interstate migration spurred by marriage laws was concentrated among gay men (Marcén and Morales, 2022) and female heads of household (Beaudin, 2017), and migration came only in the form of leaving states that did not recognize the marriages of same-sex couples. We also conducted a composition balance test and determined that population demographics were not changing within a state.

The other component of SUTVA is that there are no hidden variations of treatment—or, in our case, that marriage recognition for same-sex couples means the same in each state. In this case, SUTVA might be violated if we were interested in the outcomes of same-sex couples given that marriage recognition for same-sex couples means different things in some states (in terms of the benefits of marriage—e.g., tax break variations). However, in the context of the outcomes of people who are not accessing legal marriage recognition itself (different-sex couples), the treatment (a change in law or policy that allows same-sex couples to marry) is homogeneous across treatment groups.

The third assumption is a so-called strict exogeneity assumption. Strict exogeneity is concerned with whether treatment (in our case, the legalization of marriage for same-sex couples) is adopted endogenously. This assumption is likely violated if states legalize marriage in response to changing family formation patterns among different-sex couples. Within this context, it is worth remembering that, as pointed out by Sansone (2019), some of the most socially liberal states, such as New York and California, were not among the first to legalize marriage for same-sex couples. Iowa (a politically moderate state) was the third state (in 2009) to grant marriage licenses to same-sex couples. Sansone (2019) highlights that the expansion of marriage access to same-sex couples was largely driven by court decisions, and many of the early-legalizing states legalized marriage for same-sex couples prior to public opinion being in favor of legalization. Concurring, Aksoy and coauthors argue that legalization of marriage for same-sex couples likely changed public opinion rather than being an endogenous response to public opinion (Aksoy et al., 2020). These facts increase the likelihood that the broader population (i.e., people other than those seeking to form same-sex couples) would not be able to predict or foresee the exact timing of marriage access for same-sex couples within their state, thereby increasing the likelihood that strict exogeneity is satisfied.

In addition to the three assumptions underlying difference-in-differences models, recent literature has demonstrated that, in staggered settings (i.e., when states adopt a policy, such as legalization of marriage for same-sex couples, at different times), the classic difference-in-differences models may produce biased estimates of the desired treatment effect. The classic model is especially likely to be biased or even give wrong-signed estimates when treatment effects vary over time. Several solutions have been proposed that circumvent these issues. We made use of Sun and Abraham's (2021) interaction-weighted estimator (which circumvents the issues of the classic model) implemented through the *eventstudyinteract* command in Stata (Sun, 2022). An attractive feature of the Sun and Abraham approach, in addition to recovering a trustworthy estimate of the desired treatment effect, is that it allowed us to visually inspect the trends in outcomes before treatment, thus providing some suggestive evidence either in favor of or against the crucial parallel trends assumption.

Although there remains no statistical test of this assumption (because the actual outcomes of treated units absent treatment are never realized), it is common practice to use event study models to visually inspect the likelihood that the assumption is satisfied. Event study models are regression models that include numerous treatment lags and leads, allowing one to explore whether treatment and control groups were comparable (i.e., a null difference) on outcome dynamics pre-treatment and to explore dynamic effects post-treatment.

A difference-in-differences approach would take the following form:

$$Y_{ist} = \alpha + \beta D_{ist} + x_{ist} + S_s + T_t + \varepsilon_{ist},$$

where Y_{ist} represents the outcome of interest of individual *i*, in state *s*, at time *t*. *D* takes the value 1 if the individual resides in a state and period in which marriage for same-sex couples has already been legalized and takes the value 0 if the individual resides in a state and period in which marriage for same-sex couples has not yet been legalized. *x* corresponds to a series of additional control variables, which we included to take into consideration, among other things, the broader marriage market. In practice, we included time-varying controls at the state level for sex ratios, sex-specific shares of race and ethnicity groups, sex-specific shares of age groups, sex-specific shares of education groups, female labor force participation rate, unemployment rate, the natural log of earnings, the proportion of the state's population that is foreign-born, and whether the state legally recognizes civil unions. We also included state fixed effects (S_s) and time fixed effects (T_t). In addition, individual-level models control for own education, sex, race, labor force participation status, the natural log of family income, and a quadratic in age.[2] Standard errors are clustered at the level of treatment—U.S. state (Bertrand, Duflo, and Mullainathan, 2004). Under assumptions described above, β captures the effect of legalization of marriage for same-sex couples on the outcome of interest.

[2] Specifications using the MTF data contain only race and sex indicators as individual-level controls.

In practice, the interaction-weighted event study approach involves estimating a model for state treatment cohorts of the following form:

$$Y_{ist} = \alpha + \sum_{\tau=-q}^{-1} \gamma_\tau D_{s\tau} + \sum_{\tau=0}^{m} \delta_\tau D_{s\tau} + x_{ist} + \varepsilon_{ist},$$

where the notation takes the same form as before. Treatment occurs in year 0, and leads and lags are denoted as q and m, respectively. Leads and lags are binned at five years prior to and five years after treatment. $\tau = -1$ is omitted. The coefficients indexed from q (γ_τ) allow one to explore whether treatment and control states were trending similarly prior to treatment, while the coefficients indexed by m (γ_τ) allow one to explore dynamic effects in the post-treatment period. This model is estimated using the *reghdfe* command in Stata (Correia, 2023). Graphical representation of the event study model (as is provided in Appendix D) allows one to visually inspect the plausibility of the parallel trends/parallel paths assumption. Interpretation of an event study model is discussed in Appendix D.

Estimation

Parameterization of Outcomes

With the exception of MTF, individual-level models employ an indicator variable for the outcome of interest (married, divorced, cohabiting, had a recent birth). For MTF, we transformed the Likert-scale outcomes into a binary variable, looking at positive sentiment, with additional specification checks to analyze shifts in the tails (very positive, very negative).

State-level models use the natural log of the state rate of the outcome in question. Generally, these rates are percentages; the CDC rate for marriage licenses is per 1,000 residents.

Parameterization of Legal Recognition

Table C.1 details the year of marriage recognition for each state and the case, law, or referendum that led to that practice.

TABLE C.1
State History of Marriage Recognition for Same-Sex Couples

State	Year	Source
Alabama	2015	*Searcy v. Strange*, 81 F. Supp. 3d 1285 (D. Ala. 2015) (in effect from February 9 to March 3, 2015, only), effectively abrogated by *Ex parte State ex rel. Alabama Pol'y Inst.*, 200 So. 3d 495 (Ala. 2015); *Obergefell v. Hodges*, 576 U.S. 644 (2015) (June onward)
Alaska[a]	2014	*Hamby v. Parnell*, 56 F. Supp. 3d 1056 (D. Alaska 2014)
Arizona	2014	*Connolly v. Jeanes*, 73 F. Supp. 3d 1094 (D. Ariz. 2014)
Arkansas	2015	*Jernigan v. Crane*, 64 F. Supp. 3d 1260 (E.D. Ark. 2014) (decision stayed pending appeal); *Obergefell v. Hodges*, 576 U.S. 644 (2015)
California[b]	2008, 2013	*In re Marriage Cases*, 183 P.3d 384 (Cal. 2008) (effective from June to November 2008); *Hollingsworth v. Perry*, 570 U.S. 693 (2013) (effective June 2013 onward)
Colorado	2014	*Burns v. Hickenlooper*, Civil Action No. 14-cv-01817-RM-KLM, 2014 WL 3634834, 2014 U.S. Dist. LEXIS 100894 (D. Colo. July 23, 2014), stayed pending appeal, and stay dissolved by 10th Circuit after denial of writ of certiorari in *Kitchen v. Herbert*, 574 U.S. 874 (2014) and *Smith v. Bishop*, 574 U.S. 875 (2014). See also *Burns v. Hickenlooper*, No. 14-cv-01817-RM-KLM, 2014 WL 5312541, 2014 U.S. Dist. LEXIS 148123 (D. Colo. Oct. 17, 2014) (issuing permanent injunction and recognizing dissolution of stay as of Oct. 3, 2014)
Connecticut	2008	*Kerrigan v. Commissioner of Pub. Health*, 957 A.2d 407 (Conn. 2008)
Delaware	2013	79 Del. Laws Ch. 19 (2013) (H.B. 75)
District of Columbia	2010	Religious Freedom and Civil Marriage Equality Amendment Act of 2009, 57 D.C. Reg. 27 (Mar. 3, 2010)
Florida	2015	*Brenner v. Scott*, 999 F. Supp. 2d 1278 (N.D. Fla. 2014)
Georgia	2015	*Obergefell v. Hodges*, 576 U.S. 644 (2015)
Hawai'i	2013	Hawai'i Marriage Equality Act of 2013, 2014 Haw. Sess. Laws 1 (S.B. 1)
Idaho	2014	*Latta v. Otter*, 19 F. Supp. 3d 1054 (D. Idaho 2014), aff'd, 771 F.3d 456 (9th Cir. 2014)
Illinois	2014	Religious Freedom and Marriage Fairness Act, 2013 Ill. Laws 7141 (S.B. 10)
Indiana	2014	*Baskin v. Bogan*, 12 F. Supp. 3d 1144 (S.D. Ind. 2014), aff'd 766 F.3d 648 (7th Cir. 2014)
Iowa	2009	*Varnum v. Brien*, 763 N.W. 2d 862 (Iowa 2009)
Kansas	2015	*Marie v. Moser*, 65 F. Supp. 3d 1175 (D. Kan. 2014), stayed pending appeal, see *Moser v. Marie*, 135 S. Ct. 511 (2014), cert. denied, 574 U.S. 1006 (2014) (preventing state from enforcing ban); *Obergefell v. Hodges*, 576 U.S. 644 (2015).
Kentucky	2015	*Obergefell v. Hodges*, 576 U.S. 644 (2015)
Louisiana	2015	*Obergefell v. Hodges*, 576 U.S. 644 (2015)

Table C.1—Continued

State	Year	Source
Maine	2012	An Act to Allow Marriage Licenses for Same-Sex Couples and Protect Religious Freedom, 2013 Me. Laws 1125 (enacted by ballot initiative 2012 Maine Question 1)
Maryland	2013	Civil Marriage Protection Act, 2012 Md. Laws 9 (H.B. 438) (confirmed by 2012 Referendum Question 6)
Massachusetts	2004	*Goodridge v. Department of Public Health*, 798 N.E. 2d 941 (Mass. 2003)
Michigan	2015	*Obergefell v. Hodges*, 576 U.S. 644 (2015)
Minnesota	2013	2013 Minn. Laws 404 (S.F. 925, H.F. 1054)
Mississippi	2015	*Obergefell v. Hodges*, 576 U.S. 644 (2015)
Missouri	2015	*Obergefell v. Hodges*, 576 U.S. 644 (2015)
Montana	2014	*Rolando v. Fox*, 23 F. Sup 3d 1227 (D. Mont. 2014)
Nebraska	2015	*Obergefell v. Hodges*, 576 U.S. 644 (2015)
Nevada	2014	*Latta v. Otter*, 771 F.3d 456 (9th Cir. 2014) (vacating *Sevcik v. Sandoval*, 911 F. Supp. 2d 996 (D. Nev. 2012)
New Hampshire	2010	2009 N.H. Laws 60 (H.B. 436)
New Jersey	2013	*Garden State Equality v. Dow*, 82 A.3d 336 (N.J. Super. Ct. Law Div. 2013)
New Mexico	2013	*Griego v. Oliver*, 316 P.3d 865 (N.M. 2013)
New York	2011	N.Y. Marriage Equality Act, 2011 N.Y. Laws 749 (Ch. 95, A.B. 8354)
North Carolina	2014	*General Synod of the United Church of Christ v. Resinger*, 12 F. Supp. 3d 790 (W.D. N.C. 2014)
North Dakota	2015	*Obergefell v. Hodges*, 576 U.S. 644 (2015)
Ohio	2015	*Obergefell v. Hodges*, 576 U.S. 644 (2015)
Oklahoma	2014	*Bishop v. United States*, 760 F.3d 1070 (10th Cir. 2014) (mandate stayed pending disposition of cert.) *Smith v. Bishop*, 574 U.S. 875 (2014) (denying cert.) *Bishop v. Smith*, Nos. 14-5003 & 14-5006, 2014 WL 4960523, 2014 U.S. App. LEXIS 19305 (10th Cir. Oct. 6, 2014) (lifting stay of mandate).
Oregon	2014	*Geiger v. Kitzhaber*, 994 F. Supp. 2d 1128 (2014)
Pennsylvania	2014	*Whitewood v. Wolf*, 992 F. Supp. 2d 410 (2014)
Rhode Island	2013	2013 R.I. Pub. Laws 15 (Ch. 5) (H.B. 5015)
South Carolina	2014	*Condon v. Haley*, 21 F. Supp. 3d 572 (2014)
South Dakota	2015	*Obergefell v. Hodges*, 576 U.S. 644 (2015)
Tennessee	2015	*Obergefell v. Hodges*, 576 U.S. 644 (2015)
Texas	2015	*Obergefell v. Hodges*, 576 U.S. 644 (2015)

Table C.1—Continued

State	Year	Source
Utah	2014	*Kitchen v. Herbert*, 755 F.3d 1193 (10th Cir. 2014) (stayed pending disposition of any writ of certiorari); *Kitchen v. Herbert*, 574 U.S. 874 (2014) (denying cert.).
Vermont	2009	2009 Vt. Acts & Resolves 33 (Act No. 3, S. 115)
Virginia	2014	*Bostic v. Schaefer*, 760 F.3d 352 (4th Cir. 2014)
Washington	2012	2012 Wash. Sess. Laws 199 (S.S.B. 6239, approved via 2012 Wash. Referendum 74)
West Virginia	2014	*McGee v. Cole*, 66 F. Supp. 3d 747 (S.D.W.V. 2014)
Wisconsin	2014	*Wolf v. Walker*, 986 F. Supp. 2d 982 (W.D. Wisc. 2014); *Wolf v. Walker*, 26 F. Supp. 3d 866 (W.D. Wisc. 2014), aff'd *Baskin v. Bogan*, 766 F.3d 648 (7th Cir. 2014)
Wyoming	2014	*Guzzo v. Mead*, No. 14–CV–200–SWS, 2014 WL 5317797, 2014 U.S. Dist. LEXIS 148481 (D. Wyo. Oct. 17, 2014)

NOTE: The Williams Institute compiled this list of recognition years. The dates were confirmed by obtaining the text of the source case, referendum, or legislation. The empirical analysis presented in Chapter 3 diverges in two cases (see below).

[a] *Hamby v. Parnell* was partially resolved in 2014, and marriage licenses were recorded as being granted to same-sex couples as early as October 2014. We consider 2014 a partially treated year in our analysis.

[b] California permitted (in June 2008) and then disallowed (in November 2008) the issuing of marriage licenses to same-sex couples. It is the only state to have multiple treatment periods (with the second one starting in 2013). We code California as treated continuously starting in 2013 (keeping 2008 as untreated).

Analytic Sample

As discussed in Chapter 3, critics of *Obergefell* focused on potential harms to different-sex couples. To mirror this focus, we generally constrained our analyses to a sample with the potential to form a different-sex couple. None of the data sources used contained a measure of sexual orientation during our analytic period. We discuss the considerations for each data source in turn.

American Community Survey

In the ACS, we can identify the sex of the partner in a cohabiting relationship or marriage in 2008 and later. We excluded from all analyses (regardless of outcome) those who were cohabiting with or married to a same-sex partner. We recognize that this may mischaracterize coupled bisexual individuals, as well as LGBT individuals who are single or in noncohabiting relationships; however, for the age range and period of focus, these individuals are expected to be a relatively small portion of the population. Prior to 2008, data administrators recoded the sex of individuals, relationship status, or marital status of people who were in same-sex couples. Therefore, we excluded all people who have had their sex or marital status recoded or imputed. Note that the ACS does not currently (as of February 2024) measure sexual orientation or gender identity. Baseline descriptive statistics are shown in Table C.2.

Current Population Survey

In the CPS, we can identify the sex of the partner in a cohabiting relationship or marriage. We excluded from all analyses (regardless of outcome) those who were cohabiting with or married to a same-sex partner. We recognize that this may mischaracterize coupled bisexual individuals, as well as LGBT individuals who are single or in noncohabiting relationships; however, for the age range and period of focus, these individuals are expected to be a relatively small portion of the population. The CPS raises an additional complication: The gender of the partner in a "married, spouse absent" relationship (approximately 1.4 percent of the sample) is unrecorded. We tested sensitivity to this type of situation by alternately coding such individuals as being married to a same-sex partner (and excluding them from the sample) and as being married to a different-sex partner (and including them). Results from the latter are used in the main analysis; results from the former are available upon request. Note that the CPS does not currently (as of February 2024) measure sexual orientation or gender identity. Baseline descriptive statistics are shown in Table C.3.

Centers for Disease Control and Prevention

In the CDC data, only state totals for marriage licenses issued are reported; there is no disaggregation by partner gender or sex. We contacted state health and vital records agencies in an attempt to access more-disaggregated data, as in Dillender (2014). Thirty-one states responded to our request. Of those, several had inconsistencies in their reported data that were substantial enough that we had little confidence in their reliability. For example, some states reported marriages between same-sex couples before it was legally recognized, and others reported the exact same number of marriages and civil unions for each year. One state responded to our further inquiries by stating, "After discussing it with my manager and looking over the data again, it is obvious that many of the years are missing a significant amount of data, and feel it would be biased to use any [state] marriage data at this time." Therefore, analyses using CDC data include all marriages rather than just those among different-sex couples. Baseline descriptive statistics are shown in Table C.4.

Panel Study of Income Dynamics

The PSID did not track partner gender until 2015 and did not do so systematically until 2017; same-sex couples were categorized as main study nonfamilial relationships. Backdating those in same-sex couples in 2017 to our analysis period, we found that there were 159 same-sex partnerships, less than 2 percent of the relationships and partnerships in the analytic sample. This is likely an incomplete picture of same-sex partnerships within the sample, so we elected to include all respondents and interpret the results among the general population. Baseline descriptive statistics are shown in Table C.5.

Monitoring the Future

In the MTF main study, respondents are not asked about sexual orientation, and, as high school students, they are generally not in legally recognized relationships. Therefore, the sample for the marriage attitudes analyses includes individuals who may identify as LGBT individuals. The number of youth identifying as LGBT individuals has increased in recent years, and our MTF sample likely reflects this growth (Jones, 2022). These facts may limit the generalizability of this group's attitudes to other subpopulations; however, we believe that individuals who are just entering adulthood and are thus on the precipice of family formation are an important group for study. Baseline descriptive statistics are shown in Table C.6.

TABLE C.2

Sample Characteristics, American Community Survey, 2000

	Individual	State	
Characteristic	Outcome	Outcome	ln(Outcome)
Currently married	62%	60%	−0.51
New marriage	5%	5%	−3.08
Cohabitation	4%	4%	−3.13
Divorced unconditional	10%	11%	−2.23
Divorced conditional	14%	15%	−1.89
New divorce unconditional	1%	1%	−4.36
New divorce conditional	1%	2%	−3.99
Max *N*	276,032	50	50

SOURCE: Features data from the ACS (Ruggles et al., 2023).

NOTE: ln(Outcome) = natural log of the outcome. The sample excludes those in same-sex relationships. Cells give the mean of the outcome of interest at the level of aggregation (individual, state) specified. In regression models, state-level analyses use the ln(outcome) rather than the rate, so both are presented for interpretability. *Max N* refers to the largest sample size across outcomes (conditional outcomes will use a smaller sample).

TABLE C.3

Sample Characteristics, Current Population Survey, 2000

	Individual	State	
Characteristic	Outcome	Outcome	ln(Outcome)
Currently married	62%	61%	−0.51
Cohabitation	3%	3%	−3.46
Divorced unconditional	10%	10%	−2.30
Divorced conditional	14%	15%	−1.92
Max *N*	95,986	50	50

SOURCE: Features data from the CPS (Flood et al., 2023).

NOTE: ln(Outcome) = natural log of the outcome. The sample excludes those in same-sex relationships. Cells give the mean of the outcome of interest at the level of aggregation (individual, state) specified. In regression models, state-level analyses use the ln(outcome) rather than the rate, so both are presented for interpretability. *Max N* refers to the largest sample size across outcomes (conditional outcomes will use a smaller sample).

TABLE C.4

Sample Characteristics, Centers for Disease Control and Prevention, 2000

	State	
Characteristic	**Outcome**	**ln(Outcome)**
New marriages per 1,000	9.8	2.1
Max *N*	50	50

SOURCE: Features data from CDC Vital Statistics (CDC, undated).

NOTE: ln(Outcome) = natural log of the outcome. Data are aggregated at the state level. Cells give the mean of the outcome of interest. In regression models, state-level analyses use the ln(outcome) rather than the rate, so both are presented for interpretability. *Max N* refers to the largest sample size across outcomes.

TABLE C.5

Sample Characteristics, Panel Study of Income Dynamics, 2000

	Individual
Characteristic	**Outcome**
Currently married	59%
Marriage entry unconditional	2%
Divorced unconditional	15%
Divorce entry unconditional	1%
Max *N*	7,128

SOURCE: Features data from the PSID (Institute for Social Research, 2023).

NOTE: Cells give the mean of the outcome of interest. PSID analyses are conducted only at the individual level. *Max N* refers to the largest sample size across outcomes.

TABLE C.6

Sample Characteristics, Monitoring the Future, 2000

Outcome	Individual Mean
Agree or mostly agree: "Most people will have fuller and happier lives if they choose legal marriage rather than staying single or just living with someone."	33%
Quite or extremely important: "Having a good marriage and family life"	90%
Disagree or mostly disagree: "One sees so few good or happy marriages that one questions it as a way of life."	47%
Disagree or mostly disagree: "It is usually a good idea for a couple to live together before getting married in order to find out whether they really get along."	27%
Max *N*	2,208

SOURCE: Features data and statements from the MTF study (Schulenberg et al., 2023).

NOTE: MTF analyses are conducted only at the individual level. *Max N* refers to the largest sample size across outcomes.

APPENDIX D

Event Study Figures

In this appendix, we present event study figures (Figures D.1–D.31) to summarize analysis results. Each figure presents analyses for an outcome of interest (marriage, divorce, cohabitation, and attitudes toward marriage and/or family formation). The horizontal axis in each figure represents time relative to the legal issuance of marriage licenses to same-sex couples (legalization); legalization takes effect at time 0. The vertical axis represents the average change in the outcome variable. Each figure presents analyses from six models: a TWFE model, a TWFE model that includes state-level market controls and individual-level controls when applicable, a TWFE model that includes both state-level market and individual controls and treatment cohort–specific linear time trends, an interaction-weighted estimator model, an interaction-weighted estimator model with market and individual controls, and an interaction-weighted estimator model with market and individual controls and cohort-specific linear time trends.

The figures present coefficient estimates for each year relative to legalization (year = 0) from each estimated model. Coefficient estimates from different specifications are represented by the different shapes in the figure (e.g., circles, triangles, squares) and summarize the estimated average change in the outcome in treated states relative to control states. These coefficients should be interpreted relative to the missing coefficient in the figure: the coefficient from the year prior to the policy change (year = –1). This form of interpretation induces such statements as "Relative to just before the policy change, marriage grew by 1 percent more in states allowing same-sex couples to marry." Each coefficient estimate is presented with a 95-percent confidence interval, represented in the figures by vertical lines. Confidence intervals indicate the range of values that is *likely* to contain the true population-level parameter of the change in outcome (i.e., the true value estimated by the coefficient). Confidence intervals help determine whether an estimate is statistically significant. If the confidence interval range includes 0, then the estimate is not statistically different from 0 for a given level of precision.

Reported estimates for years prior to legalization help assess the parallel trends (paths) assumption discussed earlier. To have valid estimates from the difference-in-differences methodology, all estimates for the periods before legalization should be statistically indistinguishable from 0 (i.e., their confidence interval range includes 0). This indicates that control and treated states had similar patterns in the outcome variable prior to legalization of marriage for same-sex couples. For the TWFE model, we include the results of a statistical test that all pre–treatment period coefficients are 0 in each figure note.

When interpreting event study figures, one should consider statistical significance in addition to economic magnitude of estimates relative to the outcome's baseline, prior to the policy change. To interpret Figure D.1, for example, note that estimates after legalization (on the right-hand side of the graph) range from –0.01 to 0.01, and all estimates have confidence intervals that contain 0. This means that estimates are not statistically distinguishable from 0. An estimate of 0.01, which is a 1–percentage point change, off a baseline marriage proportion of 60 percent is arguably not economically meaningful. Therefore, this data source and the models suggest that the percentage of married individuals did not noticeably change in response to legalization.

When the confidence interval range does not include 0, then one can conclude that the estimated coefficient is statistically different from 0, often referred to by the phrase *statistically significant.* Consider, in Figure D.2, the estimates from Sun and Abraham's (2021) interaction-weighted estimator model with controls and cohort trends, represented by purple circles and confidence intervals. When we examine the pre-period estimates (years –5 to –2), we observe coefficients that are close to 0 and confidence intervals that include 0. Therefore, we do not observe differences in an individual's likelihood of being married between treated and control states (states that did and did not legalize marriage for same-sex couples), relative to the year before legalization, that are statistically distinguishable from 0. Now consider the estimated coefficient for year 3 after legalization, which is greater than 0 and has a confidence interval that does not include 0. This is true for all three interaction-weighted estimator specifications for this outcome-data-year combination; we would describe this point estimate as "robust" to various controls. In this case, we found statistically significant evidence that, three years after legalization of marriage for same-sex couples, individuals in treated states are more likely than those in control states to be married, relative to the baseline.

Marriage

Currently Married

FIGURE D.1
Event Study of Currently Married, American Community Survey, State

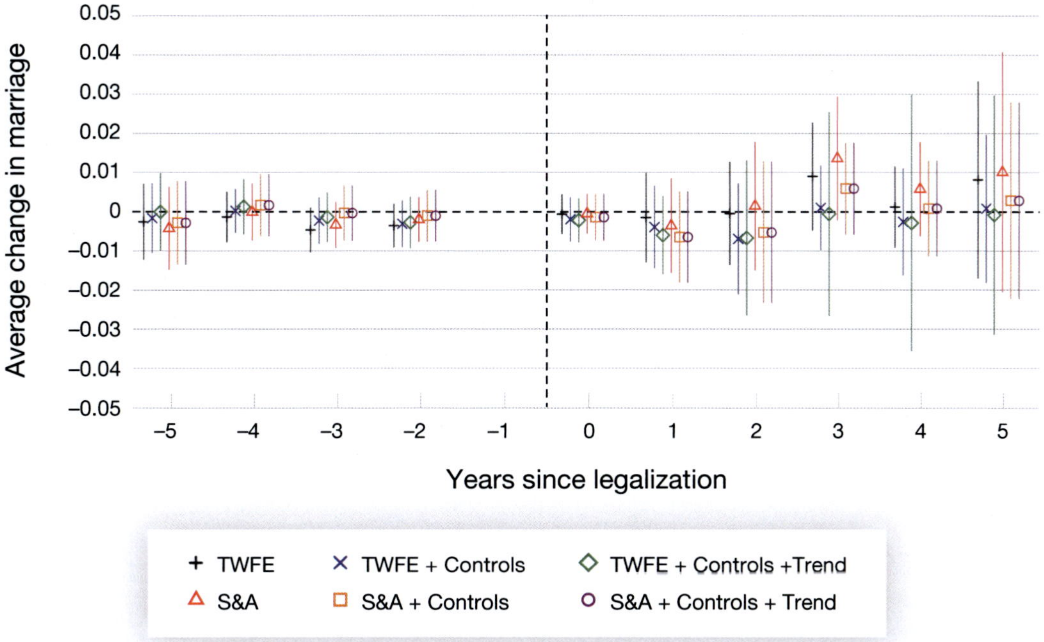

SOURCE: Data are from ACS, 2000–2014 (Ruggles et al., 2023).

NOTE: The dependent variable is the natural log of the percentage of respondents currently married in a state-year. Models are TWFE and Sun and Abraham's (2021) interaction-weighted estimator (S&A). The three specifications for each model are (1) no controls, (2) controlling for state-level market characteristics, and (3) controlling for state-level market characteristics and cohort-specific linear trends. State-level controls include sex ratios; sex-specific shares of race and ethnicity groups, education groups, and age groups; female labor force participation rate; proportion of the population that is foreign-born; logged median earnings; the unemployment rate; and whether the state recognizes civil unions. Bars represent 95-percent confidence intervals. The average percentage of respondents currently married in a state was 60 percent in 2000. Joint significance tests of the pre-period coefficients in the TWFE models found no statistically significant pre-trend variation between treated and control states ($p = 0.589$, $p = 0.840$, and $p = 0.826$ for specifications 1, 2, and 3, respectively). For more information on the models used, see Appendix C. Individuals who are separated but not divorced are considered currently married.

FIGURE D.2

Event Study of Currently Married, American Community Survey, Individual

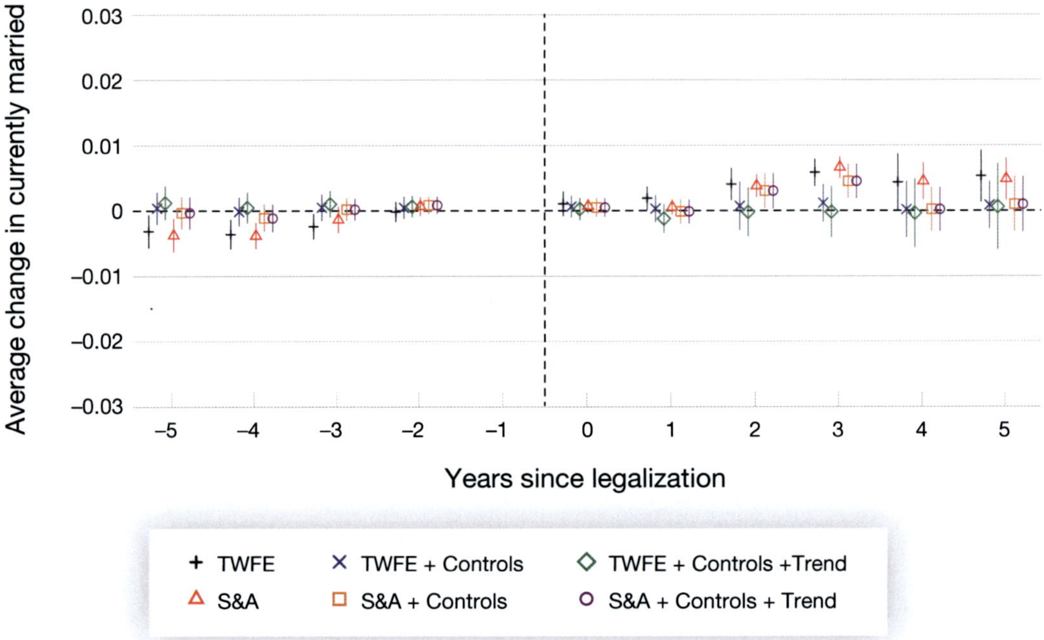

SOURCE: Data are from the ACS, 2000–2014 (Ruggles et al., 2023).

NOTE: S&A = interaction-weighted estimator. The dependent variable is an indicator for being currently married in a state-year. Models are TWFE and Sun and Abraham's (2021) interaction-weighted estimator (S&A). The three specifications for each model are (1) no controls, (2) controlling for individual- and state-level market characteristics, and (3) controlling for individual- and state-level market characteristics and cohort-specific linear trends. Individual-level controls include education, race, labor force participation status, logged family income, and a quadratic in age. State-level controls include sex ratios; sex-specific shares of race and ethnicity groups, education groups, and age groups; female labor force participation rate; proportion of the population that is foreign-born; logged median earnings; the unemployment rate; and whether the state recognizes civil unions. Bars represent 95-percent confidence intervals. In 2000, 62 percent of respondents were currently married. Joint significance tests of the pre-period coefficients in the TWFE models identified statistically significant pre-trend variation between treated and control states in the specification with no controls ($p = 0.036$) and no statistically significant pre-trend variation for specifications 2 and 3 ($p = 0.958$ and $p = 0.865$, respectively). For more information on the models used, see Appendix C. Individuals who are separated but not divorced are considered currently married.

FIGURE D.3

Event Study of Currently Married, Current Population Survey, State

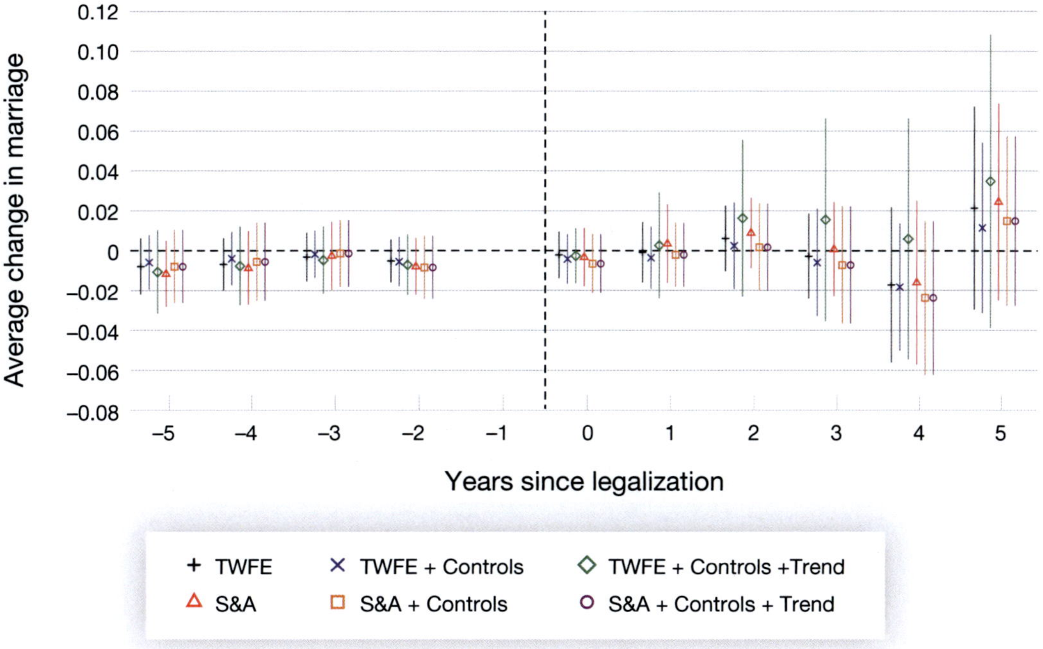

SOURCE: Data are from the CPS, 2000–2014 (Flood et al., 2023).

NOTE: The dependent variable is the natural log of the percentage of respondents currently married in a state-year. Models are TWFE and Sun and Abraham's (2021) interaction-weighted estimator (S&A). The three specifications for each model are (1) no controls, (2) controlling for state-level market characteristics, and (3) controlling for state-level market characteristics and cohort-specific linear trends. State-level controls include sex ratios; sex-specific shares of race and ethnicity groups, education groups, and age groups; female labor force participation rate; proportion of the population that is foreign-born; logged median earnings; the unemployment rate; and whether the state recognizes civil unions. Bars represent 95 percent confidence intervals. The average percentage of respondents currently married in a state was 61 percent in 2000. Joint significance tests of the pre-period coefficients in the TWFE models found no statistically significant pre-trend variation between treated and control states ($p = 0.638$, $p = 0.707$, and $p = 0.725$ for specifications 1, 2, and 3, respectively). For more information on the models used, see Appendix C. Individuals who are separated but not divorced are considered currently married.

FIGURE D.4
Event Study of Currently Married, Current Population Survey, Individual

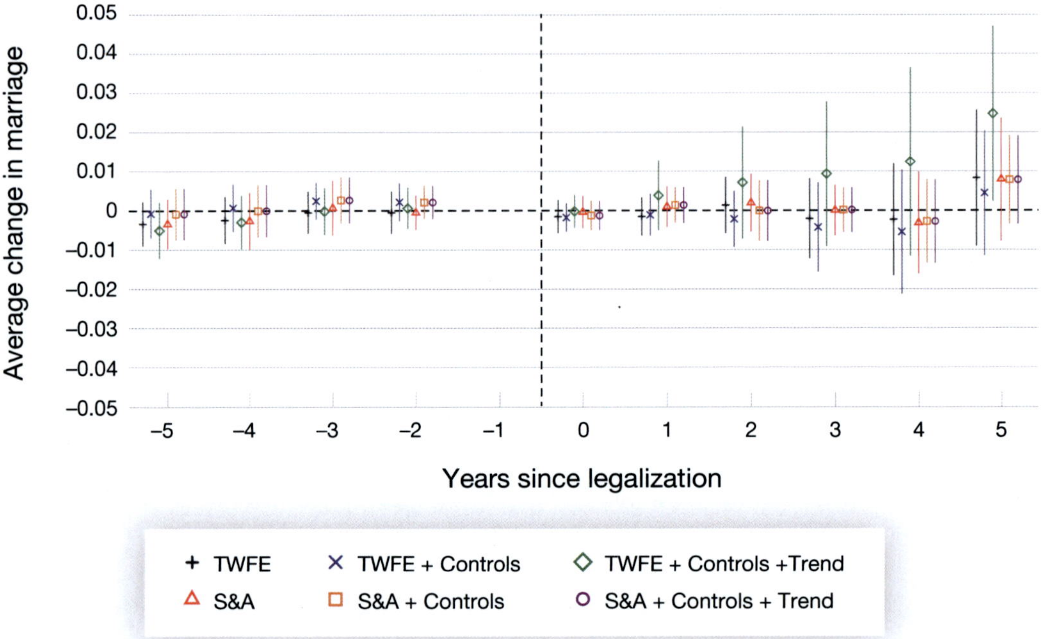

SOURCE: Data are from the CPS, 2000–2014 (Flood et al., 2023).

NOTE: The dependent variable is an indicator for being currently married in a state-year. Models are TWFE and Sun and Abraham's (2021) interaction-weighted estimator (S&A). The three specifications for each model are (1) no controls, (2) controlling for individual- and state-level market characteristics, and (3) controlling for individual- and state-level market characteristics and cohort-specific linear trends. Individual-level controls include education, race, labor force participation status, logged family income, and a quadratic in age. State-level controls include sex ratios; sex-specific shares of race and ethnicity groups, education groups, and age groups; female labor force participation rate; proportion of the population that is foreign-born; logged median earnings; the unemployment rate; and whether the state recognizes civil unions. Bars represent 95-percent confidence intervals. In 2000, 62 percent of respondents were currently married. Joint significance tests of the pre-period coefficients in the TWFE models found no statistically significant pre-trend variation between treated and control states (p = 0.741, p = 0.756, and p = 0.452 for specifications 1, 2, and 3, respectively). For more information on the models used, see Appendix C. Individuals who are separated but not divorced are considered currently married.

FIGURE D.5

Event Study of Currently Married, Panel Study of Income Dynamics, Individual

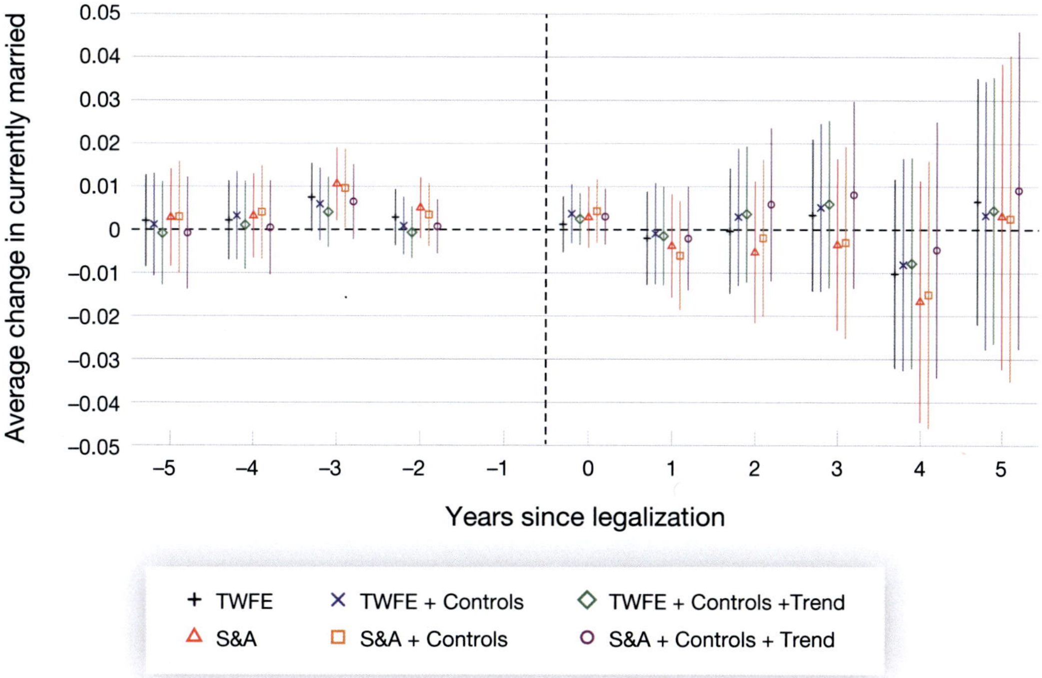

SOURCE: Data are from the PSID, 2000–2014 (Institute for Social Research, 2023).

NOTE: The dependent variable is an indicator for being currently married in a state-year, derived from the PSID Marriage History File. Models are TWFE and Sun and Abraham's (2021) interaction-weighted estimator (S&A). The three specifications for each model are (1) no controls, (2) controlling for individual- and state-level market characteristics, and (3) controlling for individual- and state-level market characteristics and cohort-specific linear trends. Individual-level controls include education, race, labor force participation status, logged family income, and a quadratic in age. State-level controls include sex ratios; sex-specific shares of race and ethnicity groups, education groups, and age groups; female labor force participation rate; proportion of the population that is foreign-born; logged median earnings; the unemployment rate; and whether the state recognizes civil unions. Bars represent 95-percent confidence intervals. In 2000, 59 percent of respondents were currently married. Joint significance tests of the pre-period coefficients in the TWFE models found no statistically significant pre-trend variation between treated and control states (p = 0.094, p = 0.394, and p = 0.437 for specifications 1, 2, and 3, respectively). For more information on the models used, see Appendix C. Individuals who are separated but not divorced are considered currently married. The sample may include same-sex couples.

New Marriages

FIGURE D.6

Event Study of New Marriages, American Community Survey, State

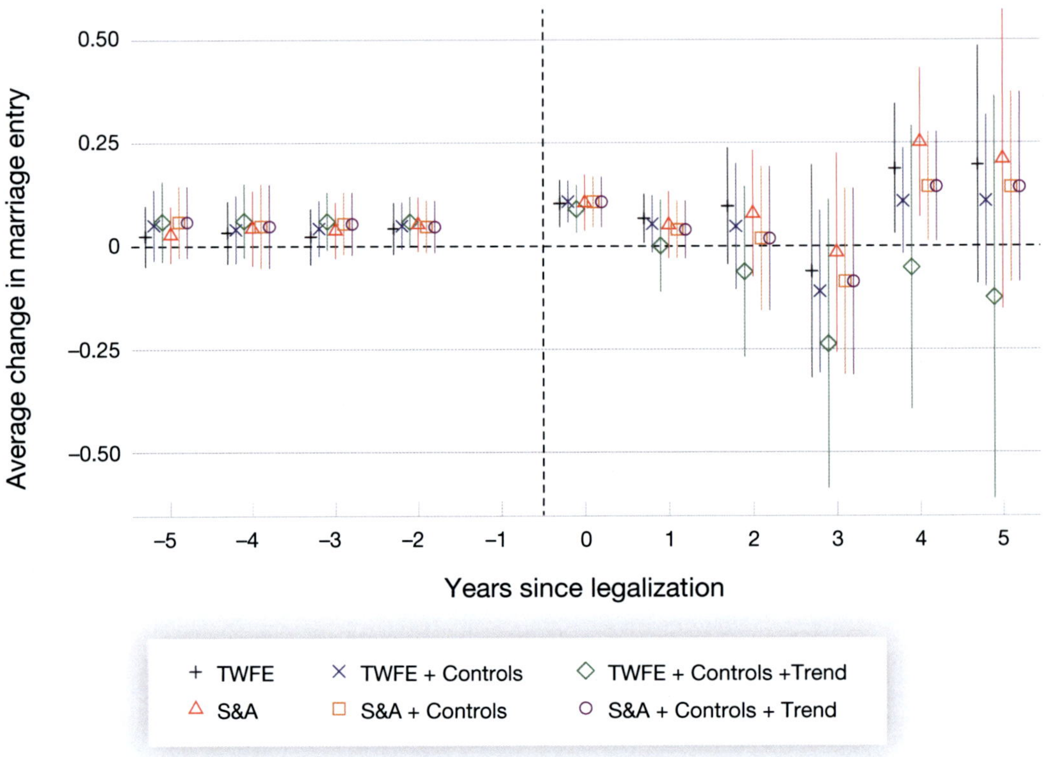

SOURCE: Data are from the ACS, 2000–2014 (Ruggles et al., 2023).

NOTE: The dependent variable is the natural log of the percentage of respondents newly married (in the past year) in a state-year. Models are TWFE and Sun and Abraham's (2021) interaction-weighted estimator (S&A). The three specifications for each model are (1) no controls, (2) controlling for state-level market characteristics, and (3) controlling for state-level market characteristics and cohort-specific linear trends. State-level controls include sex ratios; sex-specific shares of race and ethnicity groups, education groups, and age groups; female labor force participation rate; proportion of the population that is foreign-born; logged median earnings; the unemployment rate; and whether the state recognizes civil unions. Bars represent 95-percent confidence intervals. The average percentage of respondents newly married (in the past year) in a state was 5 percent in 2000. Joint significance tests of the pre-period coefficients in the TWFE models found no statistically significant pre-trend variation between treated and control states (p = 0.796, p = 0.552, and p = 0.467 for specifications 1, 2, and 3, respectively). For more information on the models used, see Appendix C.

FIGURE D.7

Event Study of New Marriages, American Community Survey, Individual

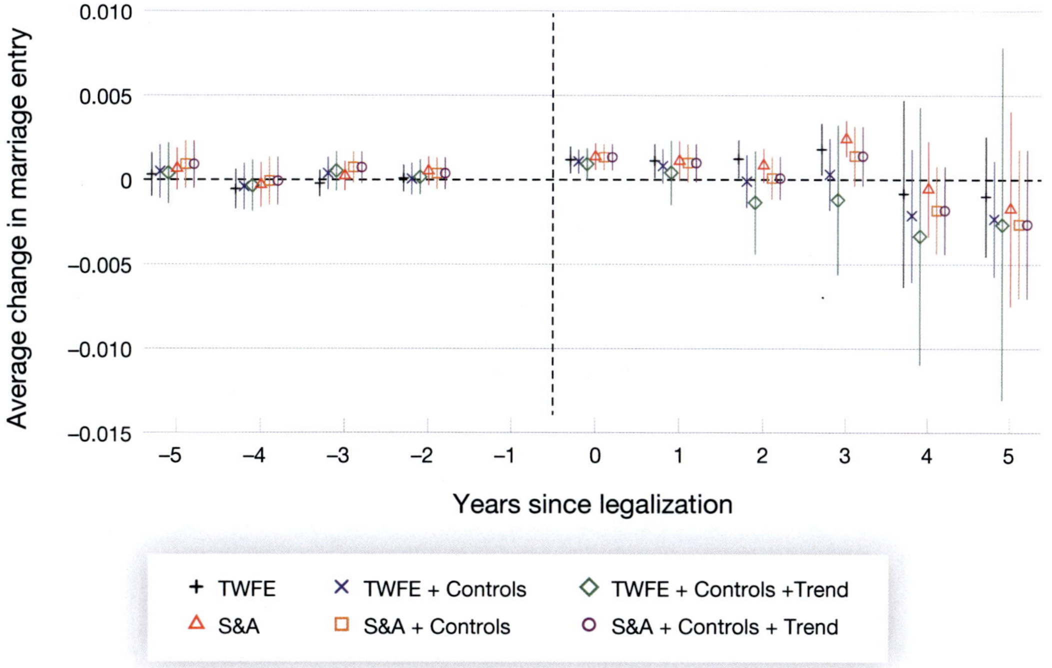

SOURCE: Data are from the ACS, 2000–2014 (Ruggles et al., 2023).

NOTE: The dependent variable is an indicator for being newly married (in the past year) in a state-year. Models are TWFE and Sun and Abraham's (2021) interaction-weighted estimator (S&A). The three specifications for each model are (1) no controls, (2) controlling for individual- and state-level market characteristics, and (3) controlling for individual- and state-level market characteristics and cohort-specific linear trends. Individual-level controls include education, race, labor force participation status, logged family income, and a quadratic in age. State-level controls include sex ratios; sex-specific shares of race and ethnicity groups, education groups, and age groups, female labor force participation rate; proportion of the population that is foreign-born; logged median earnings; the unemployment rate; and whether the state recognizes civil unions. Bars represent 95-percent confidence intervals. In 2000, 5 percent of respondents were newly married (in the past year). Joint significance tests of the pre-period coefficients in the TWFE models found no statistically significant pre-trend variation between treated and control states ($p = 0.759$, $p = 0.532$, and $p = 0.479$ for specifications 1, 2, and 3, respectively). For more information on the models used, see Appendix C.

FIGURE D.8
Event Study of New Marriages, Panel Study of Income Dynamics, Individual

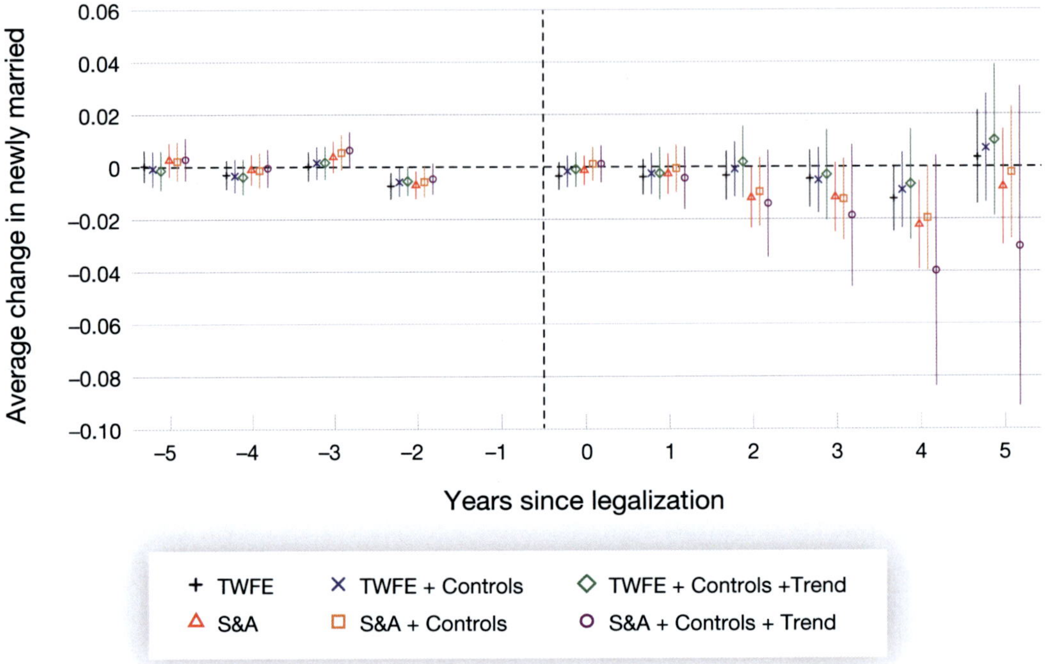

SOURCE: Data are from the PSID, 2000–2014 (Institute for Social Research, 2023).

NOTE: The dependent variable is an indicator for being newly married (in the past year) in a state-year, derived from the PSID Marriage History File. Models are TWFE and Sun and Abraham's (2021) interaction-weighted estimator (S&A). The three specifications for each model are (1) no controls, (2) controlling for individual- and state-level market characteristics, and (3) controlling for individual- and state-level market characteristics and cohort-specific linear trends. Individual-level controls include education, race, labor force participation status, logged family income, and a quadratic in age. State-level controls include sex ratios; sex-specific shares of race and ethnicity groups, education groups, and age groups; female labor force participation rate; proportion of the population that is foreign-born; logged median earnings; the unemployment rate; and whether the state recognizes civil unions. Bars represent 95-percent confidence intervals. In 2000, 2 percent of respondents were newly married (in the past year). Joint significance tests of the pre-period coefficients in the TWFE models identified statistically significant pre-trend variation between treated and control states in the specification with no controls ($p = 0.013$) and no statistically significant pre-trend variation for specifications 2 and 3 ($p = 0.095$ and $p = 0.107$, respectively). For more information on the models used, see Appendix C. The sample may include same-sex couples.

FIGURE D.9
Event Study of New Marriages, Centers for Disease Control and Prevention, State

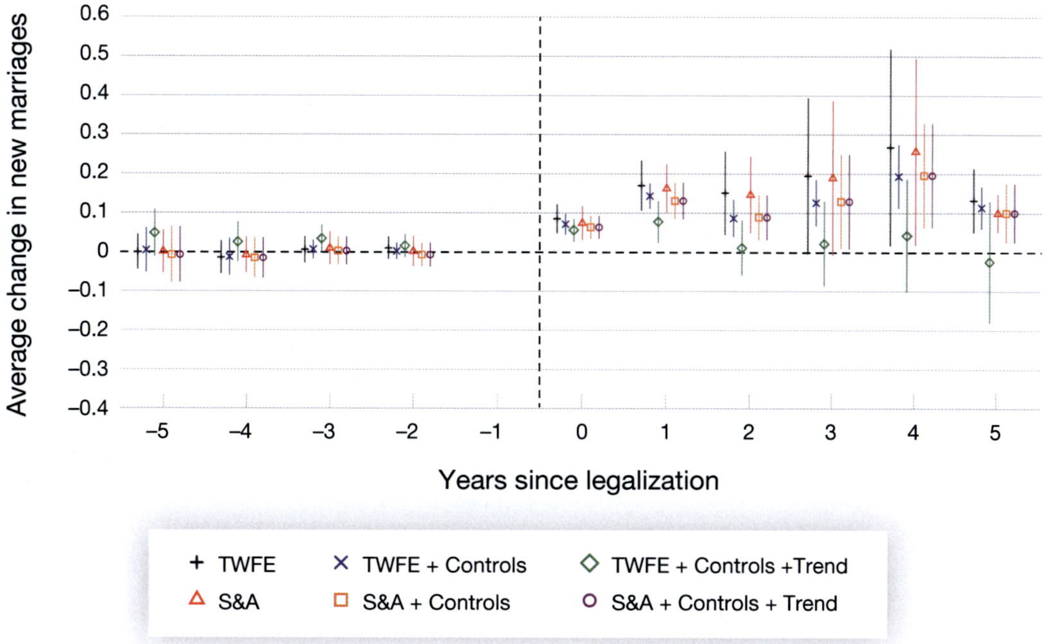

SOURCE: Data are from the CDC, 2000–2014 (CDC, undated).

NOTE: The dependent variable is the rate of new marriages per 1,000 residents in a state-year. Models are TWFE and Sun and Abraham's (2021) interaction-weighted estimator (S&A). The three specifications for each model are (1) no controls, (2) controlling for state-level market characteristics, and (3) controlling for state-level market characteristics and cohort-specific linear trends. State-level controls include sex ratios; sex-specific shares of race and ethnicity groups, education groups, and age groups; female labor force participation rate; proportion of the population that is foreign-born; logged median earnings; the unemployment rate; and whether the state recognizes civil unions. Bars represent 95-percent confidence intervals. In 2000, the average rate of new marriages for states was 9.8 per 1,000 residents. Joint significance tests of the pre-period coefficients in the TWFE models found no statistically significant pre-trend variation between treated and control states ($p = 0.390$, $p = 0.583$, and $p = 0.211$ for specifications 1, 2, and 3, respectively). For more information on the models used, see Appendix C.

Cohabitation

FIGURE D.10
Event Study of Currently Cohabiting, American Community Survey, State

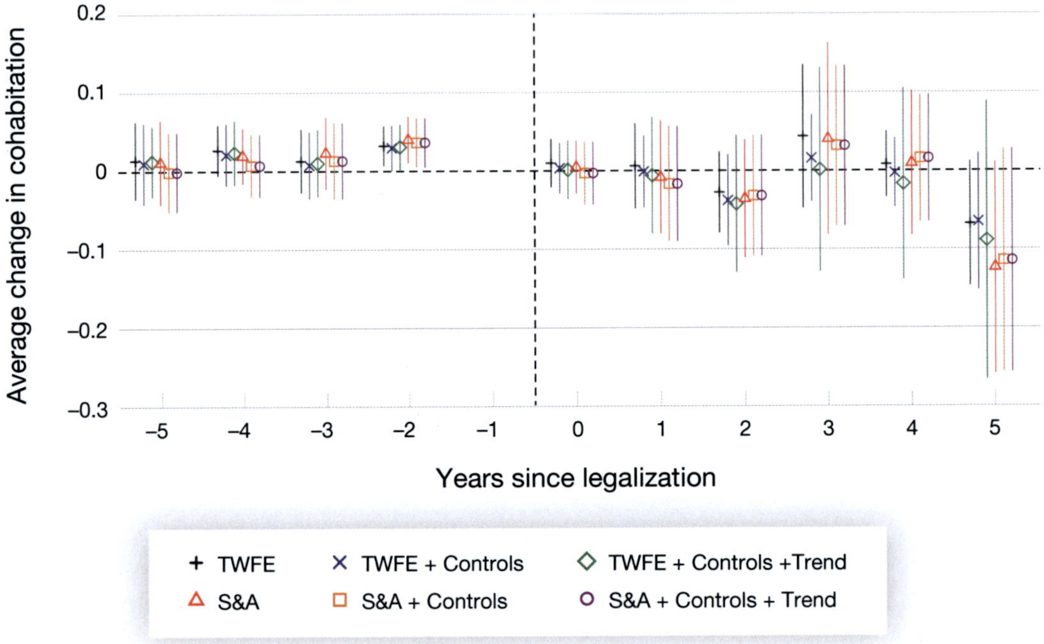

SOURCE: Data are from the ACS, 2000–2014 (Ruggles et al., 2023).

NOTE: The dependent variable is the natural log of the percentage of respondents currently cohabiting with an unmarried partner in a state-year. Models are TWFE and Sun and Abraham's (2021) interaction-weighted estimator (S&A). The three specifications for each model are (1) no controls, (2) controlling for state-level market characteristics, and (3) controlling for state-level market characteristics and cohort-specific linear trends. State-level controls include sex ratios; sex-specific shares of race and ethnicity groups, education groups, and age groups; female labor force participation rate; proportion of the population that is foreign-born; logged median earnings; the unemployment rate; and whether the state recognizes civil unions. Bars represent 95-percent confidence intervals. The average percentage of respondents currently cohabiting with an unmarried partner in a state was 4 percent in 2000. Joint significance tests of the pre-period coefficients in the TWFE models identified statistically significant pre-trend variation between treated and control states in the specification with no controls ($p = 0.017$) and no statistically significant pre-trend variation for specifications 2 and 3 ($p = 0.129$ and $p = 0.142$, respectively). For more information on the models used, see Appendix C.

FIGURE D.11
Event Study of Currently Cohabiting, American Community Survey, Individual

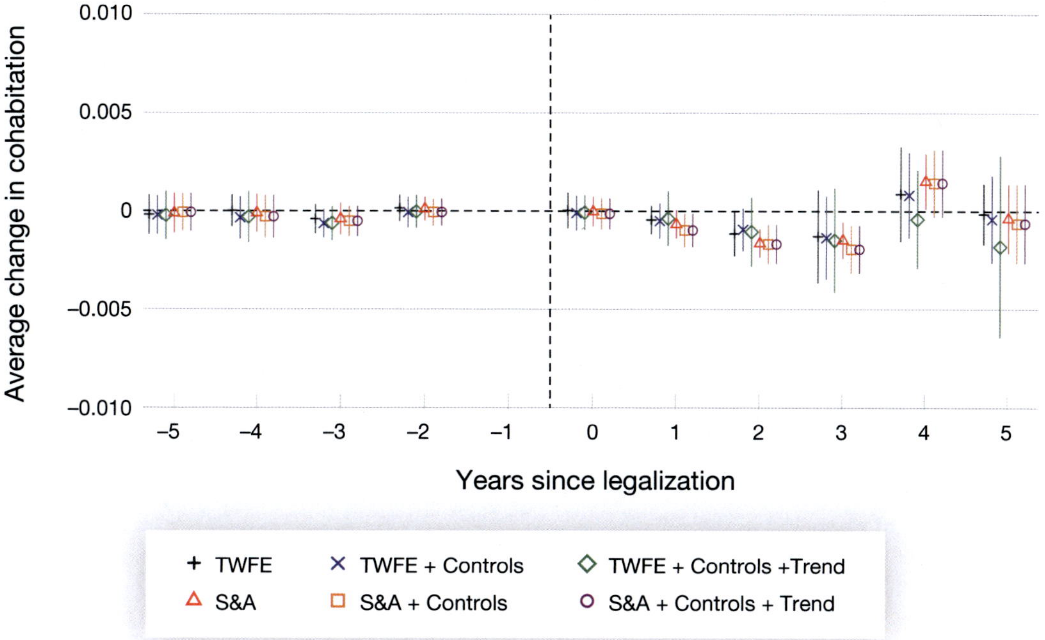

SOURCE: Data are from the ACS, 2000–2014 (Ruggles et al., 2023).

NOTE: The dependent variable is an indicator for currently cohabiting with an unmarried partner in a state-year. Models are TWFE and Sun and Abraham's (2021) interaction-weighted estimator (S&A). The three specifications for each model are (1) no controls, (2) controlling for individual- and state-level market characteristics, and (3) controlling for individual- and state-level market characteristics and cohort-specific linear trends. Individual-level controls include education, race, labor force participation status, logged family income, and a quadratic in age. State-level controls include sex ratios; sex-specific shares of race and ethnicity groups, education groups, and age groups; female labor force participation rate; proportion of the population that is foreign-born; logged median earnings; the unemployment rate; and whether the state recognizes civil unions. Bars represent 95-percent confidence intervals. In 2000, 4 percent of respondents were cohabiting with an unmarried partner. Joint significance tests of the pre-period coefficients in the TWFE models found no statistically significant pre-trend variation between treated and control states (p = 0.691, p = 0.594, and p = 0.646 for specifications 1, 2, and 3, respectively). For more information on the models used, see Appendix C.

FIGURE D.12

Event Study of Currently Cohabiting, Current Population Survey, State

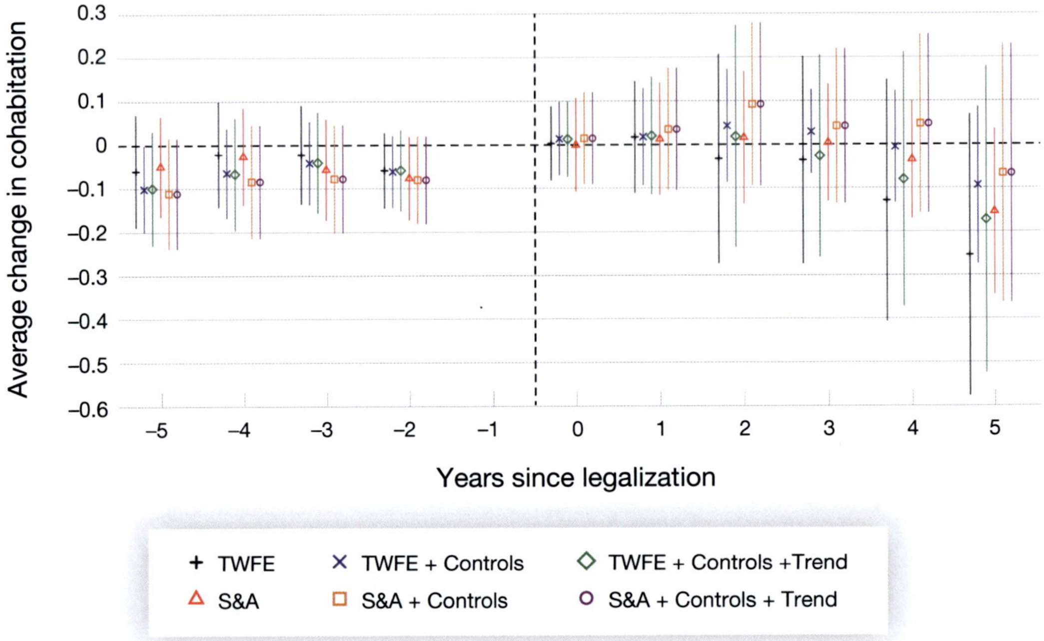

SOURCE: Data are from the CPS, 2000–2014 (Flood et al., 2023).

NOTE: The dependent variable is the natural log of the percentage of respondents currently cohabiting with an unmarried partner in a state-year. Models are TWFE and Sun and Abraham's (2021) interaction-weighted estimator (S&A). The three specifications for each model are (1) no controls, (2) controlling for state-level market characteristics, and (3) controlling for state-level market characteristics and cohort-specific linear trends. State-level controls include sex ratios; sex-specific shares of race and ethnicity groups, education groups, and age groups; female labor force participation rate; proportion of the population that is foreign-born; logged median earnings; the unemployment rate; and whether the state recognizes civil unions. Bars represent 95-percent confidence intervals. The average percentage of respondents currently cohabiting with an unmarried partner in a state was 3 percent in 2000. Joint significance tests of the pre-period coefficients in the TWFE models found no statistically significant pre-trend variation between treated and control states ($p = 0.261$, $p = 0.258$, and $p = 0.449$ for specifications 1, 2, and 3, respectively). For more information on the models used, see Appendix C.

FIGURE D.13

Event Study of Currently Cohabiting, Current Population Survey, Individual

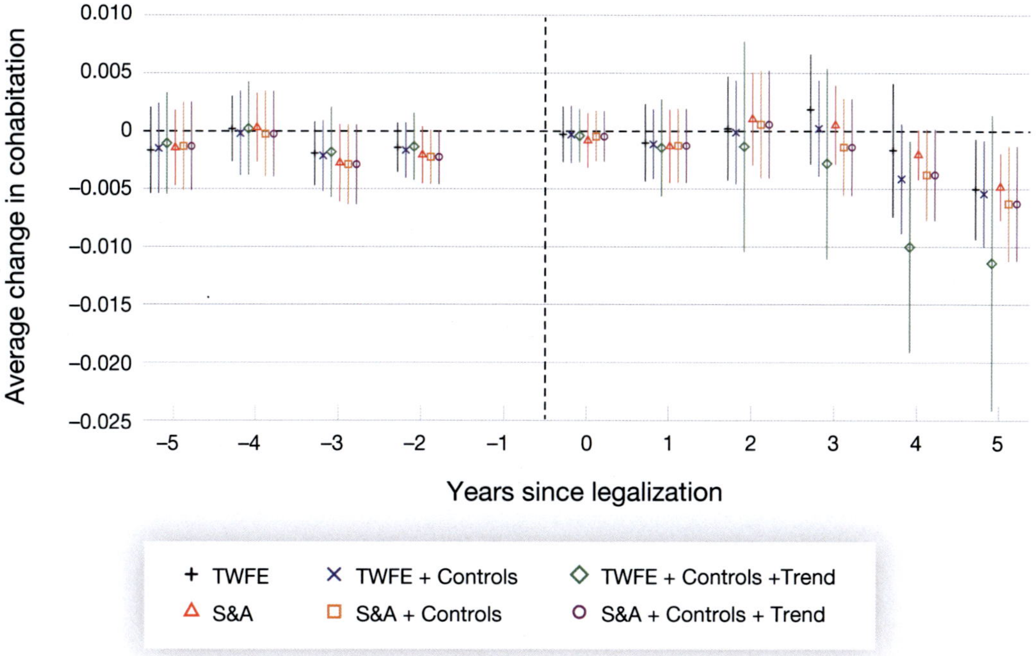

SOURCE: Data are from the CPS, 2000–2014 (Flood et al., 2023).

NOTE: The dependent variable is an indicator for currently cohabiting with an unmarried partner in a state-year. Models are TWFE and Sun and Abraham's (2021) interaction-weighted estimator (S&A). The three specifications for each model are (1) no controls, (2) controlling for individual- and state-level market characteristics, and (3) controlling for individual- and state-level market characteristics and cohort-specific linear trends. Individual-level controls include education, race, labor force participation status, logged family income, and a quadratic in age. State-level controls include sex ratios; sex-specific shares of race and ethnicity groups, education groups, and age groups; female labor force participation rate; proportion of the population that is foreign-born; logged median earnings; the unemployment rate; and whether the state recognizes civil unions. Bars represent 95-percent confidence intervals. In 2000, 3 percent of respondents were currently cohabiting with an unmarried partner. Joint significance tests of the pre-period coefficients in the TWFE models found no statistically significant pre-trend variation between treated and control states ($p = 0.244$, $p = 0.257$, and $p = 0.395$ for specifications 1, 2, and 3, respectively). For more information on the models used, see Appendix C.

Divorce

Currently Divorced

FIGURE D.14

Event Study of Currently Divorced, American Community Survey, State, Unconditional

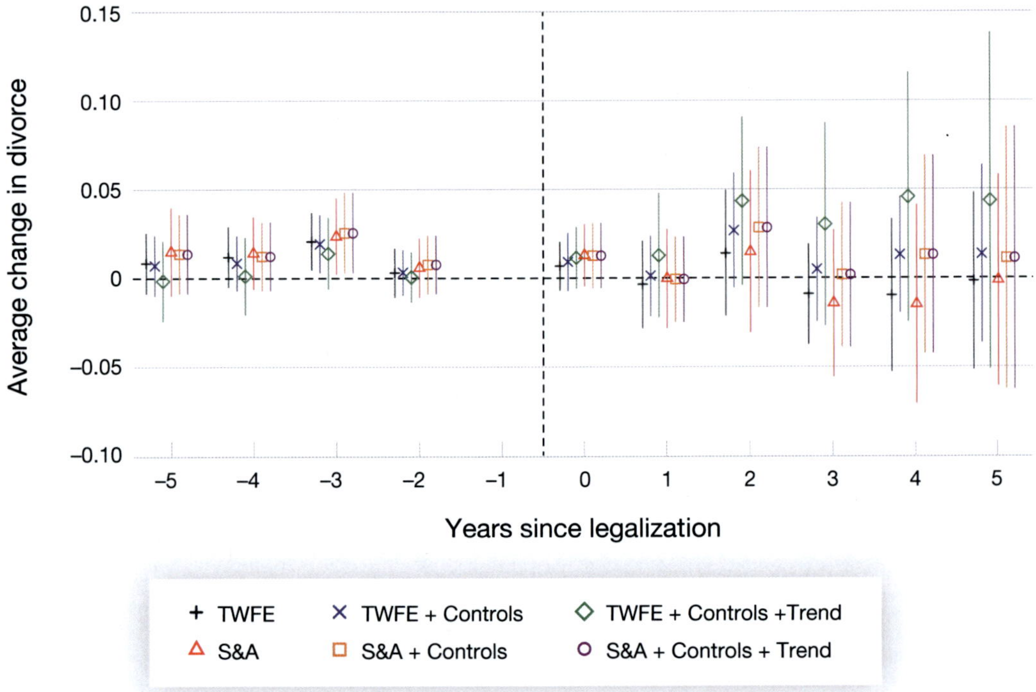

SOURCE: Data are from the ACS, 2000–2014 (Ruggles et al., 2023).

NOTE: The dependent variable is the natural log of the percentage of respondents currently divorced in a state-year. Models are TWFE and Sun and Abraham's (2021) interaction-weighted estimator (S&A). The three specifications for each model are (1) no controls, (2) controlling for state-level market characteristics, and (3) controlling for state-level market characteristics and cohort-specific linear trends. State-level controls include sex ratios; sex-specific shares of race and ethnicity groups, education groups, and age groups; female labor force participation rate; proportion of the population that is foreign-born; logged median earnings; the unemployment rate; and whether the state recognizes civil unions. Bars represent 95-percent confidence intervals. The average percentage of respondents currently divorced in a state was 11 percent in 2000. Joint significance tests of the pre-period coefficients in the TWFE models found no statistically significant pre-trend variation between treated and control states ($p = 0.142$, $p = 0.230$, and $p = 0.408$ for specifications 1, 2, and 3, respectively). For more information on the models used, see Appendix C. The sample includes all respondents not cohabiting with or married to a same-sex partner.

FIGURE D.15

Event Study of Currently Divorced, American Community Survey, State, Conditional

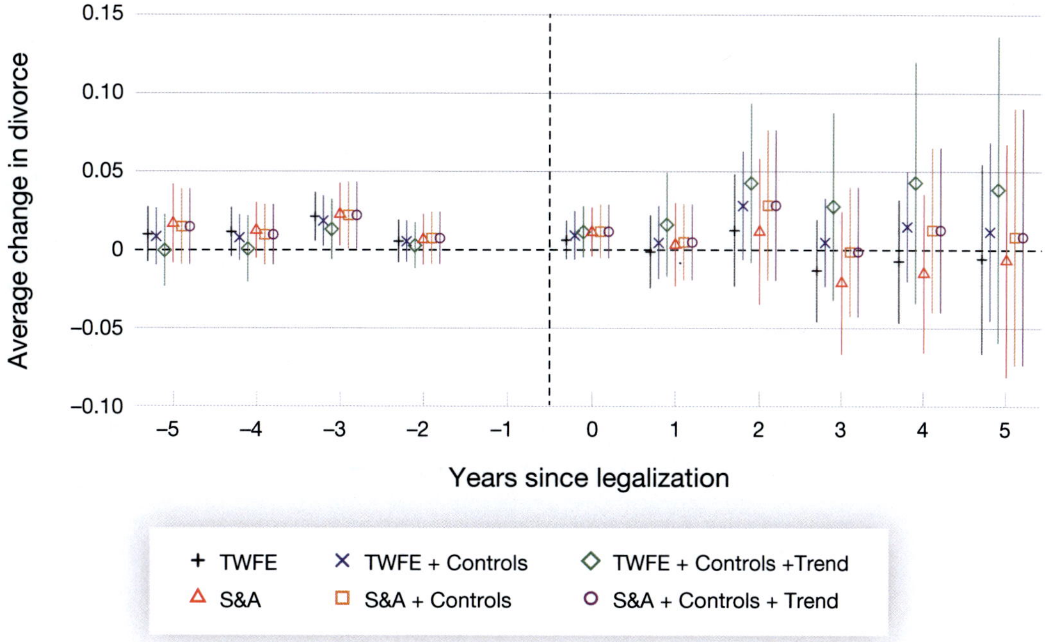

SOURCE: Data are from the ACS, 2000–2014 (Ruggles et al., 2023).

NOTE: The dependent variable is the natural log of the percentage of respondents currently divorced in a state-year. The sample consists of married respondents not cohabiting with or married to a same-sex partner. Models are TWFE and Sun and Abraham's (2021) interaction-weighted estimator (S&A). The three specifications for each model are (1) no controls, (2) controlling for state-level market characteristics, and (3) controlling for state-level market characteristics and cohort-specific linear trends. State-level controls include sex ratios; sex-specific shares of race and ethnicity groups, education groups, and age groups; female labor force participation rate; proportion of the population that is foreign-born; logged median earnings; the unemployment rate; and whether the state recognizes civil unions. Bars represent 95-percent confidence intervals. The average percentage of married respondents currently divorced in a state was 15 percent in 2000. Joint significance tests of the pre-period coefficients in the TWFE models found no statistically significant pre-trend variation between treated and control states ($p = 0.142$, $p = 0.230$, and $p = 0.408$ for specifications 1, 2, and 3, respectively). For more information on the models used, see Appendix C.

FIGURE D.16

Event Study of Currently Divorced, American Community Survey, Individual, Unconditional

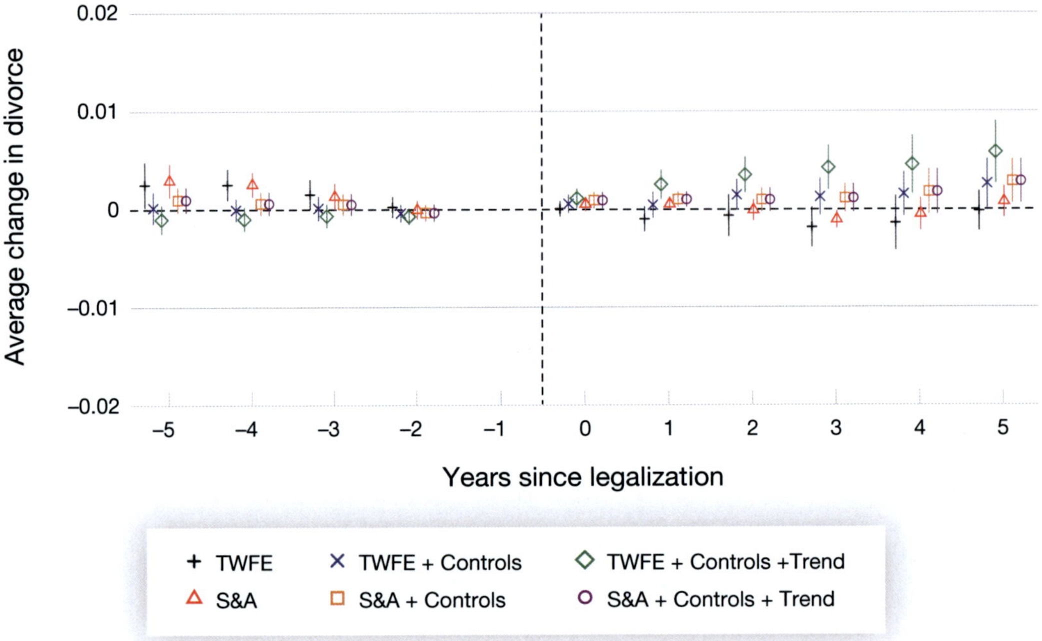

SOURCE: Data are from the ACS, 2000–2014 (Ruggles et al., 2023).

NOTE: The dependent variable is an indicator for being currently divorced in a state-year. Models are TWFE and Sun and Abraham's (2021) interaction-weighted estimator (S&A). The three specifications for each model are (1) no controls, (2) controlling for individual- and state-level market characteristics, and (3) controlling for individual- and state-level market characteristics and cohort-specific linear trends. Individual-level controls include education, race, labor force participation status, logged family income, and a quadratic in age. State-level controls include sex ratios; sex-specific shares of race and ethnicity groups, education groups, and age groups; female labor force participation rate; proportion of the population that is foreign-born; logged median earnings; the unemployment rate; and whether the state recognizes civil unions. Bars represent 95-percent confidence intervals. In 2000, 10 percent of respondents were currently divorced. Joint significance tests of the pre-period coefficients in the TWFE models identified statistically significant pre-trend variation between treated and control states in the specification with no controls ($p = 0.009$) and no statistically significant pre-trend variation for specifications 2 and 3 ($p = 0.664$ and $p = 0.432$, respectively). For more information on the models used, see Appendix C. The sample includes all respondents not cohabiting with or married to a same-sex partner.

FIGURE D.17

Event Study of Currently Divorced, American Community Survey, Individual, Conditional

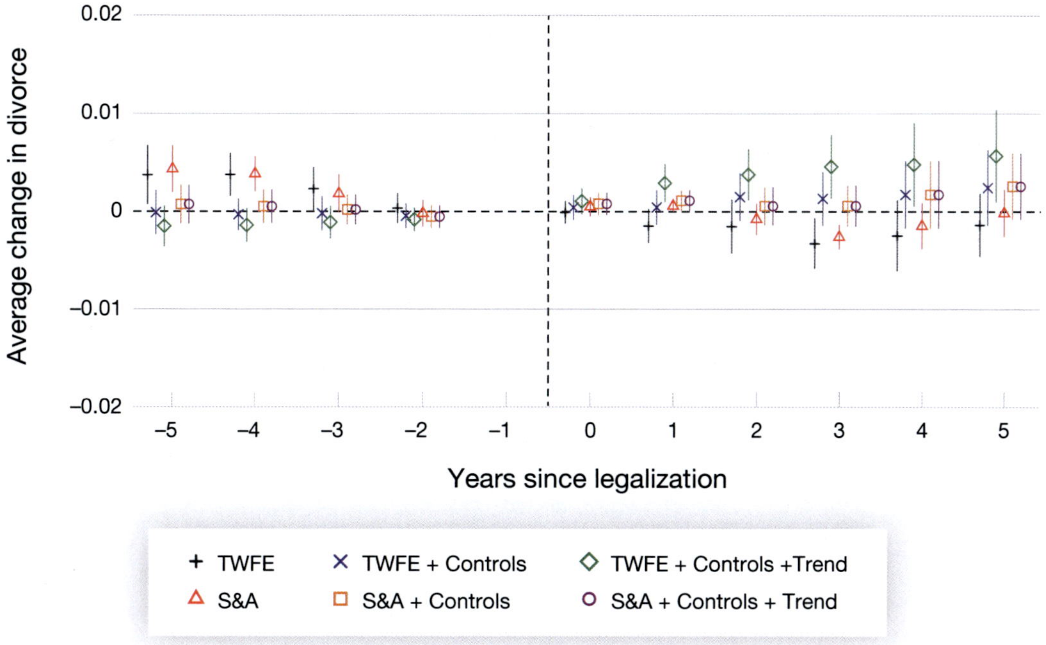

SOURCE: Data are from the ACS, 2000–2014 (Ruggles et al., 2023).

NOTE: The dependent variable is an indicator for being currently divorced in a state-year. The sample consists of married respondents not cohabiting with or married to a same-sex partner. Models are TWFE and Sun and Abraham's (2021) interaction-weighted estimator (S&A). The three specifications for each model are (1) no controls, (2) controlling for individual- and state-level market characteristics, and (3) controlling for individual- and state-level market characteristics and cohort-specific linear trends. Individual-level controls include education, race, labor force participation status, logged family income, and a quadratic in age. State-level controls include sex ratios; sex-specific shares of race and ethnicity groups, education groups, and age groups; female labor force participation rate; proportion of the population that is foreign-born; logged median earnings; the unemployment rate; and whether the state recognizes civil unions. Bars represent 95-percent confidence intervals. In 2000, 14 percent of married respondents were currently divorced. Joint significance tests of the pre-period coefficients in the TWFE models identified statistically significant pre-trend variation between treated and control states in the specification with no controls ($p = 0.011$) and no statistically significant pre-trend variation for specifications 2 and 3 ($p = 0.918$ and $p = 0.485$, respectively). For more information on the models used, see Appendix C.

FIGURE D.18

Event Study of Currently Divorced, Current Population Survey, State, Unconditional

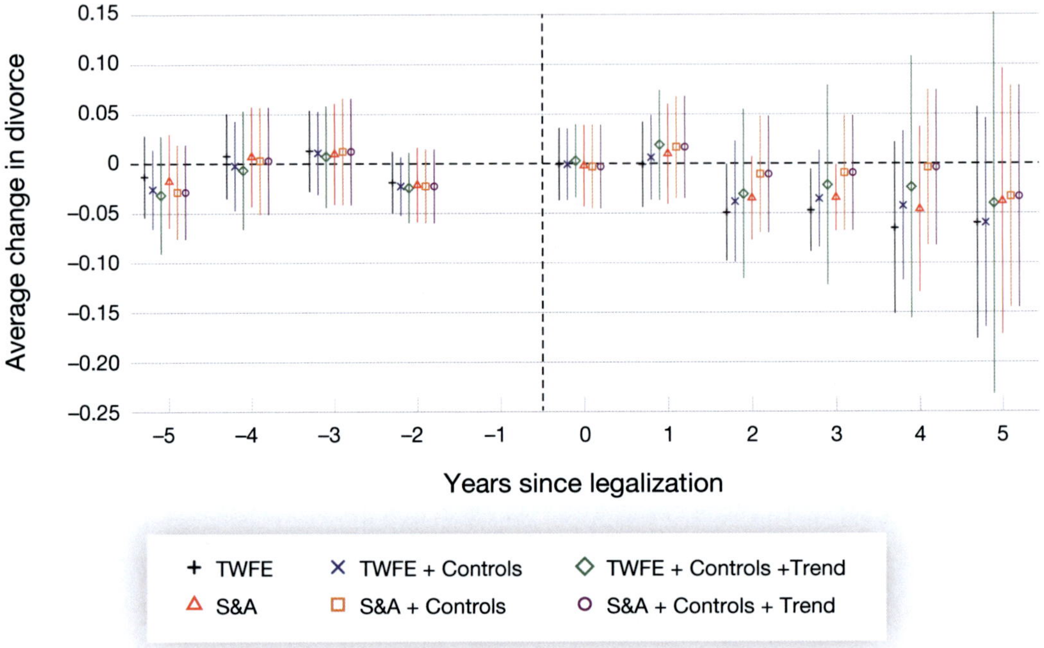

SOURCE: Data are from the CPS, 2000–2014 (Flood et al., 2023).

NOTE: The dependent variable is the natural log of the percentage of respondents currently divorced in a state-year. Models are TWFE and Sun and Abraham's (2021) interaction-weighted estimator (S&A). The three specifications for each model are (1) no controls, (2) controlling for state-level market characteristics, and (3) controlling for state-level market characteristics and cohort-specific linear trends. State-level controls include sex ratios; sex-specific shares of race and ethnicity groups, education groups, and age groups; female labor force participation rate; proportion of the population that is foreign-born; logged median earnings; the unemployment rate; and whether the state recognizes civil unions. Bars represent 95-percent confidence intervals. The average percentage of respondents currently divorced in a state was 10 percent in 2000. Joint significance tests of the pre-period coefficients in the TWFE models found no statistically significant pre-trend variation between treated and control states (p = 0.076, p = 0.066, and p = 0.114 for specifications 1, 2, and 3, respectively). For more information on the models used, see Appendix C. The sample includes all respondents not cohabiting with or married to a same-sex partner.

FIGURE D.19

Event Study of Currently Divorced, Current Population Survey, State, Conditional

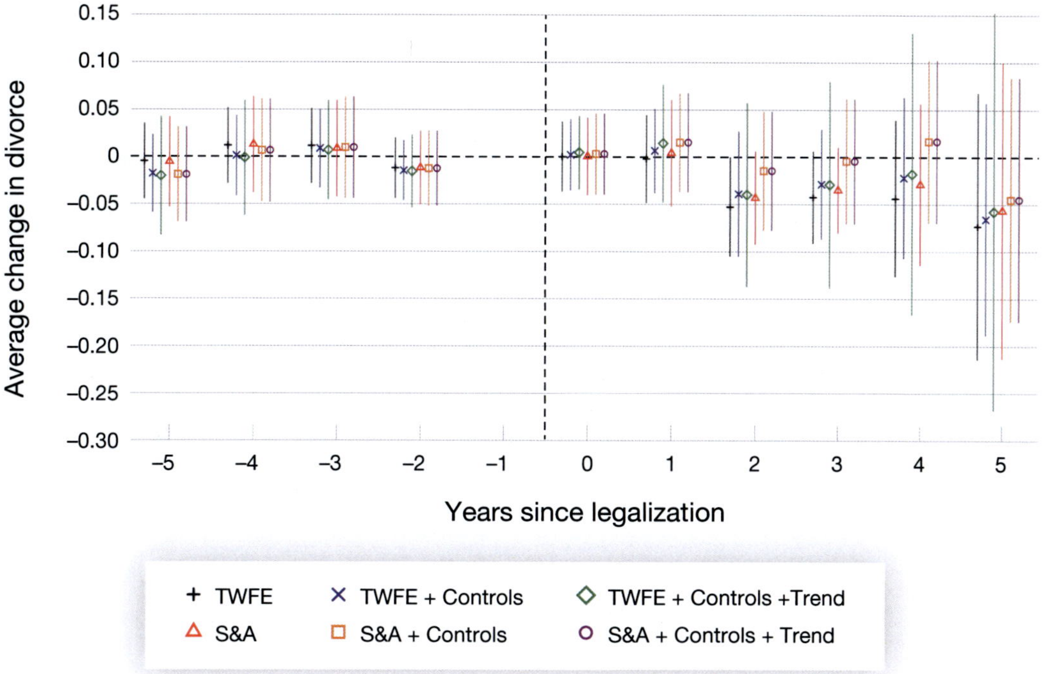

SOURCE: Data are from the CPS, 2000–2014 (Flood et al., 2023).

NOTE: The dependent variable is the natural log of the percentage of respondents currently divorced in a state-year. The sample consists of married respondents not cohabiting with or married to a same-sex partner. Models are TWFE and Sun and Abraham's (2021) interaction-weighted estimator (S&A). The three specifications for each model are (1) no controls, (2) controlling for state-level market characteristics, and (3) controlling for state-level market characteristics and cohort-specific linear trends. State-level controls include sex ratios; sex-specific shares of race and ethnicity groups, education groups, and age groups; female labor force participation rate; proportion of the population that is foreign-born; logged median earnings; the unemployment rate; and whether the state recognizes civil unions. Bars represent 95-percent confidence intervals. The average percentage of married respondents currently divorced in a state was 15 percent in 2000. Joint significance tests of the pre-period coefficients in the TWFE models found no statistically significant pre-trend variation between treated and control states ($p = 0.276$, $p = 0.261$, and $p = 0.355$ for specifications 1, 2, and 3, respectively). For more information on the models used, see Appendix C.

FIGURE D.20

Event Study of Currently Divorced, Current Population Survey, Individual, Unconditional

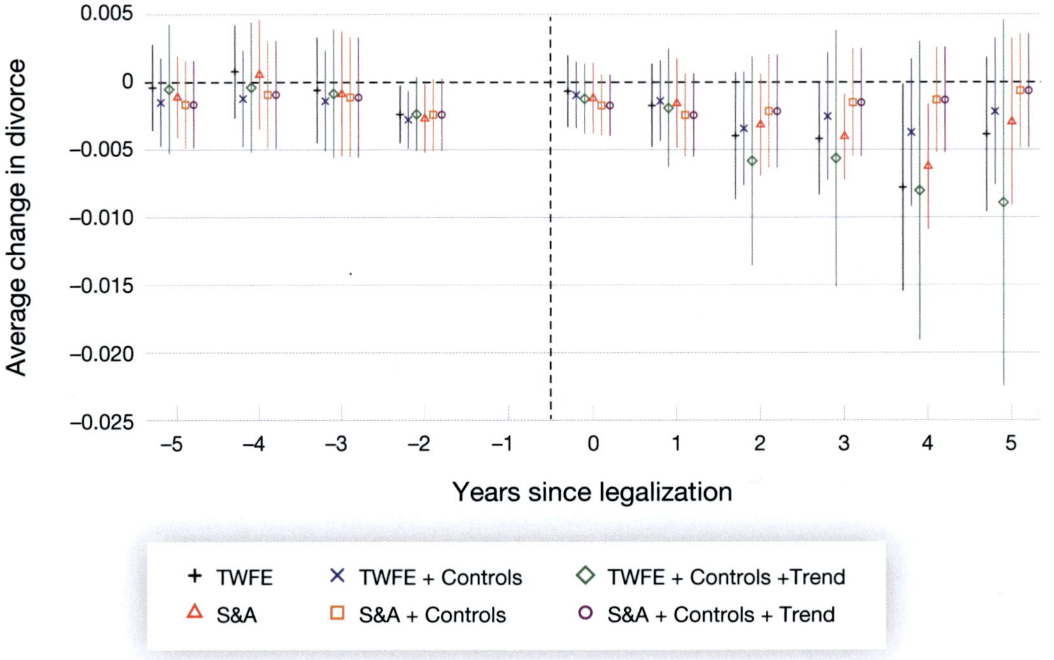

SOURCE: Data are from the CPS, 2000–2014 (Flood et al., 2023).

NOTE: The dependent variable is an indicator for being currently divorced in a state-year. Models are TWFE and Sun and Abraham's (2021) interaction-weighted estimator (S&A). The three specifications for each model are (1) no controls, (2) controlling for individual- and state-level market characteristics, and (3) controlling for individual- and state-level market characteristics and cohort-specific linear trends. Individual-level controls include education, race, labor force participation status, logged family income, and a quadratic in age. State-level controls include sex ratios; sex-specific shares of race and ethnicity groups, education groups, and age groups; female labor force participation rate; proportion of the population that is foreign-born; logged median earnings; the unemployment rate; and whether the state recognizes civil unions. Bars represent 95-percent confidence intervals. In 2000, 10 percent of respondents were currently divorced. Joint significance tests of the pre-period coefficients in the TWFE models found no statistically significant pre-trend variation between treated and control states ($p = 0.077$, $p = 0.081$, and $p = 0.247$ for specifications 1, 2, and 3, respectively). For more information on the models used, see Appendix C. The sample includes all respondents not cohabiting with or married to a same-sex partner.

FIGURE D.21

Event Study of Currently Divorced, Current Population Survey, Individual, Conditional

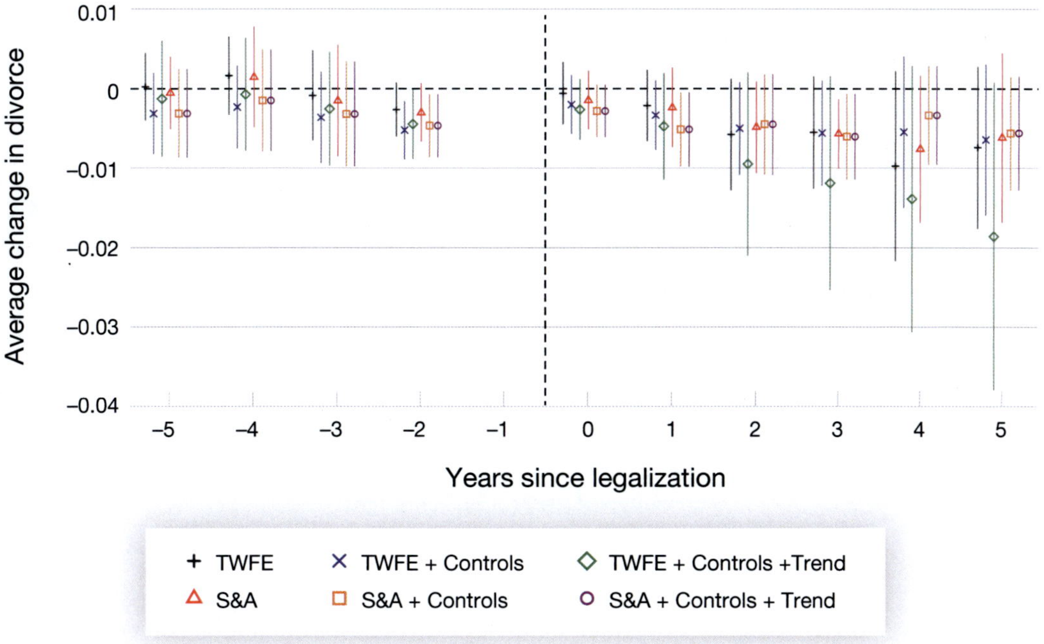

SOURCE: Data are from the CPS, 2000–2014 (Flood et al., 2023).

NOTE: The dependent variable is an indicator for being currently divorced in a state-year. The sample consists of married respondents not cohabiting with or married to a same-sex partner. Models are TWFE and Sun and Abraham's (2021) interaction-weighted estimator (S&A). The three specifications for each model are (1) no controls, (2) controlling for individual- and state-level market characteristics, and (3) controlling for individual- and state-level market characteristics and cohort-specific linear trends. Individual-level controls include education, race, labor force participation status, logged family income, and a quadratic in age. State-level controls include sex ratios; sex-specific shares of race and ethnicity groups, education groups, and age groups; female labor force participation rate; proportion of the population that is foreign-born; logged median earnings; the unemployment rate; and whether the state recognizes civil unions. Bars represent 95-percent confidence intervals. In 2000, 14 percent of married respondents were currently divorced. Joint significance tests of the pre-period coefficients in the TWFE models identified statistically significant pre-trend variation between treated and control states in specification 2 (p = 0.029) and no statistically significant pre-trend variation for specifications 1 and 3 (p = 0.246 and p = 0.138, respectively). For more information on the models used, see Appendix C.

FIGURE D.22

Event Study of Currently Divorced, Panel Study of Income Dynamics, Individual, Unconditional

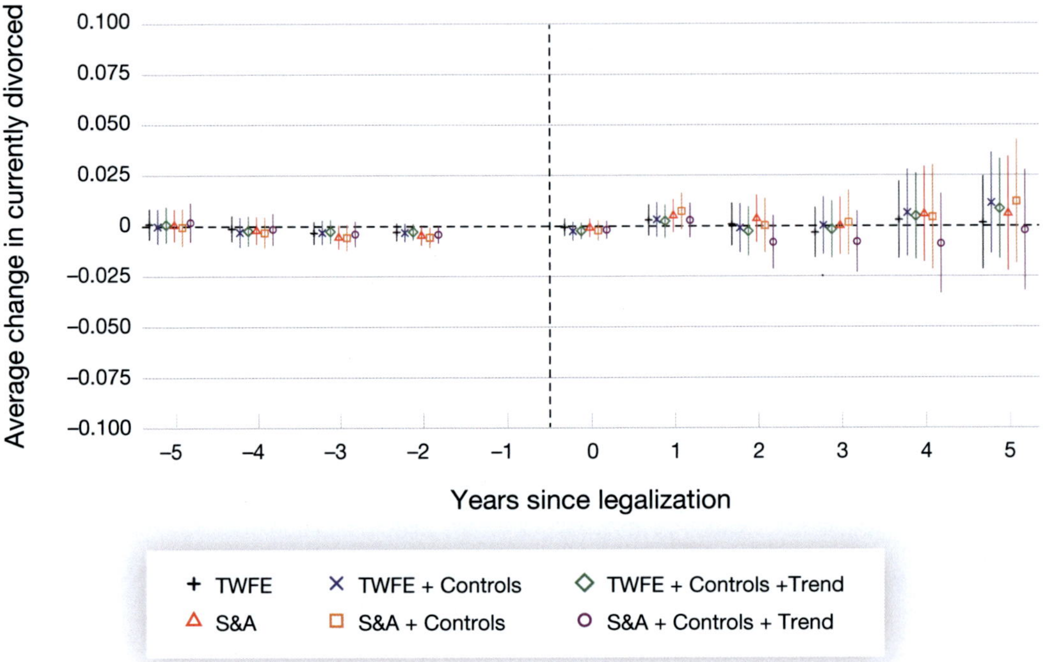

SOURCE: Data are from the PSID, 2000–2014 (Institute for Social Research, 2023).

NOTE: The dependent variable is an indicator for being currently divorced in a state-year, derived from the PSID Marriage History File. Models are TWFE and Sun and Abraham's (2021) interaction-weighted estimator (S&A). The three specifications for each model are (1) no controls, (2) controlling for individual- and state-level market characteristics, and (3) controlling for individual- and state-level market characteristics and cohort-specific linear trends. Individual-level controls include education, race, labor force participation status, logged family income, and a quadratic in age. State-level controls include sex ratios; sex-specific shares of race and ethnicity groups, education groups, and age groups; female labor force participation rate; proportion of the population that is foreign-born; logged median earnings; the unemployment rate; and whether the state recognizes civil unions. Bars represent 95-percent confidence intervals. In 2000, 15 percent of respondents were currently divorced. Joint significance tests of the pre-period coefficients in the TWFE models found no statistically significant pre-trend variation between treated and control states (p = 0.415, p = 0.551, and p = 0.514 for specifications 1, 2, and 3, respectively). For more information on the models used, see Appendix C. The sample may include same-sex couples.

FIGURE D.23

Event Study of New Divorces, American Community Survey, State, Unconditional

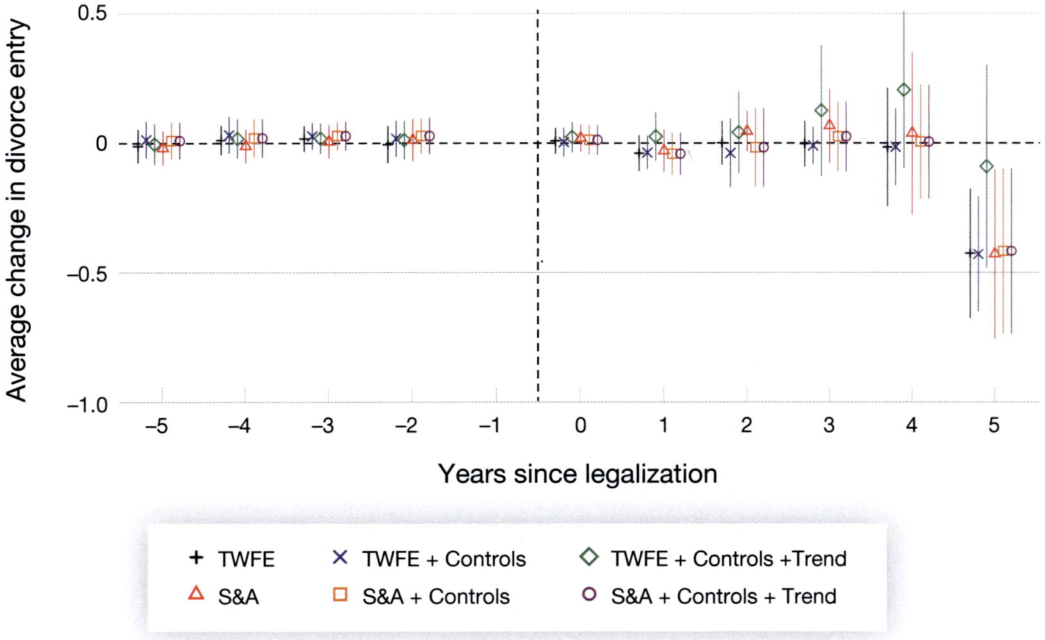

SOURCE: Data are from the ACS, 2000–2014 (Ruggles et al., 2023).

NOTE: The dependent variable is the natural log of the percentage of respondents newly divorced (in the past year) in a state-year. Models are TWFE and Sun and Abraham's (2021) interaction-weighted estimator (S&A). The three specifications for each model are (1) no controls, (2) controlling for state-level market characteristics, and (3) controlling for state-level market characteristics and cohort-specific linear trends. State-level controls include sex ratios; sex-specific shares of race and ethnicity groups, education groups, and age groups; female labor force participation rate; proportion of the population that is foreign-born; logged median earnings; the unemployment rate; and whether the state recognizes civil unions. Bars represent 95-percent confidence intervals. The average percentage of respondents newly divorced (in the past year) in a state was 1 percent in 2000. Joint significance tests of the pre-period coefficients in the TWFE models found no statistically significant pre-trend variation between treated and control states (p = 0.848, p = 0.807, and p = 0.921 for specifications 1, 2, and 3, respectively). For more information on the models used, see Appendix C. The sample includes all respondents not cohabiting with or married to a same-sex partner.

FIGURE D.24
Event Study of New Divorces, American Community Survey, State, Conditional

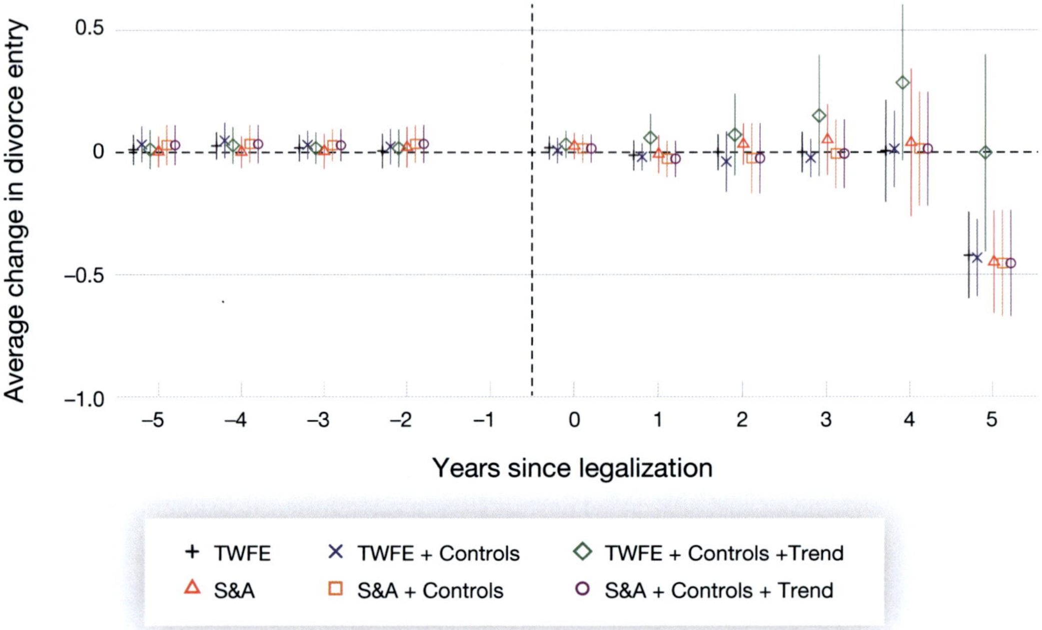

SOURCE: Data are from the ACS, 2000–2014 (Ruggles et al., 2023).

NOTE: The dependent variable is the natural log of the percentage of respondents newly divorced (in the past year) in a state-year. The sample consists of married respondents not cohabiting with or married to a same-sex partner. Models are TWFE and Sun and Abraham's (2021) interaction-weighted estimator (S&A). The three specifications for each model are (1) no controls, (2) controlling for state-level market characteristics, and (3) controlling for state-level market characteristics and cohort-specific linear trends. State-level controls include sex ratios; sex-specific shares of race and ethnicity groups, education groups, and age groups; female labor force participation rate; proportion of the population that is foreign-born; logged median earnings; the unemployment rate; and whether the state recognizes civil unions. Bars represent 95-percent confidence intervals. The average percentage of married respondents newly divorced in a state was 2 percent in 2000. Joint significance tests of the pre-period coefficients in the TWFE models found no statistically significant pre-trend variation between treated and control states ($p = 0.885$, $p = 0.739$, and $p = 0.948$ for specifications 1, 2, and 3, respectively). For more information on the models used, see Appendix C.

FIGURE D.25

Event Study of New Divorces, American Community Survey, Individual, Unconditional

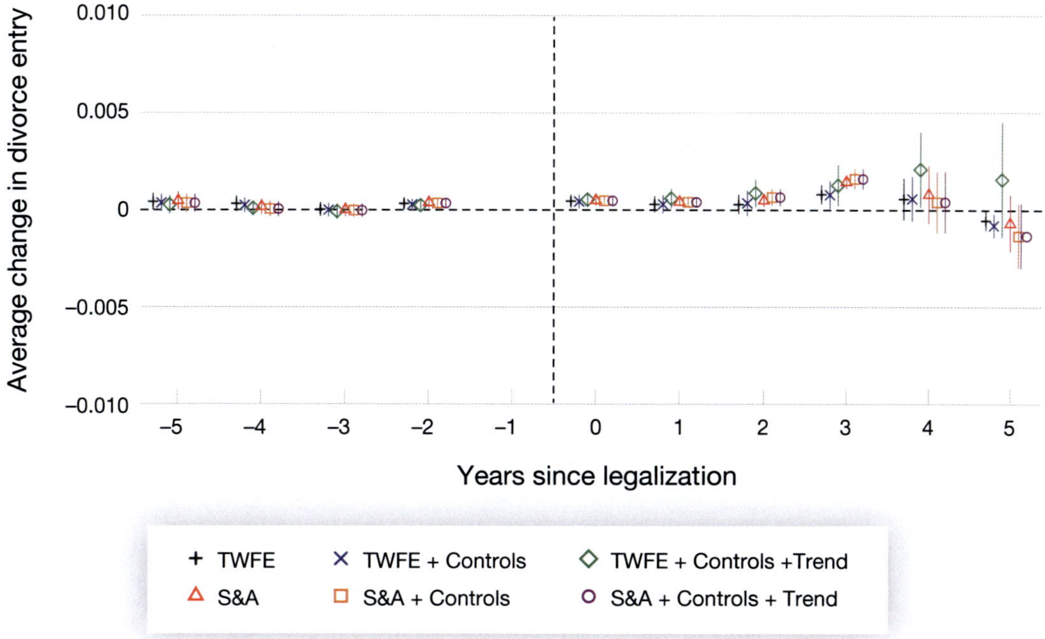

SOURCE: Data are from the ACS, 2000–2014 (Ruggles et al., 2023).

NOTE: The dependent variable is an indicator for being newly divorced (in the past year) in a state-year. Models are TWFE and Sun and Abraham's (2021) interaction-weighted estimator (S&A). The three specifications for each model are (1) no controls, (2) controlling for individual- and state-level market characteristics, and (3) controlling for individual- and state-level market characteristics and cohort-specific linear trends. Individual-level controls include education, race, labor force participation status, logged family income, and a quadratic in age. State-level controls include sex ratios; sex-specific shares of race and ethnicity groups, education groups, and age groups; female labor force participation rate; proportion of the population that is foreign-born; logged median earnings; the unemployment rate; and whether the state recognizes civil unions. Bars represent 95-percent confidence intervals. In 2000, 1 percent of respondents were newly divorced (in the past year). Joint significance tests of the pre-period coefficients in the TWFE models identified statistically significant pre-trend variation between treated and control states for all specifications ($p = 0.011$, $p = 0.010$, and $p = 0.005$ for specifications 1, 2, and 3, respectively). For more information on the models used, see Appendix C. The sample includes all respondents not cohabiting with or married to a same-sex partner.

FIGURE D.26

Event Study of New Divorces, American Community Survey, Individual, Conditional

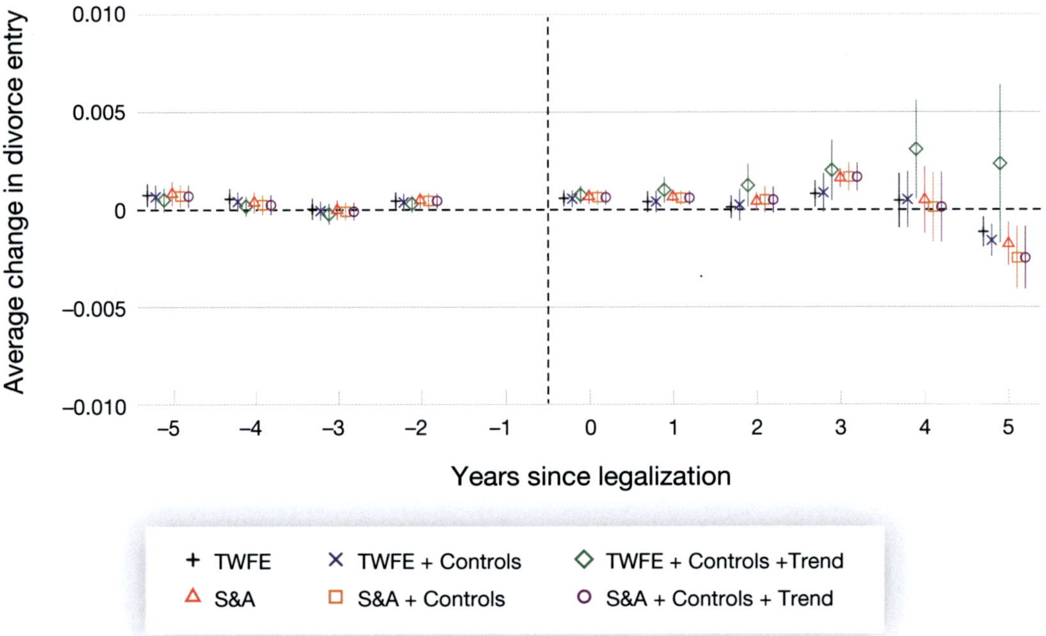

SOURCE: Data are from the ACS, 2000–2014 (Ruggles et al., 2023).

NOTE: The dependent variable is an indicator for being newly divorced (in the past year) in a state-year. The sample consists of married respondents not cohabiting with or married to a same-sex partner. Models are TWFE and Sun and Abraham's (2021) interaction-weighted estimator (S&A). The three specifications for each model are (1) no controls, (2) controlling for individual- and state-level market characteristics, and (3) controlling for individual- and state-level market characteristics and cohort-specific linear trends. Individual-level controls include education, race, labor force participation status, logged family income, and a quadratic in age. State-level controls include sex ratios; sex-specific shares of race and ethnicity groups, education groups, and age groups; female labor force participation rate; proportion of the population that is foreign-born; logged median earnings; the unemployment rate; and whether the state recognizes civil unions. Bars represent 95-percent confidence intervals. In 2000, 1 percent of married respondents were newly divorced (in the past year). Joint significance tests of the pre-period coefficients in the TWFE models identified statistically significant pre-trend variation between treated and control states for all specifications ($p < 0.001$ for all specifications). For more information on the models used, see Appendix C.

FIGURE D.27
Event Study of New Divorces, Panel Study of Income Dynamics, Individual, Unconditional

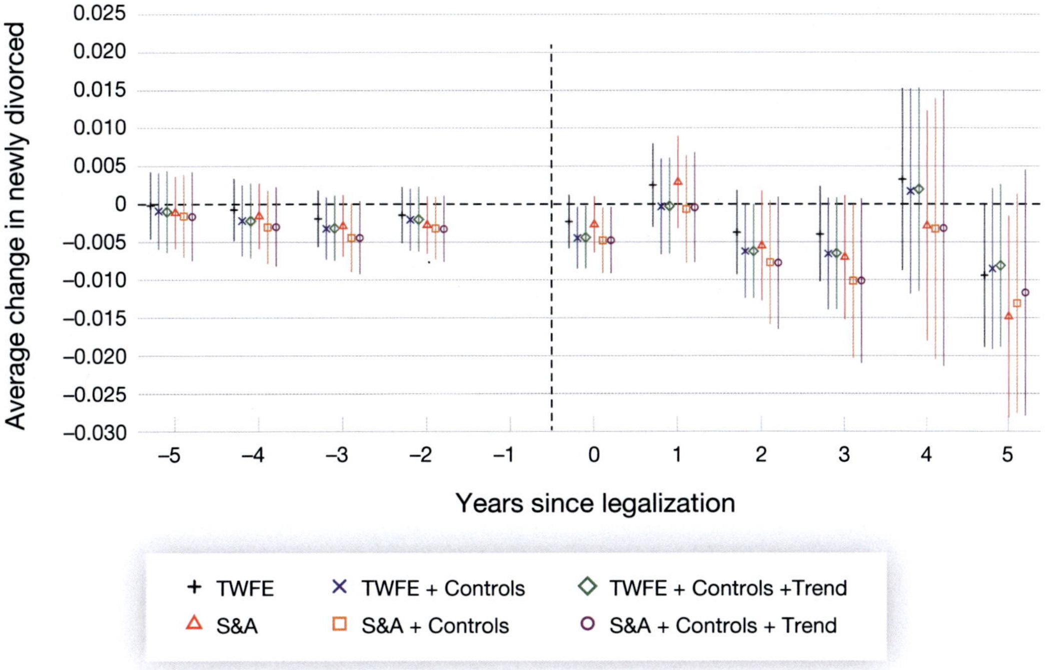

SOURCE: Data are from the PSID, 2000–2014 (Institute for Social Research, 2023).

NOTE: The dependent variable is an indicator for being newly divorced (in the past year) in a state-year, derived from the PSID Marriage History File. Models are TWFE and Sun and Abraham's (2021) interaction-weighted estimator (S&A). The three specifications for each model are (1) no controls, (2) controlling for individual- and state-level market characteristics, and (3) controlling for individual- and state-level market characteristics and cohort-specific linear trends. Individual-level controls include education, race, labor force participation status, logged family income, and a quadratic in age. State-level controls include sex ratios; sex-specific shares of race and ethnicity groups, education groups, and age groups; female labor force participation rate; proportion of the population that is foreign-born; logged median earnings; the unemployment rate; and whether the state recognizes civil unions. Bars represent 95-percent confidence intervals. In 2000, 1 percent of respondents were newly divorced (in the past year). Joint significance tests of the pre-period coefficients in the TWFE models found no statistically significant pre-trend variation between treated and control states ($p = 0.841$, $p = 0.607$, and $p = 0.660$ for specifications 1, 2, and 3, respectively). For more information on the models used, see Appendix C. The sample may include same-sex couples.

Marriage Attitudes

FIGURE D.28

Event Study of Marriage Attitudes, Fuller Lives with Marriage, Monitoring the Future Main Study, Individual

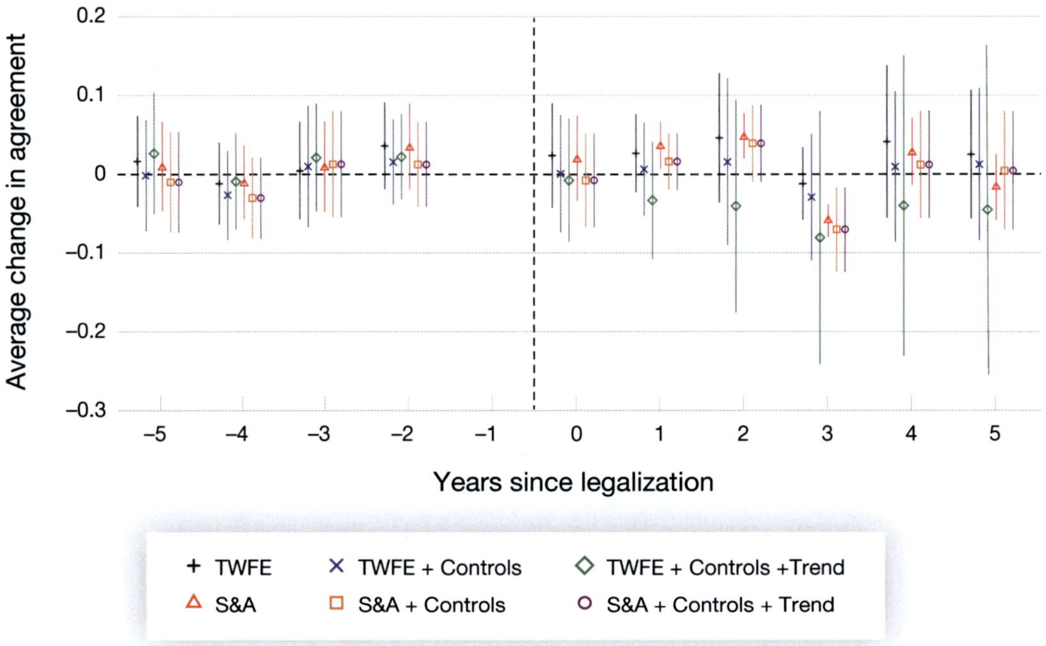

SOURCE: Data are from the MTF study (Schulenberg et al., 2023).

NOTE: The dependent variable is an indicator for agreeing or mostly agreeing with the statement: "Most people will have fuller and happier lives if they choose legal marriage rather than staying single, or just living with someone." Models are TWFE and Sun and Abraham's (2021) interaction-weighted estimator (S&A). The three specifications for each model are (1) no controls, (2) controlling for individual- and state-level market characteristics, and (3) controlling for individual- and state-level market characteristics and cohort-specific linear trends. Individual-level controls include race and sex. State-level controls include sex ratios; sex-specific shares of race and ethnicity groups, education groups, and age groups; female labor force participation rate; proportion of the population that is foreign-born; logged median earnings; the unemployment rate; and whether the state recognizes civil unions. Bars represent 95-percent confidence intervals. In 2000, 33 percent of respondents agreed or mostly agreed with the statement: "Most people will have fuller and happier lives if they choose legal marriage rather than staying single, or just living with someone." Joint significance tests of the pre-period coefficients in the TWFE models found no statistically significant pre-trend variation between treated and control states (p = 0.421, p = 0.347, and p = 0.426 for specifications 1, 2, and 3, respectively). For more information on the models used, see Appendix C. The sample consists of U.S. high school seniors, excluding those who attend school in Hawai'i, Alaska, California, and U.S. territories. The sample may include individuals who identify as LGBTQ.

FIGURE D.29

Event Study of Marriage Attitudes, Importance of Marriage and Family Life, Monitoring the Future Main Study, Individual

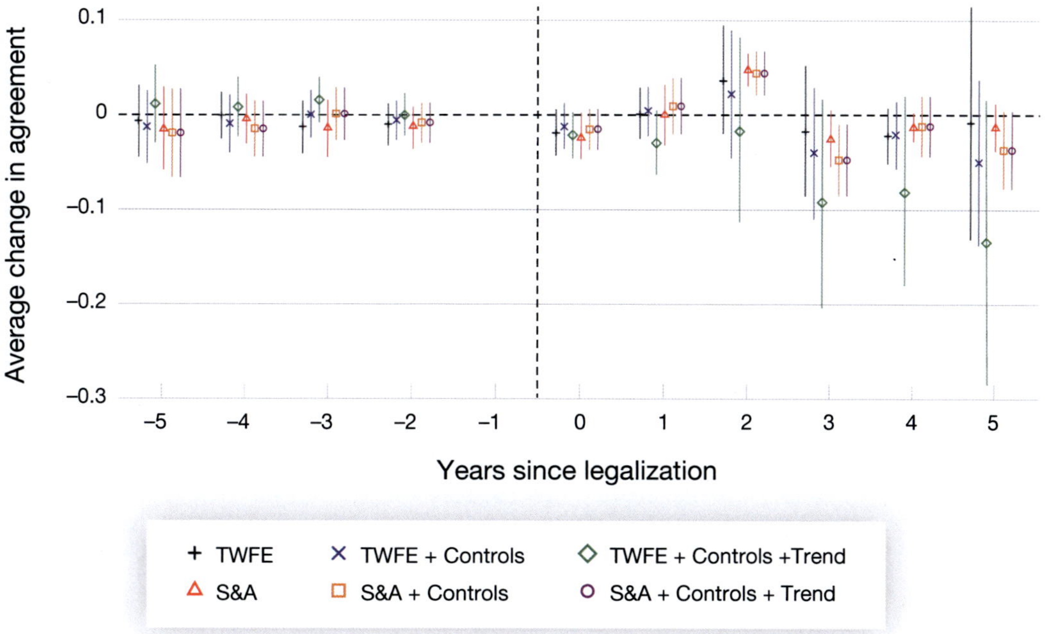

SOURCE: Data are from the MTF study (Schulenberg et al., 2023).

NOTE: The dependent variable is an indicator for identifying "Having a good marriage and family life" as quite important or extremely important. Models are TWFE and Sun and Abraham's (2021) interaction-weighted estimator (S&A). The three specifications for each model are (1) no controls, (2) controlling for individual- and state-level market characteristics, and (3) controlling for individual- and state-level market characteristics and cohort-specific linear trends. Individual-level controls include race and sex. State-level controls include sex ratios; sex-specific shares of race and ethnicity groups, education groups, and age groups; female labor force participation rate; proportion of the population that is foreign-born; logged median earnings; the unemployment rate; and whether the state recognizes civil unions. Bars represent 95-percent confidence intervals. In 2000, 90 percent of respondents identified "Having a good marriage and family life" as quite important or extremely important. Joint significance tests of the pre-period coefficients in the TWFE models found no statistically significant pre-trend variation between treated and control states (p = 0.727, p = 0.777, and p = 0.640 for specifications 1, 2, and 3, respectively). For more information on the models used, see Appendix C. The sample consists of U.S. high school seniors, excluding those who attend school in Hawai'i, Alaska, and U.S. territories. The sample may include individuals who identify as LGBTQ.

FIGURE D.30

Event Study of Marriage Attitudes, Disagree with Questioning Marriage as a Way of Life, Monitoring the Future Main Study, Individual

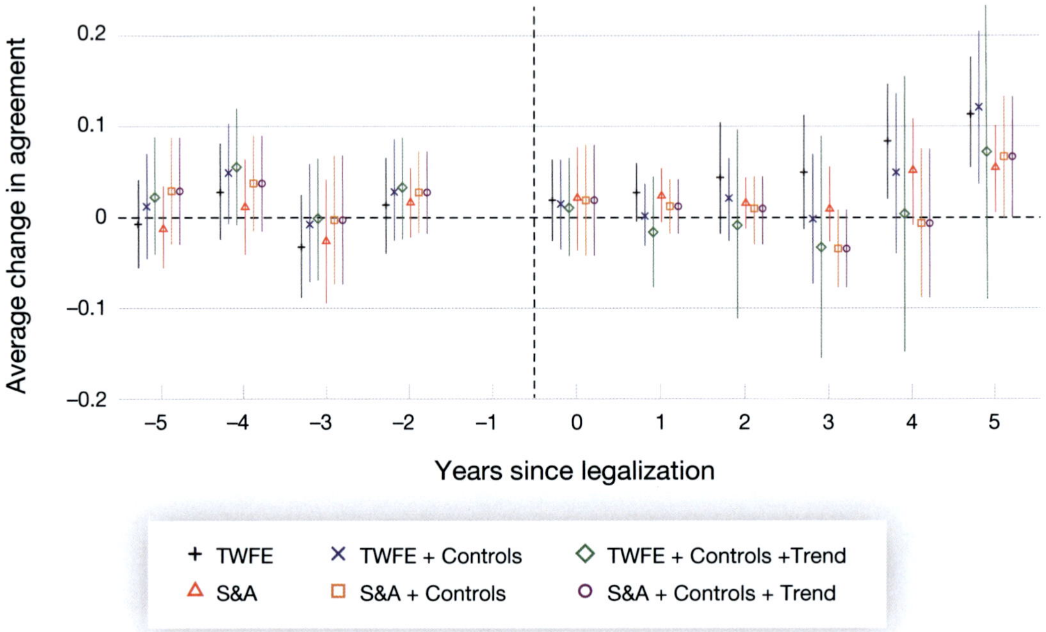

SOURCE: Data are from the MTF study (Schulenberg et al., 2023).

NOTE: The dependent variable is an indicator for disagreeing or mostly disagreeing with the statement: "One sees so few good or happy marriages that one questions it as a way of life." Models are TWFE and Sun and Abraham's (2021) interaction-weighted estimator (S&A). The three specifications for each model are (1) no controls, (2) controlling for individual- and state-level market characteristics, and (3) controlling for individual- and state-level market characteristics and cohort-specific linear trends. Individual-level controls include race and sex. State-level controls include sex ratios; sex-specific shares of race and ethnicity groups, education groups, and age groups; female labor force participation rate; proportion of the population that is foreign-born; logged median earnings; the unemployment rate; and whether the state recognizes civil unions. Bars represent 95-percent confidence intervals. In 2000, 47 percent of respondents disagreed or mostly disagreed with the statement: "One sees so few good or happy marriages that one questions it as a way of life." Joint significance tests of the pre-period coefficients in the TWFE models found no statistically significant pre-trend variation between treated and control states ($p = 0.167$, $p = 0.210$, and $p = 0.219$ for specifications 1, 2, and 3, respectively). For more information on the models used, see Appendix C. Sample consists of U.S. high school seniors, excluding those who attend school in Hawai'i, Alaska, California, and U.S. territories. The sample may include individuals who identify as LGBTQ.

FIGURE D.31

Event Study of Marriage Attitudes, Disagree That It Is a Good Idea to Live Together Before Marriage, Monitoring the Future Main Study, Individual

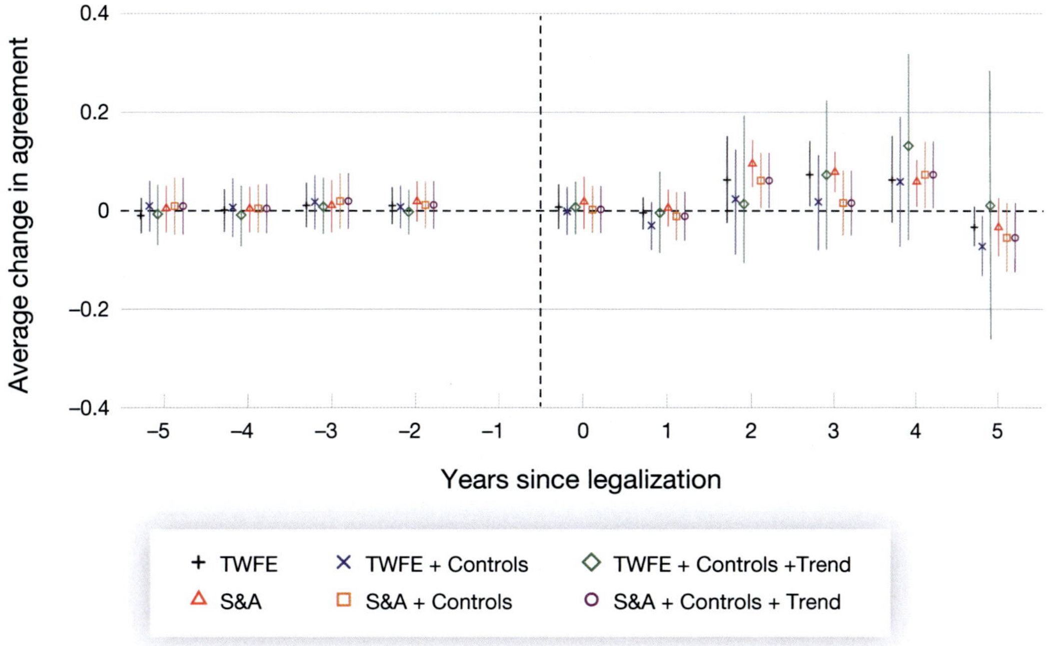

SOURCE: Data are from the MTF study (Schulenberg et al., 2023).

NOTE: The dependent variable is an indicator for disagreeing or mostly disagreeing with the statement: "It is usually a good idea for a couple to live together before getting married in order to find out whether they really get along." Models are TWFE and Sun and Abraham's (2021) interaction-weighted estimator (S&A). The three specifications for each model are (1) no controls, (2) controlling for individual- and state-level market characteristics, and (3) controlling for individual- and state-level market characteristics and cohort-specific linear trends. Individual-level controls include race and a quadratic in age. State-level controls include sex ratios; sex-specific shares of race and ethnicity groups, education groups, and age groups; female labor force participation rate; proportion of the population that is foreign-born; logged median earnings; the unemployment rate; and whether the state recognizes civil unions. Bars represent 95-percent confidence intervals. In 2000, 27 percent of respondents disagreed or mostly disagreed with the statement: "It is usually a good idea for a couple to live together before getting married in order to find out whether they really get along." Joint significance tests of the pre-period coefficients in the TWFE models found no statistically significant pre-trend variation between treated and control states ($p = 0.849$, $p = 0.973$, and $p = 0.950$ for specifications 1, 2, and 3, respectively). For more information on the models used, see Appendix C. The sample consists of U.S. high school seniors, excluding those who attend school in Hawai'i, Alaska, California, and U.S. territories. The sample may include individuals who identify as LGBTQ.

Additional Analyses

In this section, we provide additional robustness checks using the state-level currently married analysis in the ACS as an exemplar. We have run these checks on all outcome-analysis level combinations but provide only the one outcome in the interest of brevity.

Fully Balanced Panel

In a staggered difference-in-differences model, states might be included for different numbers of post-treatment years. In particular, later-adopting states will contribute to only the first few event study coefficients. This means that (1) earlier years' coefficients tend to be estimated with more precision and (2) separating out duration effects from cohort effects (i.e., timing of policy change) can be challenging. In Figure D.32, we use a consistent sample

FIGURE D.32

Event Study of Currently Married, American Community Survey, State: Fully Balanced Panel

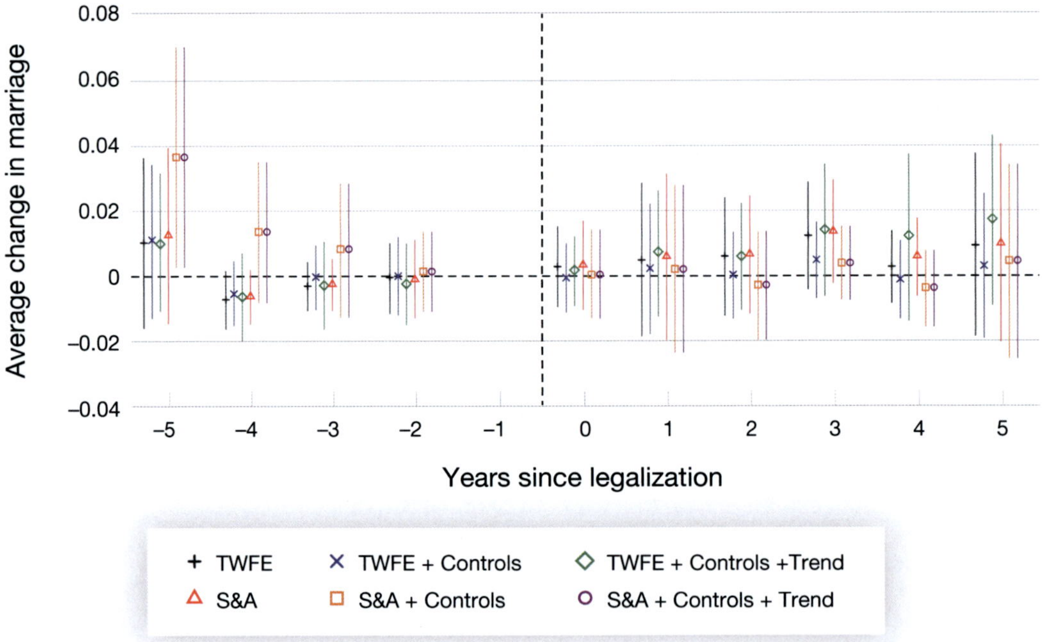

SOURCE: Data are from ACS, 2000–2014 (Ruggles et al., 2023).

NOTE: The dependent variable is the natural log of the percentage of respondents currently married in a state-year. Models are TWFE and Sun and Abraham's (2021) interaction-weighted estimator (S&A). The three specifications for each model are (1) no controls, (2) controlling for state-level market characteristics, and (3) controlling for state-level market characteristics and cohort-specific linear trends. State-level controls include sex ratios; sex-specific shares of race and ethnicity groups, education groups, and age groups; female labor force participation rate; proportion of the population that is foreign-born; logged median earnings; the unemployment rate; and whether the state recognizes civil unions. Bars represent 95-percent confidence intervals. The average percentage of respondents currently married in a state was 60 percent in 2000. For more information on the models used, see Appendix C. Individuals who are separated but not divorced are considered currently married.

of states to explore duration apart from cohort effects. In comparison with the estimates in Figure D.1, the Figure D.32 coefficient estimates from TWFE grow over time and have a larger magnitude. However, the conclusions are qualitatively the same: In the ACS, no statistically significant effects on marriage stock are detectable in a state-level analysis.

Early Versus Late Adopters

One potential concern with staggered difference-in-differences is the potential for early adopters to dominate the overall treatment effect. In our case, the latest adopters (2014, just before the *Obergefell* decision) have a truncated treatment window: We can look at only same-year effects. However, comparing these estimates in Figure D.33 is nonetheless instructive. Early adopters have same-year effects that center precisely on 0 with no statistical significance. Later adopters have same-year effects centered slightly above 0, with similar statistical imprecision.

California

As shown in Table C.1 in Appendix C, California briefly issued marriage licenses to same-sex couples in 2008. A state constitutional amendment halted the practice until 2013. In our main analyses, we use 2013 as the definition of treatment for California. In the plots in Figure D.34, we show that our results from the analysis in Figure D.1 are not sensitive to changing this timing (treating California in 2008) or excluding California from our analysis altogether.

FIGURE D.33

Event Study of Currently Married, American Community Survey, State: Timing of Policy Adoption

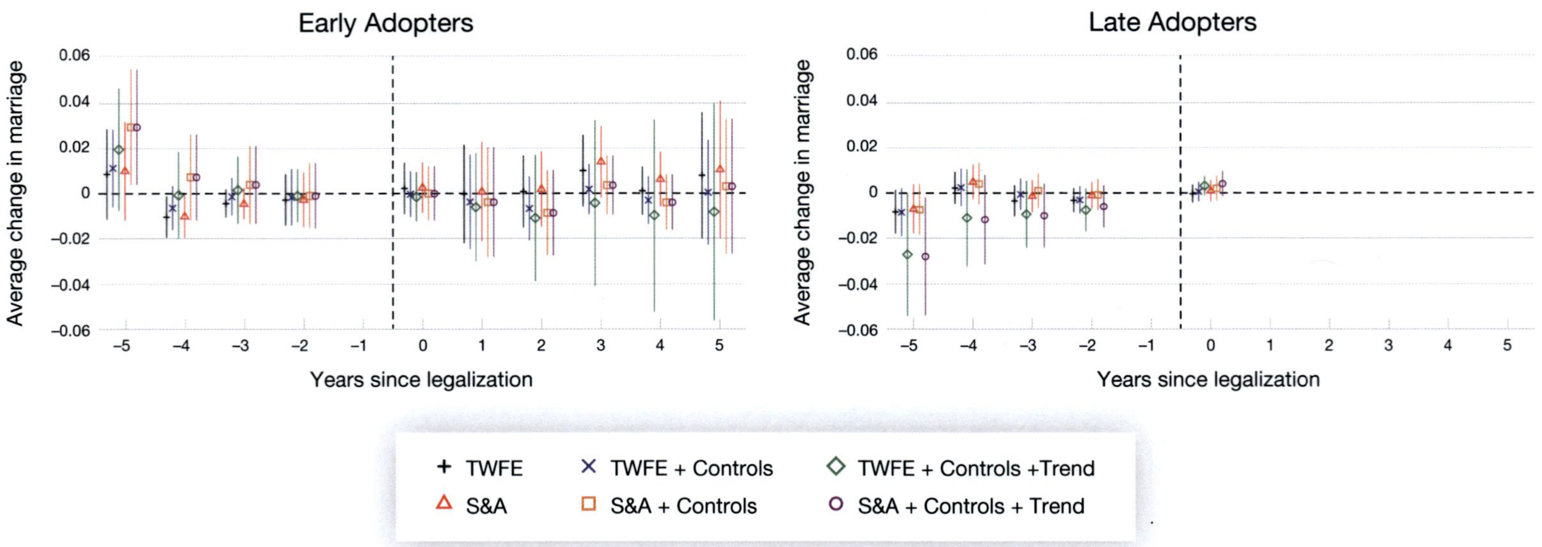

SOURCE: Data are from ACS, 2000–2014 (Ruggles et al., 2023).

NOTE: The dependent variable is the natural log of the percentage of respondents currently married in a state-year. Early adopters are states that legalized in 2012 or earlier, and late adopters are states that legalized in 2013 or 2014. Models are TWFE and Sun and Abraham's (2021) interaction-weighted estimator (S&A). The three specifications for each model are (1) no controls, (2) controlling for state-level market characteristics, and (3) controlling for state-level market characteristics and cohort-specific linear trends. State-level controls include sex ratios; sex-specific shares of race and ethnicity groups, education groups, and age groups; female labor force participation rate; proportion of the population that is foreign-born; logged median earnings; the unemployment rate; and whether the state recognizes civil unions. Bars represent 95-percent confidence intervals. The average percentage of respondents currently married in a state was 60 percent in 2000. For more information on the models used, see Appendix C. Individuals who are separated but not divorced are considered currently married.

FIGURE D.34

Event Study of Currently Married, American Community Survey, State: Sensitivity to California Policy Timing

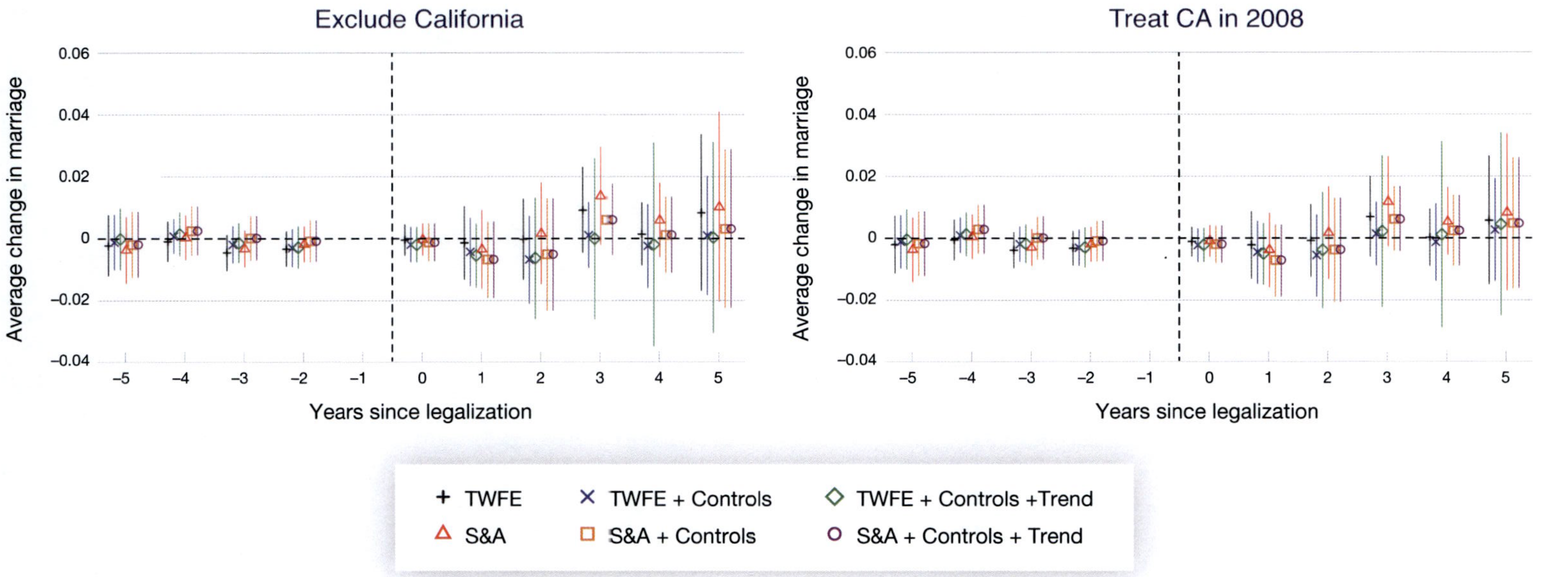

SOURCE: Data are from ACS, 2000–2014 (Ruggles et al., 2023).

NOTE: The dependent variable is the natural log of the percentage of respondents currently married in a state-year. *Exclude California* drops California from the analysis, and *Treat CA in 2008* codes California as part of the 2008 treatment cohort, with treatment never turning back off. Models are TWFE and Sun and Abraham's (2021) interaction-weighted estimator (S&A). The three specifications for each model are (1) no controls, (2) controlling for state-level market characteristics, and (3) controlling for state-level market characteristics and cohort-specific linear trends. State-level controls include sex ratios; sex-specific shares of race and ethnicity groups, education groups, and age groups; female labor force participation rate; proportion of the population that is foreign-born; logged median earnings; the unemployment rate; and whether the state recognizes civil unions. Bars represent 95-percent confidence intervals. The average percentage of respondents currently married in a state was 60 percent in 2000. For more information on the models used, see Appendix C. Individuals who are separated but not divorced are considered currently married.

Abbreviations

ACS	American Community Survey
CDC	Centers for Disease Control and Prevention
CPS	Current Population Survey
LGBT	lesbian, gay, bisexual, and transgender
LGBTQ	lesbian, gay, bisexual, transgender, and queer or questioning
MTF	Monitoring the Future
NHIS	National Health Interview Survey
PRISMA	Preferred Reporting Items for Systematic Reviews and Meta-Analyses
PSID	Panel Study of Income Dynamics
S&A	interaction-weighted estimator
STI	sexually transmitted infection
SUTVA	stable unit treatment values assumption
TWFE	two-way fixed effects

References

57 D.C. Reg. 27, Religious Freedom and Civil Marriage Equality Amendment Act of 2009, 2010.

57 Opinions of the Attorney General 71, Maryland, 1972.

70 Delaware Laws Ch. 375, 1996.

79 Delaware Laws Ch. 19, 2013.

Adams-Cohen, Nicholas Joseph, "Policy Change and Public Opinion: Measuring Shifting Political Sentiment with Social Media Data," *American Politics Research*, Vol. 48, No. 5, September 2020.

Aftab, Ammar, and Sara Imanpour, "Quasi Experimental Study of Same-Sex Marriage Laws & Sexually Transmitted Infections," *Public Health in Practice*, Vol. 4, December 2022.

Aizer, Ayal A., Ming-Hui Chen, Ellen P. McCarthy, Mallika L. Mendu, Sophia Koo, Tyler J. Wilhite, Powell L. Graham, Toni K. Choueiri, Karen E. Hoffman, Neil E. Martin, Jim C. Hu, and Paul L. Nguyen, "Marital Status and Survival in Patients with Cancer," *Journal of Clinical Oncology*, Vol. 31, No. 31, November 1, 2013.

Aksoy, Cevat G., Christopher S. Carpenter, Ralph De Haas, and Kevin D. Tran, "Do Laws Shape Attitudes? Evidence from Same-Sex Relationship Recognition Policies in Europe," *European Economic Review*, Vol. 124, May 2020.

Alabama Constitution Art. I, § 36.03, 2006.

Alabama Laws 98-500, Alabama Marriage Protection Act, 1998.

Alaska Constitution Art. I, § 25, 1998.

Alaska Laws Ch. 21, An Act Clarifying a Statute Relating to Persons Who May Legally Marry, Relating to Same-Sex Marriage, and Providing for an Effective Date, 1996.

Allen, Doug, "More Heat Than Light: A Critical Assessment of the Same-Sex Parenting Literature, 1995–2013," *Marriage & Family Review*, Vol. 51, No. 2, 2015.

Allen, Douglas W., and Joseph Price, "Same-Sex Marriage and Negative Externalities: A Critique, Replication, and Correction of Langbein and Yost," *Economic Journal Watch*, Vol. 12, No. 2, May 2015.

Alliance Defending Freedom, "Marriage Is the Future," webpage, undated. As of March 11, 2024:
https://adflegal.org/issues/marriage

Alm, James, M. V. Lee Badgett, and Leslie A. Whittington, "Wedding Bell Blues: The Income Tax Consequences of Legalizing Same-Sex Marriage," *National Tax Journal*, Vol. 53, No. 2, June 2000.

Alm, James, J. Sebastian Leguizamon, and Susane Leguizamon, "Revisiting the Income Tax Effects of Legalizing Same-Sex Marriages," *Journal of Policy Analysis and Management*, Vol. 33, No. 2, Spring 2014.

Alonso-Villar, Olga, and Coral del Río, "Poverty Among Same-Sex Couple Families in the United States: Is There a Premium for Married Couples?" *Journal of Economic Inequality*, August 18, 2023.

American Psychological Association, *Lesbian & Gay Parenting*, 2005.

Anderson, D. Mark, Kyutaro Matsuzawa, and Joseph J. Sabia, "Marriage Equality Laws and Youth Mental Health," *Journal of Law & Economics*, Vol. 64, No. 1, February 2021.

Aneshensel, Carol S., Carolyn M. Rutter, and Peter A. Lachenbruch, "Social Structure, Stress, and Mental Health: Competing Conceptual and Analytic Models," *American Sociological Review*, Vol. 56, No. 2, April 1991.

Arizona Constitution Art. XXX, § 1, 2008.

Arizona Legis. Serv. Ch. 348, 1996.

Arkansas Constitutional Amendment 83, 2004.

Arkansas Laws Act 144, 1997.

Aron, A., E. N. Aron, M. Tudor, and G. Nelson, "Close Relationships as Including Other in the Self," *Journal of Personality and Social Psychology*, Vol. 60, No. 2, 1991.

Avery, Alison, Justin Chase, Linda Johansson, Samantha Litvak, Darrel Montero, and Michael Wydra, "America's Changing Attitudes Toward Homosexuality, Civil Unions, and Same-Gender Marriage: 1977–2004," *Social Work*, Vol. 52, No. 1, January 2007.

Bachman, Jerald G., Katherine N. Wadsworth, Patrick M. O'Malley, John Schulenberg, and Lloyd D. Johnston, "Marriage, Divorce, and Parenthood During the Transition to Young Adulthood: Impacts on Drug Use and Abuse," in J. Schulenberg, J. L. Maggs, and K. Hurrelmann, eds., *Health Risks and Developmental Transitions During Adolescence*, Cambridge University Press, 1997.

Badgett, M. V. Lee, "The Wage Effects of Sexual Orientation Discrimination," *Industrial and Labor Relations Review*, Vol. 48, No. 4, July 1995.

Badgett, M. V. Lee, "Left Out? Lesbian, Gay, and Bisexual Poverty in the U.S.," *Population Research and Policy Review*, Vol. 37, No. 5, October 2018.

Baehr v. Miike, 910 P.2d 112, Hawai'i, 1996.

Baker, Andrew C., David F. Larcker, and Charles C. Y. Wang, "How Much Should We Trust Staggered Difference-in-Differences Estimates?" *Journal of Financial Economics*, Vol. 144, No. 2, May 2022.

Baker v. Nelson, 191 N.W.2d 185, 1971, appeal dismissed, 409 U.S. 810, 1972.

Baker v. State, 744 A.2d 864, Vermont, 1999.

Balsam, Kimberly F., Theodore P. Beauchaine, Esther D. Rothblum, and Sondra E. Solomon, "Three-Year Follow-Up of Same-Sex Couples Who Had Civil Unions in Vermont, Same-Sex Couples Not in Civil Unions, and Heterosexual Married Couples," *Developmental Psychology*, Vol. 44, No. 1, January 2008.

Baskin v. Bogan, 766 F.3d 648, 7th Cir., 2014.

Bauermeister, José A., "How Statewide LGB Policies Go from "Under Our Skin" to "Into Our Hearts": Fatherhood Aspirations and Psychological Well-Being Among Emerging Adult Sexual Minority Men," *Journal of Youth and Adolescence*, Vol. 43, No. 8, August 2014.

Baunach, Dawn Michelle, "Decomposing Trends in Attitudes Toward Gay Marriage, 1988–2006," *Social Science Quarterly*, Vol. 92, No. 2, June 2011.

Beaudin, Laura, "Marriage Equality and Interstate Migration," *Applied Economics*, Vol. 49, No. 30, 2017.

Becker, Gary S., *A Treatise on the Family*, Harvard University Press, 2009.

Belluck, Pam, "Massachusetts Arrives at Moment for Same-Sex Marriage," *New York Times*, May 17, 2004.

Ben-Ari, Adital, "The Discovery That an Offspring Is Gay: Parents', Gay Men's, and Lesbians' Perspectives," *Journal of Homosexuality*, Vol. 30, No. 1, 1995.

Bennett, Neil G., David E. Bloom, and Patricia H. Craig, "The Divergence of Black and White Marriage Patterns," *American Journal of Sociology*, Vol. 95, No. 3, November 1989.

Bernstein, Mary, Nancy A. Naples, and Brenna Harvey, "The Meaning of Marriage to Same-Sex Families: Formal Partnership, Parenthood, Gender, and the Welfare State in International Perspective," *Social Politics: International Studies in Gender, State & Society*, Vol. 23, No. 1, Spring 2016.

Bertrand, Marianne, Esther Duflo, and Sendhil Mullainathan, "How Much Should We Trust Differences-in-Differences Estimates?" *Quarterly Journal of Economics*, Vol. 119, No. 1, February 2004.

Biblarz, Timothy J., and Evren Savci, "Lesbian, Gay, Bisexual, and Transgender Families," *Journal of Marriage and Family*, Vol. 72, No. 3, June 2010.

Biden, Joseph, "Advancing Equality for Lesbian, Gay, Bisexual, Transgender, Queer, and Intersex Individuals," Executive Order 14075, Executive Office of the President, June 15, 2022.

Bishin, Benjamin G., Thomas J. Hayes, Matthew B. Incantalupo, and Charles Anthony Smith, "Opinion Backlash and Public Attitudes: Are Political Advances in Gay Rights Counterproductive?" *American Journal of Political Science*, Vol. 60, No. 3, July 2016.

Bishop v. United States, 962 F. Supp. 2d 1252, N.D. Okla., 2014.

Bitler, Marianne, Jonah B. Gelbach, Hilary W. Hoynes, and Madeline Zavodny, "The Impact of Welfare Reform on Marriage and Divorce," *Demography*, Vol. 41, No. 2, May 1, 2004.

Black, Dan, Gary Gates, Seth Sanders, and Lowell Taylor, *The Measurement of Same-Sex Unmarried Partner Couples in the 2000 U.S. Census*, California Center for Population Research, University of California–Los Angeles, CCPR-023-07, September 2007.

Black, Dan A., Seth G. Sanders, and Lowell J. Taylor, "The Economics of Lesbian and Gay Families," *Journal of Economic Perspectives*, Vol. 21, No. 2, Spring 2007.

Blanchflower, David G., and Andrew J. Oswald, "Well-Being over Time in Britain and the USA," *Journal of Public Economics*, Vol. 88, No. 7–8, July 2004.

Blau, Francine D., Lawrence M. Kahn, and Jane Waldfogel, "Understanding Young Women's Marriage Decisions: The Role of Labor and Marriage Market Conditions," *Industrial and Labor Relations Review*, Vol. 53, No. 4, July 2000.

Boertien, Diederik, and Fabrizio Bernardi, "Same-Sex Parents and Children's School Progress: An Association That Disappeared over Time," *Demography*, Vol. 56, No. 2, April 2019.

Boertien, Diederik, and Juho Härkönen, "Why Does Women's Education Stabilize Marriages? The Role of Marital Attraction and Barriers to Divorce," *Demographic Research*, Vol. 38, 2018.

Bos, Henny M. W., Justin R. Knox, Loes van Rijn-van Gelderen, and Nanette K. Gartrell, "Same-Sex and Different-Sex Parent Households and Child Health Outcomes: Findings from the National Survey of Children's Health," *Journal of Developmental & Behavioral Pediatrics*, Vol. 37, No. 3, April 2016.

Bostic v. Schaefer, 760 F.3d 352, 4th Cir., 2014.

Bowen, Deirdre M., "All That Heaven Will Allow: A Statistical Analysis of the Coexistence of Same-Sex Marriage and Gay Matrimonial Bans," *Denver Law Review*, Vol. 91, No. 2, 2014.

Brenner v. Scott, 999 F. Supp. 2d 1278, N.D. Fla., 2014.

Brief Amicus Curiae of United States Conference of Catholic Bishops in Support of Respondents and Supporting Affirmance, *Obergefell v. Hodges*, 576 U.S. 644, 2015, Nos. 14-556, 14-562, 14-571, & 14-574.

Brodoff, Lisa, Bridget Hiedemann, and Yuqing Xue, "Marriage Equality and Activity Limitations Among Older Adults in Same-Sex Relationships," *Sexuality Research and Social Policy*, January 26, 2024.

Brown, Susan L., "Marriage and Child Well-Being: Research and Policy Perspectives," *Journal of Marriage and Family*, Vol. 72, No. 5, October 2010.

Brown, Susan L., and Alan Booth, "Cohabitation Versus Marriage: A Comparison of Relationship Quality," *Journal of Marriage and Family*, Vol. 58, No. 3, August 1996.

Buchmueller, Thomas, and Christopher S. Carpenter, "Disparities in Health Insurance Coverage, Access, and Outcomes for Individuals in Same-Sex Versus Different-Sex Relationships, 2000-2007," *American Journal of Public Health*, Vol. 100, No. 3, March 2010.

Burns v. Hickenlooper, Civil Action No. 14-cv-01817-RM-KLM, 2014 WL 3634834, 2014 U.S. Dist. LEXIS 100894, D. Colo., 2014.

Bursch, John J., Transcript of Question 1 Oral Argument at 64, *Obergefell v. Hodges*, 576 U.S. 644 (2015) (Nos. 14-556, 14-562, 14-571, and 14-574).

California Assembly Bill 205, The California Domestic Partner Rights and Responsibilities Act, Cal. Leg., 2003-04, Regular Session, enacted, 2003.

California Assembly Bill 607, Leg., 1977-78 Sess., 1997.

California Constitution Art. 1, § 7.5, 2008.

California Family Code §§ 297–299.6, 1999.

California Senate Bill 75, Domestic Partnership Act, Cal. Leg., 1999-00 Reg. Sess., enacted, 1999.

Callaway, Brantly, and Pedro H. C. Sant'Anna, "Difference-in-Differences with Multiple Time Periods," *Journal of Econometrics*, Vol. 225, No. 2, December 2021.

Capaldi, Deborah M., Hyoun K. Kim, and Lee D. Owen, "Romantic Partners' Influence on Men's Likelihood of Arrest in Early Adulthood," *Criminology*, Vol. 46, No. 2, May 2008.

Carpenter, Christopher S., "The Direct Effects of Legal Same-Sex Marriage in the United States: Evidence from Massachusetts," *Demography*, Vol. 57, No. 5, October 2020.

Carpenter, Christopher S., Samuel T. Eppink, Gilbert Gonzales, and Tara McKay, "Effects of Access to Legal Same-Sex Marriage on Marriage and Health," *Journal of Policy Analysis and Management*, Vol. 40, No. 2, March 2021.

CDC—*See* Centers for Disease Control and Prevention.

Centers for Disease Control and Prevention, National Vital Statistics System, "Marriage Rates by State: 1990, 1995, and 1999-2021," table of data, undated.

Chang, Cindy J., John K. Kellerman, Kara Binder Fehling, Brian A. Feinstein, and Edward A. Selby, "The Roles of Discrimination and Social Support in the Associations Between Outness and Mental Health Outcomes Among Sexual Minorities," *American Journal of Orthopsychiatry*, Vol. 91, No. 5, June 2021.

Charlton, Brittany M., Heather L. Corliss, Donna Spiegelman, Kerry Williams, and S. Bryn Austin, "Changes in Reported Sexual Orientation Following US States Recognition of Same-Sex Couples," *American Journal of Public Health*, Vol. 106, No. 12, December 2016.

Chen, Shuai, and Jan C. van Ours, "Subjective Well-Being and Partnership Dynamics: Are Same-Sex Relationships Different?" *Demography*, Vol. 55, No. 6, December 2018.

Cheng, Simon, and Brian Powell, "Measurement, Methods, and Divergent Patterns: Reassessing the Effects of Same-Sex Parents," *Social Science Research*, Vol. 52, July 2015.

Cherlin, Andrew J., "The Deinstitutionalization of American Marriage," *Journal of Marriage and Family*, Vol. 66, No. 4, November 2004.

Cherlin, Andrew J., "Degrees of Change: An Assessment of the Deinstitutionalization of Marriage Thesis," *Journal of Marriage and Family*, Vol. 82, No. 1, February 2020.

Cleves, Rachel Hope, "'What, Another Female Husband?': The Prehistory of Same-Sex Marriage in America," *Journal of American History*, Vol. 101, No. 4, March 2015.

Coley, Jonathan S., "Have Christian Colleges and Universities Become More Inclusive of LGBTQ Students Since *Obergefell v. Hodges*?" *Religions*, Vol. 11, No. 9, September 2020.

Colistra, Rita, and Chelsea Betts Johnson, "Framing the Legalization of Marriage for Same-Sex Couples: An Examination of News Coverage Surrounding the U.S. Supreme Court's Landmark Decision," *Journal of Homosexuality*, Vol. 68, No. 1, 2021.

Colorado Constitution Art. II, § 31, 2006.

Colorado Legis. Serv. Ch. 233, An Act Concerning Strengthening of the Marriage Relationship, 2000.

Condon v. Haley, 21 F. Supp. 3d 572, D. S.C., 2014.

Connecticut Senate Bill 899, An Act Implementing the Guarantee of Equal Protection Under the Constitution of the State for Same-Sex Couples, Legis. Serv. P.A. 09-13 (2009).

Connecticut Senate Bill 963, An Act Concerning Civil Unions, Legis. Serv. P.A. 05-10, 2005.

Connolly v. Jeanes, 73 F. Supp. 3d 1094, D. Ariz., 2014.

Coontz, Stephanie, *Marriage, a History: From Obedience to Intimacy or How Love Conquered Marriage*, Viking, 2005.

Correia, Sergio, "REGHDFE: Stata Module to Perform Linear or Instrumental-Variable Regression Absorbing Any Number of High-Dimensional Fixed Effects," Statistical Software Components S457874, Boston College Department of Economics, revised August 21, 2023.

Crowl, Alicia, Soyeon Ahn, and Jean Baker, "A Meta-Analysis of Developmental Outcomes for Children of Same-Sex and Heterosexual Parents," *Journal of GLBT Family Studies*, Vol. 4, No. 3, 2008.

Cushing-Daniels, Brendan, and Tsz-Ying Yeung, "Wage Penalties and Sexual Orientation: An Update Using the General Social Survey," *Contemporary Economic Policy*, Vol. 27, No. 2, April 2009.

de Vries, Brian, Anne M. Mason, Jean Quam, and Kimberly Acquaviva, "State Recognition of Same-Sex Relationships and Preparations for End of Life Among Lesbian and Gay Boomers," *Sexuality Research and Social Policy*, Vol. 6, No. 1, March 2009.

DeBoer v. Snyder, 973 F. Supp. 2d 757, E.D. Mich., 2014.

Delhommer, Scott M., and Daniel S. Hamermesh, "Same-Sex Couples and the Gains to Marriage: The Importance of the Legal Environment," *Journal of Policy Analysis and Management*, Vol. 40, No. 4, September 2021.

Denniston, Lyle, "Opinion Analysis: Marriage Now Open to Same-Sex Couples," *SCOTUSblog*, June 26, 2015.

Dillender, Marcus, "The Death of Marriage? The Effects of New Forms of Legal Recognition on Marriage Rates in the United States," *Demography*, Vol. 51, No. 2, April 1, 2014.

Dillender, Marcus, "Health Insurance and Labor Force Participation: What Legal Recognition Does for Same-Sex Couples," *Contemporary Economic Policy*, Vol. 33, No. 2, April 2015.

Dinno, Alexis, and Chelsea Whitney, "Same Sex Marriage and the Perceived Assault on Opposite Sex Marriage," *PLoS One*, Vol. 8, No. 6, June 2013.

Dodge, Brian, Debby Herbenick, Tsung-Chieh Fu, Vanessa Schick, Michael Reece, Stephanie Sanders, and J. Dennis Fortenberry, "Sexual Behaviors of U.S. Men by Self-Identified Sexual Orientation: Results from the 2012 National Survey of Sexual Health and Behavior," *Journal of Sexual Medicine*, Vol. 13, No. 4, April 2016.

Donovan, Todd, and Caroline Tolbert, "Do Popular Votes on Rights Create Animosity Toward Minorities?" *Political Research Quarterly*, Vol. 66, No. 4, December 2013.

Downing, Janelle, and Paulette Cha, "Same-Sex Marriage and Gains in Employer-Sponsored Insurance for US Adults, 2008–2017," *American Journal of Public Health*, Vol. 110, No. 4, April 2020.

Drabble, Laurie A., Amy A. Mericle, Cat Munroe, Angie R. Wootton, Karen F. Trocki, and Tonda L. Hughes, "Examining Perceived Effects of Same-Sex Marriage Legalization Among Sexual Minority Women: Identifying Demographic Differences and Factors Related to Alcohol Use Disorder, Depression, and Self-Perceived Health," *Sexuality Research and Social Policy*, Vol. 19, No. 3, September 2022.

Drydakis, Nick, "Sexual Orientation and Labor Market Outcomes," IZA World of Labor, July 2019.

Duncan, Greg J., Bessie Wilkerson, and Paula England, "Cleaning Up Their Act: The Effects of Marriage and Cohabitation on Licit and Illicit Drug Use," *Demography*, Vol. 43, No. 4, November 2006.

Dynes, Wayne R., and Stephen Donaldson, eds., *Homosexuality in the Ancient World*, Garland Publishing, Inc., 1992.

Ellis, Renee, Matthew Virgile, Jessica L. Holzberg, Dawn V. Nelson, Jennifer Edgar, Polly Phipps, and Robin Kaplan, *Assessing the Feasibility of Asking About Sexual Orientation and Gender Identity in the Current Population Survey: Results from Cognitive Interviews*, Center for Survey Measurement, Research and Methodology Directorate, U.S. Census Bureau, April 2, 2018.

Elwood, William N., Veronica L. Irvin, Qiankun Sun, and Nancy Breen, "Measuring the Influence of Legally Recognized Partnerships on the Health and Well-Being of Same-Sex Couples: Utility of the California Health Interview Survey," *LGBT Health*, Vol. 4, No. 2, 2017.

Eskridge, William N., Jr., "A History of Same-Sex Marriage," *Virginia Law Review*, Vol. 79, No. 7, October 1993.

Eskridge, William N., Jr., and Christopher R. Riano, *Marriage Equality: From Outlaws to In-Laws*, Yale University Press, 2020.

Everett, Bethany G., Mark L. Hatzenbuehler, and Tonda L. Hughes, "The Impact of Civil Union Legislation on Minority Stress, Depression, and Hazardous Drinking in a Diverse Sample of Sexual-Minority Women: A Quasi-Natural Experiment," *Social Science & Medicine*, Vol. 169, November 2016.

Family Research Council, "Ten Arguments from Social Science Against Same-Sex Marriage," webpage, undated. As of December 21, 2023:
https://www.frc.org/issuebrief/ten-arguments-from-social-science-against-same-sex-marriage

Fingerhut, Adam W., and Natalya C. Maisel, "Relationship Formalization and Individual and Relationship Well-Being Among Same-Sex Couples," *Journal of Social and Personal Relationships*, Vol. 27, No. 7, November 2010.

Fisher, Hayley, "The Effect of Marriage Tax Penalties and Subsidies on Marital Status," *Fiscal Studies*, Vol. 34, No. 4, December 2013.

Flood, Sarah, Miriam King, Renae Rodgers, Steven Ruggles, J. Robert Warren, Daniel Backman, Annie Chen, Grace Cooper, Stephanie Richards, Megan Schouweiler, and Michael Westberry, IPUMS Current Population Survey, dataset, version 11.0, Integrated Public Use Microdata Series, 2023.

Flores, Andrew R., and Scott Barclay, "Backlash, Consensus, Legitimacy, or Polarization: The Effect of Same-Sex Marriage Policy on Mass Attitudes," *Political Research Quarterly*, Vol. 69, No. 1, March 2016.

Flores, Andrew R., Christy Mallory, and Kerith J. Conron, *The Impact of* Obergefell v. Hodges *on the Well-Being of LGBT Adults*, Williams Institute, UCLA, June 2020.

Florida Constitution Art. I, § 2, 2008.

Florida Sess. Law Serv. Ch. 77-139, 1977.

Francis, Andrew M., and Hugo M. Mialon, "Tolerance and HIV," *Journal of Health Economics*, Vol. 29, No. 2, March 2010.

Francis, Andrew M., Hugo M. Mialon, and Handie Peng, "In Sickness and in Health: Same-Sex Marriage Laws and Sexually Transmitted Infections," *Social Science & Medicine*, Vol. 75, No. 8, October 2012.

Friedberg, Leora, and Elliott Isaac, "Same-Sex Marriage Recognition and Taxes: New Evidence About the Impact of Household Taxation," *Review of Economics and Statistics*, Vol. 106, No. 1, January 2024.

Frost, David M., Adam W. Fingerhut, and Ilan H. Meyer, "Social Change and Relationship Quality Among Sexual Minority Individuals: Does Minority Stress Still Matter?" *Journal of Marriage and Family*, Vol. 84, No. 3, June 2022.

Frost, David M., Keren Lehavot, and Ilan H. Meyer, "Minority Stress and Physical Health Among Sexual Minority Individuals," *Journal of Behavioral Medicine*, Vol. 38, No. 1, February 2015.

Frost, David M., and Ilan H. Meyer, "Minority Stress Theory: Application, Critique, and Continued Relevance," *Current Opinion in Psychology*, Vol. 51, June 2023.

Fry, Richard, and Kim Parker, *Rising Share of U.S. Adults Are Living Without a Spouse or Partner*, Pew Research Center, October 5, 2021.

Garden State Equality v. Dow, 82 A. 3d 336, N.J. Super. Ct. Law Div., 2013.

Geiger v. Kitzhaber, 994 F. Supp. 2d 1128, D. Or., 2014.

General Synod of the United Church of Christ v. Resinger, 12 F. Supp. 3d 790, W.D. N.C., 2014.

Georgia Constitution Art. 1, § IV, 2004.

Georgia Laws § 1, enacted, 1996.

Goldberg, Shoshana K., and Kerith J. Conron, "How Many Same-Sex Couples in the US Are Raising Children?" Williams Institute, UCLA, July 2018.

Goldsen, Jayn, Amanda E. B. Bryan, Hyun Jun Kim, Anna Muraco, Sarah Jen, and Karen I. Fredriksen-Goldsen, "Who Says I Do: The Changing Context of Marriage and Health and Quality of Life for LGBT Older Adults," *Gerontologist*, Vol. 57, No. S1, February 2017.

Gonzales, Gilbert, "Association of the New York State Marriage Equality Act with Changes in Health Insurance Coverage," *JAMA*, Vol. 314, No. 7, August 18, 2015.

Gonzales, Gilbert, and Lynn A. Blewett, "Disparities in Health Insurance Among Children with Same-Sex Parents," *Pediatrics*, Vol. 132, No. 4, October 2013.

Gonzales, Gilbert, and Lynn A. Blewett, "National and State-Specific Health Insurance Disparities for Adults in Same-Sex Relationships," *American Journal of Public Health*, Vol. 104, No. 2, February 2014.

Gonzales, Gilbert, and Jesse M. Ehrenfeld, "The Association Between State Policy Environments and Self-Rated Health Disparities for Sexual Minorities in the United States," *International Journal of Environmental Research and Public Health*, Vol. 15, No. 6, June 2018.

Goodridge v. Department of Public Health, 440 Mass. 309, 2003.

Goodwin, Paula Y., William D. Mosher, and Anjani Chandra, "Marriage and Cohabitation in the United States: A Statistical Portrait Based on Cycle 6 (2002) of the National Survey of Family Growth," *Vital and Health Statistics*, Series 23, No. 28, February 2010.

Griego v. Oliver, 316 P. 3d 865, N.M., 2013.

Gusmano, Michael K., Mark Schlesinger, and Tracey Thomas, "Policy Feedback and Public Opinion: The Role of Employer Responsibility in Social Policy," *Journal of Health Politics, Policy and Law*, Vol. 27, No. 5, October 2002.

Guzzo, Karen Benjamin, "How Do Marriage Market Conditions Affect Entrance into Cohabitation vs. Marriage?" *Social Science Research*, Vol. 35, No. 2, June 2006.

Guzzo v. Mead, No. 14-CV-200-SWS, WL 5317797, D. Wyo. 2014.

Haas, Stephen M., and Pamela J. Lannutti, "The Influence of Marriage and (Non)Monogamy Agreements on Relationship Quality in LGBT Relationships," in Aaron Hoy, ed., *The Social Science of Same-Sex Marriage: LGBT People and Their Relationships in the Era of Marriage Equality*, Routledge, 2022a.

Haas, Stephen M., and Pamela J. Lannutti, "Relationship Maintenance Behaviors, Resilience, and Relational Quality in Romantic Relationships of LGBTQ+ People," *Couple and Family Psychology: Research and Practice*, Vol. 11, No. 2, 2022b.

Hagendorff, Jens, Duc Duy Nguyen, and Vathunyoo Sila, "Does Marriage Equality Promote Credit Access? Evidence from Same-Sex Marriage Laws," *Journal of Corporate Finance*, Vol. 77, December 2022.

Haggerty, Benjamin B., Thomas N. Bradbury, and Benjamin R. Karney, "The Disconnected Couple: Intimate Relationships in the Context of Social Isolation," *Current Opinion in Psychology*, Vol. 43, February 2022.

Haggerty, Benjamin B., Han Du, David P. Kennedy, Thomas N. Bradbury, and Benjamin R. Karney, "Stability and Change in Newlyweds' Social Networks over the First Years of Marriage," *Journal of Family Psychology*, Vol. 37, No. 1, February 2023.

Hamby v. Parnell, 56 F. Supp 3d 1056, D. Alaska, 2014.

Hampton, Matt, and Otto Lenhart, "The Effect of the Affordable Care Act Medicaid Expansion on Marriage," *Economic Inquiry*, Vol. 60, No. 2, April 2022.

Hansen, Mary Eschelbach, Michael E. Martell, and Leanne Roncolato, "A Labor of Love: The Impact of Same-Sex Marriage on Labor Supply," *Review of Economics of the Household*, Vol. 18, No. 2, June 2020.

Hatzenbuehler, Mark L., Katie A. McLaughlin, Katherine M. Keyes, and Deborah S. Hasin, "The Impact of Institutional Discrimination on Psychiatric Disorders in Lesbian, Gay, and Bisexual Populations: A Prospective Study," *American Journal of Public Health*, Vol. 100, No. 3, March 2010.

Hatzenbuehler, Mark L., Conall O'Cleirigh, Chris Grasso, Kenneth Mayer, Steven Safren, and Judith Bradford, "Effect of Same-Sex Marriage Laws on Health Care Use and Expenditures in Sexual Minority Men: A Quasi-Natural Experiment," *American Journal of Public Health*, Vol. 102, No. 2, February 2012.

Hawai'i Act 1, 2013.

Hawai'i Constitution Art. 1, § 23, 1998.

Hawai'i House Bill 118, 19th State Leg., 1997.

Hawai'i Sess. Laws Ch. 217, 1994.

Hawai'i Sess. Laws, Hawaii Marriage Equality Act of 2013, 2014.

Herek, G. M., "Legal Recognition of Same-Sex Relationships in the United States: A Social Science Perspective," *American Psychologist*, Vol. 61, No. 6, 2006.

Hernandez v. Robles, 855 N.E.2d 1, 6, New York, 2006.

Herrando, Carolina, and Efthymios Constantinides, "Emotional Contagion: A Brief Overview and Future Directions," *Frontiers in Psychology*, Vol. 12, July 2021.

Hersch, Joni, and Leslie S. Stratton, "Household Specialization and the Male Marriage Wage Premium," *Industrial and Labor Relations Review*, Vol. 54, No. 1, October 2000.

Hetling, Andrea, Monika L. McDermott, and Mingus Mapps, "Symbolism Versus Policy Learning: Public Opinion of the 1996 U.S. Welfare Reforms," *American Politics Research*, Vol. 36, No. 3, May 2008.

Horne, Sharon G., Sharon Scales Rostosky, and Ellen D. B. Riggle, "Impact of Marriage Restriction Amendments on Family Members of Lesbian, Gay, and Bisexual Individuals: A Mixed-Method Approach," *Journal of Social Issues*, Vol. 67, No. 2, June 2011.

Hsieh, Ning, "Mental Health Disparities by Sexual Orientation in the U.S.: Current Patterns and Recent Trends," *EurAmerica*, Vol. 49, No. 2, June 2019.

Idaho Constitution Art. III, § 28, 2006.

Idaho Laws Ch. 104, 1995.

Illinois Law 504, Public Act 89–459, 1996.

Illinois Senate Bill 10, 98th Gen. Assem., 2013-15 Reg. Sess., 2013.

In re Marriage Cases, 183 P.3d 384, California, 2008.

Indiana Public Law 1-1997, § 3, 1997.

Institute for Social Research, "Panel Study of Income Dynamics," public use dataset, University of Michigan, 2023.

Iowa Ch. 1099, An Act Relating to Certain Relationships Including Certain Marriages, § 1, 1998.

Isaac, Elliott, "Suddenly Married: Joint Taxation and the Labor Supply of Same-Sex Married Couples After *U.S. v. Windsor*," *Journal of Human Resources*, Vol. 59, No. 2, March 1, 2024.

Jernigan v. Crane, 64 F. Supp 3d 1260, E.D. Ark., 2014.

Johnson, Norman J., Eric Backlund, Paul D. Sorlie, and Catherine A. Loveless, "Marital Status and Mortality: The National Longitudinal Mortality Study," *Annals of Epidemiology*, Vol. 10, No. 4, May 2000.

Jones, Jeffrey M., "LGBT Identification in U.S. Ticks Up to 7.1%," Gallup, February 17, 2022.

Joyner, Kara, Wendy Manning, and Barbara Prince, "The Qualities of Same-Sex and Different-Sex Couples in Young Adulthood," *Journal of Marriage and Family*, Vol. 81, No. 2, April 2019.

Kail, Ben Lennox, Katie L. Acosta, and Eric R. Wright, "State-Level Marriage Equality and the Health of Same-Sex Couples," *American Journal of Public Health*, Vol. 105, No. 6, June 2015.

Kansas Constitution Art. 15, § 16, 2005.

Karney, Benjamin R., Jeffrey B. Wenger, Melanie A. Zaber, and Thomas N. Bradbury, "State Minimum Wage Increases Delay Marriage and Reduce Divorce Among Low-Wage Households," *Journal of Marriage and Family*, Vol. 84, No. 4, August 2022.

Kazyak, Emily, and Mathew Stange, "Backlash or a Positive Response? Public Opinion of LGB Issues After *Obergefell v. Hodges*," *Journal of Homosexuality*, Vol. 65, No. 14, 2018.

Kearney, Melissa S., and Riley Wilson, "Male Earnings, Marriageable Men, and Nonmarital Fertility: Evidence from the Fracking Boom," *Review of Economics and Statistics*, Vol. 100, No. 4, October 2018.

Kearns, Jill N., and Kenneth E. Leonard, "Social Networks, Structural Interdependence, and Marital Quality over the Transition to Marriage: A Prospective Analysis," *Journal of Family Psychology*, Vol. 18, No. 2, 2004.

Kennedy, Heather R., and Rochelle L. Dalla, "'It May Be Legal, but It Is Not Treated Equally': Marriage Equality and Well-Being Implications for Same-Sex Couples," *Journal of Gay & Lesbian Social Services*, Vol. 32, No. 1, 2020.

Kentucky Constitution § 233A, 2004.

Kentucky Laws Ch. 258, 1998.

Kerrigan v. Commissioner of Pub. Health, 957 A.2d 407 (Conn. 2008).

Kern, Holger Lutz, "The Political Consequences of Transitions Out of Marriage in Great Britain," *Electoral Studies*, Vol. 29, No. 2, 2010.

Ketcham, Eric, and Neil G. Bennett, "Comparative Couple Stability: Same-Sex and Male-Female Unions in the United States," *Socius*, Vol. 5, 2019.

Kiecolt-Glaser, J. K., and T. L. Newton, "Marriage and Health: His and Hers," *Psychological Bulletin*, Vol. 127, No. 4, 2001.

Kimberly, Claire, and Alexa Moore, "Attitudes to Practice: National Survey of Adoption Obstacles Faced by Gay and Lesbian Prospective Parents," *Journal of Gay & Lesbian Social Services*, Vol. 27, No. 4, 2015.

Kitchen v. Herbert, 755 F.3d 1193, 10th Cir., 2014.

Klawitter, Marieka, "Meta-Analysis of the Effects of Sexual Orientation on Earnings," *Industrial Relations: A Journal of Economy and Society*, Vol. 54, No. 1, January 2015.

Knight, Ken W., Sarah E. M. Stephenson, Sue West, Martin B. Delatycki, Cheryl A. Jones, Melissa H. Little, George C. Patton, Susan M. Sawyer, S. Rachel Skinner, Michelle M. Telfer, et al., "The Kids Are OK: It Is Discrimination, Not Same-Sex Parents, That Harms Children," *Medical Journal of Australia*, Vol. 207, No. 9, November 2017.

Kowal, John F., "The Improbable Victory of Marriage Equality," Brennan Center for Justice, September 29, 2015.

Kreis, Anthony Michael, "Stages of Constitutional Grief: Democratic Constitutionalism and the Marriage Revolution," *University of Pennsylvania Journal of Constitutional Law*, Vol. 20, No. 4, 2018.

Kreitzer, Rebecca J., Allison J. Hamilton, and Caroline J. Tolbert, "Does Policy Adoption Change Opinions on Minority Rights? The Effects of Legalizing Same-Sex Marriage," *Political Research Quarterly*, Vol. 67, No. 4, December 2014.

Kurdek, Lawrence A., "What Do We Know About Gay and Lesbian Couples?" *Current Directions in Psychological Science*, Vol. 14, No. 5, October 2005.

Langbein, Laura, Brandon Ranallo-Benavidez, and Jane E. Palmer, "The Anti-Social Effects of Legalizing Same-Sex Marriage: Fact or Fiction?" *Sexuality Research and Social Policy*, Vol. 18, No. 4, December 2021.

Langbein, Laura, and Mark A. Yost, Jr., "Same-Sex Marriage and Negative Externalities," *Social Science Quarterly*, Vol. 90, No. 2, June 2009.

Langbein, Laura, and Mark A. Yost, Jr., "Still No Evidence of Negative Outcomes from Same-Sex Marriage," *Econ Journal Watch*, Vol. 12, No. 2, May 2015.

Latta v. Otter, 771 F.3d 456, 9th Cir., 2014.

LeBlanc, Allen J., David M. Frost, and Kayla Bowen, "Legal Marriage, Unequal Recognition, and Mental Health Among Same-Sex Couples," *Journal of Marriage and Family*, Vol. 80, No. 2, April 2018.

Lechner, Michael, "The Estimation of Causal Effects by Difference-in-Difference Methods," *Foundations and Trends in Econometrics*, Vol. 4, No. 3, 2011.

Levy, Brian L., and Denise L. Levy, "When Love Meets Hate: The Relationship Between State Policies on Gay and Lesbian Rights and Hate Crime Incidence," *Social Science Research*, Vol. 61, January 2017.

Lewis v. Harris, 908 A.2d 196, 208, New Jersey, 2006.

Li, Feng, and Venky Nagar, "Diversity and Performance," *Management Science*, Vol. 59, No. 3, March 2013.

Lick, David J., Laura E. Durso, and Kerri L. Johnson, "Minority Stress and Physical Health Among Sexual Minorities," *Perspectives on Psychological Science*, Vol. 8, No. 5, September 2013.

Liu, Hui, Ning Hsieh, Zhenmei Zhang, Yan Zhang, and Kenneth M. Langa, "Same-Sex Couples and Cognitive Impairment: Evidence from the Health and Retirement Study," *Journals of Gerontology Series B: Psychological Sciences and Social Sciences*, Vol. 76, No. 7, September 2021.

Logie, Carmen, "The Case for the World Health Organization's Commission on the Social Determinants of Health to Address Sexual Orientation," *American Journal of Public Health*, Vol. 102, No. 7, July 2012.

Louisiana Constitution Art. XII, § 15, 2004.

Louisiana Laws Act No. 890, 1999.

Maine H.P. 1152, An Act to Promote the Financial Security of Maine's Families and Children, 121st Leg, 2nd Reg. Sess., 2004.

Maine Laws, An Act to Allow Marriage Licenses for Same-Sex Couples and Protect Religious Freedom, 2013.

Maine Laws Ch. 65, An Act to Protect Traditional Marriage and Prohibit Same-Sex Marriage, 1997.

Maine Question 1, Citizen Initiative Same-Sex Marriage, 2012.

Manning, Wendy D., Susan L. Brown, and J. Bart Stykes, "Same-Sex and Different-Sex Cohabiting Couple Relationship Stability," *Demography*, Vol. 53, No. 4, August 2016.

Manning, Wendy D., and Lisa Carlson, "Trends in Cohabitation Prior to Marriage," *Family Profiles*, FP-21-04, National Center for Family & Marriage Research, 2021.

Manning, Wendy D., Marshal Neal Fettro, and Esther Lamidi, "Child Well-Being in Same-Sex Parent Families: Review of Research Prepared for American Sociological Association Amicus Brief," *Population Research and Policy Review*, Vol. 33, No. 4, August 2014.

Manning, Wendy D., Pamela J. Smock, and Marshal Neal Fettro, "Cohabitation and Marital Expectations Among Single Millennials in the U.S.," *Population Research and Policy Review*, Vol. 38, No. 3, June 2019.

Marcén, Miriam, and Marina Morales, "The Effect of Same-Sex Marriage Legalization on Interstate Migration in the USA," *Journal of Population Economics*, Vol. 35, No. 2, April 2022.

Marie v. Moser, 65 F. Supp. 3d 1175, D. Kan., 2014.

Marks, Loren, "Same-Sex Parenting and Children's Outcomes: A Closer Examination of the American Psychological Association's Brief on Lesbian and Gay Parenting," *Social Science Research*, Vol. 41, No. 4, July 2012.

Martell, Michael E., and Peyton Nash, "For Love and Money? Earnings and Marriage Among Same-Sex Couples," *Journal of Labor Research*, Vol. 41, No. 3, September 2020.

Martin, Joshua, and Zachary Rodriguez, "The Effect of Same-Sex Marriage Legalization on Adoptions and Family Formation in the U.S.," SSRN, December 19, 2022.

Maryland Laws, Civil Marriage Protection Act, 2012.

Maryland Laws Ch. 213, 1973.

Maryland Question 6, 2012.

Massachusetts Gen. Laws Ch. 207 § 1 & 2, 2023.

Mastekaasa, Arne, "Marriage and Psychological Well-Being: Some Evidence on Selection into Marriage," *Journal of Marriage and Family*, Vol. 54, No. 4, November 1992.

Mazrekaj, Deni, Mirjam M. Fischer, and Henny M. W. Bos, "Behavioral Outcomes of Children with Same-Sex Parents in the Netherlands," *International Journal of Environmental Research and Public Health*, Vol. 19, No. 10, May 2022.

McCabe, Sean Esteban, Tonda L. Hughes, Wendy B. Bostwick, Brady T. West, and Carol J. Boyd, "Sexual Orientation, Substance Use Behaviors and Substance Dependence in the United States," *Addiction*, Vol. 104, No. 8, August 2009.

McCarthy, Justin, "U.S. Same-Sex Marriage Support Holds at 71% High," Gallup, June 5, 2023.

McDonald, Patrick, "The Male Marriage Premium: Selection, Productivity, or Employer Preferences?" *Journal of Marriage and Family*, Vol. 82, No. 5, October 2020.

McGee v. Cole, 66 F. Supp. 3d 747 (S.D.W.V. 2014).

Metheny, Nicholas, and Rob Stephenson, "Political Environment and Perceptions of Social Inclusion After Nationwide Marriage Equality Among Partnered Men Who Have Sex with Men in the USA," *Sexuality Research and Social Policy*, Vol. 16, No. 4, December 2019.

Meyer, Ilan H., "Prejudice, Social Stress, and Mental Health in Lesbian, Gay, and Bisexual Populations: Conceptual Issues and Research Evidence," *Psychological Bulletin*, Vol. 129, No. 5, September 2003.

Michigan Comp. Laws § 551.1, Public Act 1996 No. 324, § 1, 1996.

Michigan Constitution Art. 1, § 25, 2004.

Miller, Joshua J., and Kevin A. Park, "Same-Sex Marriage Laws and Demand for Mortgage Credit," *Review of Economics of the Household*, Vol. 16, No. 2, June 2018.

Minnesota Amendment 1, Minnesota Marriage Amendment, 2012.

Minnesota House Bill 1054, 88th Reg. Sess., 2013.

Minnesota Laws Ch. 441, sec. 1, 1977.

Mississippi Constitution Art. 14, § 263A, 2004.

Mississippi Laws Ch. 301, sec. 2, 1997.

Missouri Constitution Art. 1, § 33, 2004.

Missouri Legis. Serv. Senate Bill 768, 1996.

Montana Constitution Art. XIII, § 7, 2004.

Montana Laws Ch. 424, 1997.

Mora, Ricardo, and Iliana Reggio, "Alternative Diff-in-Diffs Estimators with Several Pretreatment Periods," *Econometric Reviews*, Vol. 38, No. 5, 2019.

Movement Advancement Project, *Underneath Obergefell: A National Patchwork of Marriage Laws*, March 2022.

Nebraska Constitution Art. I, § 29, 2000.

Neuberg, Steven L., Dylan M. Smith, Jonna C. Hoffman, and Frank J. Russell, "When We Observe Stigmatized and 'Normal' Individuals Interacting: Stigma by Association," *Personality and Social Psychology Bulletin*, Vol. 20, No. 2, April 1994.

Nevada Constitution Art. I, § 21, 2000.

Nevada Question 2, 2022.

New Hampshire House Bill 436, An Act Relative to Civil Marriage and Civil Unions, 161st Leg., Gen. Ct., 2009.

New Hampshire Laws Ch. 218, sec. 1, 1987.

New Mexico Stat. § 40-1-1, 2003.

Newport, Frank, "Some Change over Time in American Attitudes Towards Homosexuality, but Negativity Remains," Gallup, March 1, 1999.

Newport, Frank, and Joy Wilke, "Most in U.S. Want Marriage, but Its Importance Has Dropped," Gallup, August 2, 2013.

New York Assembly Bill 8354, Marriage Equality Act, 234th Leg., Ann. Sess., 2011.

Nikolaou, Dimitrios, "Same-Sex Marriage Laws, LGBT Hate Crimes, and Employment Discrimination Charges," *Southern Economic Journal*, Vol. 88, No. 3, January 2022.

Nikolaou, Dimitrios, "Effects of Marriage Equality Legislation on Sexual Health of the US Population," *Health Economics*, Vol. 32, No. 1, January 2023.

North Dakota Constitution Art. XI, § 28, 2004.

North Dakota Laws Ch. 145, 1997.

Obergefell v. Hodges, Brief of 379 Employers and Organizations Representing Employers as Amici Curiae in Support of Petitioners, 2015.

Obergefell v. Hodges, Brief of Louisiana, et al. as Amici Curiae in Support of Respondents, 2015.

Obergefell v. Hodges, 576 U.S. 644, 2015.

Ofosu, Eugene K., Michelle K. Chambers, Jacqueline M. Chen, and Eric Hehman, "Same-Sex Marriage Legalization Associated with Reduced Implicit and Explicit Antigay Bias," *Proceedings of the National Academy of Sciences of the United States of America*, Vol. 116, No. 18, April 30, 2019.

Ogolsky, Brian G., J. Kale Monk, TeKisha M. Rice, and Ramona Faith Oswald, "Personal Well-Being Across the Transition to Marriage Equality: A Longitudinal Analysis," *Journal of Family Psychology*, Vol. 33, No. 4, June 2019a.

Ogolsky, Brian G., J. Kale Monk, TeKisha M. Rice, and Ramona Faith Oswald, "As the States Turned: Implications of the Changing Legal Context of Same-Sex Marriage on Well-Being," *Journal of Social and Personal Relationships*, Vol. 36, No. 10, October 2019b.

Ohio Constitution Art. XV, § 11, 2004.

Ohio House Bill 272, 125th Gen. Assem., Reg. Sess., 2004.

Oklahoma Constitution Art. 2, § 35, 2004.

Oklahoma Laws Ch. 39, 1975.

ONE Archives at the USC Libraries, "History," webpage, University of Southern California, undated. As of July 18, 2023:
https://one.usc.edu/about/history

Oregon Constitution Art. XV, § 5a, 2004.

Oregon Laws 629, 2015.

Page, Matthew J., Joanne E. McKenzie, Patrick M. Bossuyt, Isabelle Boutron, Tammy C. Hoffmann, Cynthia D. Mulrow, Larissa Shamseer, Jennifer M. Tetzlaff, Elie A. Akl, Sue E. Brennan, et al., "The PRISMA 2020 Statement: An Updated Guideline for Reporting Systematic Reviews," *BMJ*, Vol. 372, No. 71, 2021.

Paintsil, Isaac K. O., "What Did *Obergefell* Change? Clearance of Intimate Partner Violence Before and After the Legalization of Same-Sex Marriage," *Journal of Interpersonal Violence*, January 9, 2024.

Parker, Christopher S., and Matt A. Barreto, *Change They* Can't *Believe In: The Tea Party and Reactionary Politics in America*, Princeton University Press, 2013.

Pathela, Preeti, Anjum Hajat, Julia Schillinger, Susan Blank, Randall Sell, and Farzad Mostashari, "Discordance Between Sexual Behavior and Self-Reported Sexual Identity: A Population-Based Survey of New York City Men," *Annals of Internal Medicine*, Vol. 145, No. 6, September 19, 2006.

Pawelski, James G., Ellen C. Perrin, Jane M. Foy, Carole E. Allen, James E. Crawford, Mark Del Monte, Miriam Kaufman, Jonathan D. Klein, Karen Smith, Sarah Springer, et al., "The Effects of Marriage, Civil Union, and Domestic Partnership Laws on the Health and Well-Being of Children," *Pediatrics*, Vol. 118, No. 1, July 2006.

Pennsylvania House Leg. Journal, 1996.

Peplau, Letitia Anne, and Adam W. Fingerhut, "The Close Relationships of Lesbians and Gay Men," *Annual Review of Psychology*, Vol. 58, 2007.

Perrin, Paul B., Erin R. Smith, Michael A. Trujillo, Annie Rabinovitch, and Anthony E. Coy, "Differential Effects of the US Supreme Court's Same-Sex Marriage Decision on National Support for Lesbian, Gay, and Bisexual Civil Rights and Sexual Prejudice," *Sexuality Research and Social Policy*, Vol. 15, No. 3, September 2018.

Pew Research Center, *Majority of Public Favors Same-Sex Marriage, but Divisions Persist*, May 14, 2019.

Pichler, Shaun, Janell L. Blazovich, Kirsten A. Cook, Janet M. Huston, and William R. Strawser, "Do LGBT-Supportive Corporate Policies Enhance Firm Performance?" *Human Resource Management*, Vol. 57, No. 1, January 2018.

Plöderl, Martin, and Pierre Tremblay, "Mental Health of Sexual Minorities. A Systematic Review," *International Review of Psychiatry*, Vol. 27, No. 5, 2015.

Pollard, Michael S., and Italo Lopez-Garcia, "Exploring the Social Security Benefit Implications of Same-Sex Marriage," in Aaron Hoy, ed., *The Social Science of Same-Sex Marriage: LGBT People and Their Relationships in the Era of Marriage Equality*, Routledge, 2022.

Psihountas, Debbie, Richard Dippel, and George Slusarz, "Federal Discrimination of Married Same-Sex Couples," *Journal of Accounting, Ethics & Public Policy*, Vol. 14, No. 2, 2013.

Public Law 104-193, Personal Responsibility and Work Opportunity Reconciliation Act of 1996, August 22, 1996.

Public Law 104-199, Defense of Marriage Act, September 21, 1996.

Public Law 117-228, Respect for Marriage Act, December 13, 2022.

Raifman, Julia, Ellen Moscoe, S. Bryn Austin, and Margaret McConnell, "Difference-in-Differences Analysis of the Association Between State Same-Sex Marriage Policies and Adolescent Suicide Attempts," *JAMA Pediatrics*, Vol. 171, No. 4, April 2017.

Reczek, Corinne, "Sexual- and Gender-Minority Families: A 2010 to 2020 Decade in Review," *Journal of Marriage and Family*, Vol. 82, No. 1, February 2020.

Reczek, Corinne, Hui Liu, and Russell Spiker, "A Population-Based Study of Alcohol Use in Same-Sex and Different-Sex Unions," *Journal of Marriage and Family*, Vol. 76, No. 3, June 2014.

Reczek, Corinne, Russell Spiker, Hui Liu, and Robert Crosnoe, "Family Structure and Child Health: Does the Sex Composition of Parents Matter?" *Demography*, Vol. 53, No. 5, October 2016.

Reczek, Corinne, Russell Spiker, Hui Liu, and Robert Crosnoe, "The Promise and Perils of Population Research on Same-Sex Families," *Demography*, Vol. 54, No. 6, December 2017.

Reed, W. Robert, and Kathleen Harford, "The Marriage Premium and Compensating Wage Differentials," *Journal of Population Economics*, Vol. 2, No. 4, December 1989.

Regnerus, Mark, "How Different Are the Adult Children of Parents Who Have Same-Sex Relationships? Findings from the New Family Structures Study," *Social Science Research*, Vol. 41, No. 4, July 2012.

Republican National Committee, *Republican Platform 2016*, 2020. As of December 22, 2023: https://prod-cdn-static.gop.com/docs/Resolution_Platform_2020.pdf

Rhode Island Gen. Laws §§ 5-1-1 to 5-2-11, 2003.

Rhode Island House Bill 5015, 2013-14 Leg. Sess., 2013.

Riggle, Ellen D. B., Sharon S. Rostosky, and Sharon G. Horne, "Marriage Amendments and Lesbian, Gay, and Bisexual Individuals in the 2006 Election," *Sexuality Research and Social Policy*, Vol. 6, No. 1, March 2009.

Riggle, Ellen D. B., Sharon S. Rostosky, and Sharon G. Horne, "Psychological Distress, Well-Being, and Legal Recognition in Same-Sex Couple Relationships," *Journal of Family Psychology*, Vol. 24, No. 1, 2010.

Riggle, Ellen D. B., Robert E. Wickham, Sharon S. Rostosky, Esther D. Rothblum, and Kimberly F. Balsam, "Impact of Civil Marriage Recognition for Long-Term Same-Sex Couples," *Sexuality Research and Social Policy*, Vol. 14, No. 2, June 2017.

Robles, T. F., R. B. Slatcher, J. M. Trombello, and M. M. McGinn, "Marital Quality and Health: A Meta-Analytic Review," *Psychological Bulletin*, Vol. 140, No. 1, 2014.

Rolando v. Fox, 23 F. Sup 3d 1227, D. Mont., 2014.

Rosenfeld, Michael J., "Couple Longevity in the Era of Same-Sex Marriage in the United States," *Journal of Marriage and Family*, Vol. 76, No. 5, October 2014.

Rosenfeld, Michael J., "Moving a Mountain: The Extraordinary Trajectory of Same-Sex Marriage Approval in the United States," *Socius*, Vol. 3, 2017.

Rostosky, Sharon Scales, and Ellen D. B. Riggle, "Same-Sex Relationships and Minority Stress," *Current Opinion in Psychology*, Vol. 13, February 2017.

Ruggles, Steven, Sarah Flood, Matthew Sobek, Daniel Backman, Annie Chen, Grace Cooper, Stephanie Richards, Renae Rogers, and Megan Schouweiler, "American Community Survey," version 14.0, Integrated Public Use Microdata Series, IPUMS USA, 2023.

Sanbonmatsu, Kira, "Gender Backlash in American Politics?" *Politics & Gender*, Vol. 4, No. 4, December 2008.

Sansone, Dario, "Pink Work: Same-Sex Marriage, Employment and Discrimination," *Journal of Public Economics*, Vol. 180, December 2019.

Schaller, Jessamyn, "For Richer, If Not for Poorer? Marriage and Divorce over the Business Cycle," *Journal of Population Economics*, Vol. 26, No. 3, July 2013.

Scherer, Zachary, "Key Demographic and Economic Characteristics of Same-Sex and Opposite-Sex Couples Differed," U.S. Census Bureau, November 22, 2022.

Schneebaum, Alyssa, and Nina Schubert, "Marriage (In)equality: Does the Sexual Orientation Wage Gap Persist Across Marital Status?" Vienna University of Economics and Business, Department of Economics Working Paper Series No. 254, December 1, 2017.

Schulenberg, John E., Richard A. Miech, Lloyd D. Johnston, Patrick M. O'Malley, Jerald G. Bachman, and Megan E. Patrick, "Monitoring the Future: Restricted-Use Panel Data, United States, 1976-2019," dataset, Inter-University Consortium for Political and Social Research, March 27, 2023.

Schumm, Walter R., "A Review and Critique of Research on Same-Sex Parenting and Adoption," *Psychological Reports*, Vol. 119, No. 3, December 2016.

Scott, Mindy E., Erin Schelar, Jennifer Manlove, and Carol Cui, *Young Adult Attitudes About Relationships and Marriage: Times May Have Changed, but Expectations Remain High*, Child Trends, Publication No. 2009-30, July 2009.

Searcy v. Strange, 81 F. Supp. 3d 1285, D. Ala., 2015.

Seror, Avner, and Rohit Ticku, "Legalized Same-Sex Marriage and Coming Out in America: Evidence from Catholic Seminaries," Chapman University, ESI Working Paper 21-07, April 20, 2021.

Siegel, Magdalena, Constanze Assenmacher, Nathalie Meuwly, and Martina Zemp, "The Legal Vulnerability Model for Same-Sex Parent Families: A Mixed Methods Systematic Review and Theoretical Integration," *Frontiers in Psychology*, Vol. 12, March 16, 2021.

Skinner, Alexandra, Michael D. Stein, Lorraine T. Dean, Catherine E. Oldenburg, Matthew J. Mimiaga, Philip A. Chan, Kenneth H. Mayer, and Julia Raifman, "Same-Sex Marriage Laws, Provider-Patient Communication, and PrEP Awareness and Use Among Gay, Bisexual, and Other Men Who Have Sex with Men in the United States," *AIDS and Behavior*, Vol. 27, No. 6, June 2023.

Solazzo, Alexa, Bridget Gorman, and Justin Denney, "Does Sexual Orientation Complicate the Relationship Between Marital Status and Gender with Self-Rated Health and Cardiovascular Disease?" *Demography*, Vol. 57, No. 2, April 1, 2020.

Solomon, Sondra E., Esther D. Rothblum, and Kimberly F. Balsam, "Pioneers in Partnership: Lesbian and Gay Male Couples in Civil Unions Compared with Those Not in Civil Unions and Married Heterosexual Siblings," *Journal of Family Psychology*, Vol. 18, No. 2, 2004.

Solomon, Sondra E., Esther D. Rothblum, and Kimberly F. Balsam, "Money, Housework, Sex, and Conflict: Same-Sex Couples in Civil Unions, Those Not in Civil Unions, and Heterosexual Married Siblings," *Sex Roles: A Journal of Research*, Vol. 52, No. 9–10, May 2005.

South Carolina Constitution Art. XVII, § 15, 2006.

South Carolina Laws Act 327, 1996.

South Dakota Constitution Art. XXI, § 9, 2006.

South Dakota Laws Ch. 161, 1996.

Sprigg, Peter, "The Top Ten Harms of Same-Sex 'Marriage,'" pamphlet, Family Research Council, EF11B30, 2011.

Stoutenborough, James W., Donald P. Haider-Markel, and Mahalley D. Allen, "Reassessing the Impact of Supreme Court Decisions on Public Opinion: Gay Civil Rights Cases," *Political Research Quarterly*, Vol. 59, No. 3, September 2006.

Stutzer, Alois, and Bruno S. Frey, "Does Marriage Make People Happy, or Do Happy People Get Married?" *Journal of Socio-Economics*, Vol. 35, No. 2, April 2006.

Sun, Liyang, "EVENTSTUDYINTERACT: Stata Module to Implement the Interaction Weighted Estimator for an Event Study," Statistical Software Components S458978, Boston College Department of Economics, revised September 11, 2022.

Sun, Liyang, and Sarah Abraham, "Estimating Dynamic Treatment Effects in Event Studies with Heterogeneous Treatment Effects," *Journal of Econometrics*, Vol. 225, No. 2, December 2021.

Swank, Eric, "Marriage and Political Engagement Across Sexual Identities," in Aaron Hoy, ed., *The Social Science of Same-Sex Marriage: LGBT People and Their Relationships in the Era of Marriage Equality*, Routledge, 2022.

Tankard, Margaret E., and Elizabeth Levy Paluck, "The Effect of a Supreme Court Decision Regarding Gay Marriage on Social Norms and Personal Attitudes," *Psychological Science*, Vol. 28, No. 9, September 2017.

Tasker, Fiona, "Lesbian Mothers, Gay Fathers, and Their Children: A Review," *Journal of Developmental & Behavioral Pediatrics*, Vol. 26, No. 3, June 2005.

Tasker, Fiona, "Same-Sex Parenting and Child Development: Reviewing the Contribution of Parental Gender," *Journal of Marriage and Family*, Vol. 72, No. 1, February 2010.

Tatum, Alexander K., "The Interaction of Same-Sex Marriage Access with Sexual Minority Identity on Mental Health and Subjective Wellbeing," *Journal of Homosexuality*, Vol. 64, No. 5, 2017.

Taylor, Danielle, "Fifteen Percent of Same-Sex Couples Have Children in Their Household," U.S. Census Bureau, September 17, 2020.

Taylor, Melanie A., "A Comprehensive Study of Mass Murder Precipitants and Motivations of Offenders," *International Journal of Offender Therapy and Comparative Criminology*, Vol. 62, No. 2, February 2018.

Tennessee Constitution Art. XI, § 18, 2006.

Tennessee Senate Bill 2305, 99th Gen. Assem., 2nd Reg. Sess., 1996.

Texas Constitution Art. 1, § 32, 2005.

Texas Sess. Laws Ch. 7, 1997.

TFP Student Action, "10 Reasons Why Homosexual 'Marriage' Is Harmful and Must Be Opposed," 2013. As of March 11, 2024:
https://www.catholichawaii.org/media/223462/10reasonswhyhomosexualmarriageisharmful.pdf

Thornton, Arland, and Linda Young-DeMarco, "Four Decades of Trends in Attitudes Toward Family Issues in the United States: The 1960s Through the 1990s," *Journal of Marriage and Family*, Vol. 63, No. 4, November 2001.

Trandafir, Mircea, "The Effect of Same-Sex Marriage Laws on Different-Sex Marriage: Evidence from the Netherlands," *Demography*, Vol. 51, No. 1, February 2014a.

Trandafir, Mircea, "Reply to Comment on 'The Effect of Same-Sex Marriage Laws on Different-Sex Marriage: Evidence from the Netherlands,'" *Demography*, Vol. 51, No. 6, December 2014b.

Trandafir, Mircea, "Legal Recognition of Same-Sex Couples and Family Formation," *Demography*, Vol. 52, No. 1, February 2015.

Trocki, Karen F., Amy A. Mericle, Laurie A. Drabble, Jamie L. Klinger, Cindy B. Veldhuis, Tonda L. Hughes, and Katherine J. Karriker-Jaffe, "Investigating Differential Protective Effects of Marriage on Substance Use by Sexual Identity Status," *International Journal of Alcohol and Drug Research*, Vol. 8, No. 2, 2020.

Tumin, Dmitry, and Rhiannon A. Kroeger, "Private Health Insurance Coverage Among Same-Sex Couples After *Obergefell v. Hodges*," *LGBT Health*, Vol. 7, No. 5, July 2020.

U.S. Census Bureau, "American Community Survey: 2015 One Year Estimates Public Use Microdata," webpage, 2015. As of December 21, 2023: https://www.census.gov/programs-surveys/acs/microdata/documentation/2015.html

U.S. Census Bureau, "Agency Information Collection Activities; Submission to the Office of Management and Budget (OMB) for Review and Approval; Comment Request; American Community Survey Methods Panel: 2024 Sexual Orientation and Gender Identity Test," *Federal Register*, Vol. 88, No. 180, September 19, 2023.

Utah Constitution Art. 1, § 29, 2004.

Utah Senate Bill 24, 2004 Gen. Sess., 2004.

Vakili, Keyvan, and Laurina Zhang, "High on Creativity: The Impact of Social Liberalization Policies on Innovation," *Strategic Management Journal*, Vol. 39, No. 7, July 2018.

Varnum v. Brien, 763 N.W.2d 862, Iowa, 2009.

Vermont House Bill 847, An Act Relating to Civil Unions, 1999-00 General Assembly, Adj. Sess., enacted, 2000.

Vermont Senate Bill 115, An Act to Protect Religious Freedom and Promote Equality in Civil Marriage, 70th Bienn. Sess., 2009.

Virginia Acts 195, 2020.

Virginia Constitution Art. 1, § 15-a, 2006.

Virginia Laws Ch. 354, 1997.

Walters, Suzanna Danuta, *All the Rage: The Story of Gay Visibility in America*, University of Chicago Press, 2003.

Washington, Referendum Measure No. 74, 2012.

Washington State House Bill 1130, 55th Leg., Reg. Sess., 1998.

West Virginia House Bill 2199, 76th Leg., 2001.

Whitewood v. Wolf, 992 F. Supp. 2d 410, M.D. Penn., 2014.

Wight, Richard G., Allen J. LeBlanc, and M. V. Lee Badgett, "Same-Sex Legal Marriage and Psychological Well-Being: Findings from the California Health Interview Survey," *American Journal of Public Health*, Vol. 103, No. 2, February 2013.

Wight, Richard G., Allen J. LeBlanc, Brian de Vries, and Roger Detels, "Stress and Mental Health Among Midlife and Older Gay-Identified Men," *American Journal of Public Health*, Vol. 102, No. 3, March 2012.

Windsor v. United States, 570 U.S. 744, 2013.

Wisconsin Constitution Art. XIII, § 13, 2006.

Wisconsin Stat. Ann. § 765.001, 1975.

Wolf v. Walker, 986 F. Supp. 2d 982, W.D. Wisc., 2014.

Wyoming Laws Ch. 70, 1977.

Yu, Eunice, and Jianguo Liu, "Environmental Impacts of Divorce," *Proceedings of the National Academy of Sciences*, Vol. 104, No. 51, December 18, 2007.

Zhang, Yun, Haimei Huang, Min Wang, Jiawen Zhu, Sumin Tan, Weiyi Tian, Jinli Mo, Li Jiang, Jieling Mo, Wei Pan, and Chuanyi Ning, "Family Outcome Disparities Between Sexual Minority and Heterosexual Families: A Systematic Review and Meta-Analysis," *BMJ Global Health*, Vol. 8, No. 3, March 2023.

Zhu, Jessie Y., and Wally Smieliauskas, "Evidence on the Economic Consequences of Marriage Equality and LGBT Human Rights," *Journal of Business Ethics*, Vol. 178, No. 1, June 2022.

Zissimopoulos, Julie M., Benjamin R. Karney, and Amy J. Rauer, "Marriage and Economic Well Being at Older Ages," *Review of Economics of the Household*, Vol. 13, No. 1, March 2015.